TENNIS
Styles
and Stylists

Paul Metzler

The Macmillan Company

Acknowledgments

It is not possible to recall the many books, magazines and articles which, together with personal observation and memory, have helped to make up this story. To those authors whose books are to hand, I should like to make grateful acknowledgment.

S. Powell Blackmore. *Lawn Tennis Up-To-Date*. Methuen, London, 1921

J. Pamly Paret. *Lawn Tennis Library*. American Lawn Tennis Inc., 1927

W. T. Tilden. *Aces, Places and Faults*. Robert Hale, London, 1938

D. C. Coombe. *History of the Davis Cup*. Hennel Locke, London, 1949

J. G. Smyth. *British Sports—Lawn Tennis*. Batsford, London, 1953

M. Brady. *Encyclopedia of Lawn Tennis*. Robert Hale, London, 1958

L. Hoad and J. Pollard. *The Lew Hoad Story*. Horwitz, Sydney, 1959

Lord Aberdare. *Story of Tennis*. Stanley Paul, London, 1959

R. Laver and J. Pollard. *How to Play Winning Tennis*. Pelham, London, 1964

D. Macauley and J. G. Smyth. *Behind the Scenes at Wimbledon*. Collins, London, 1965.

My thanks are also due to the secretaries of the All England Lawn Tennis Club, the Lawn Tennis Association of Australia and State L.T.A.s for providing past records—and to Mr Donald Richards of the Melbourne Herald Feature Service for providing many of the photographs.

Special thanks are conveyed to Adrian Quist and to John Abernethy, editor for the publishers, for their suggestions and help.

P.M.

The Macmillan Company
866 Third Avenue, New York, N.Y. 10022

Library of Congress Catalog Card Number: 77-114328

First published in Australia in 1969 by Angus & Robertson Ltd., Sydney

FIRST AMERICAN EDITION 1970

Printed in the United States of America

Contents

Foreword

Paul Metzler's book is one of the best on tennis I've ever read.
His analysis of styles of play is first-class and his descriptions of
players intensely interesting. I've played against many of the
stars he discusses, and I think he has described them most
accurately.

He is not an international with a name well known in tennis
circles, but there is no doubt in my mind that he writes with
authority. After earlier years of top-class competitive play he is
still a fine player and stylist, as I know from the enjoyable sets
I've played with him. He has the ability to sum up a person's
game in an instant and to recognize or recall dozens of players
from their style alone. And as for the game's early days, beyond
the reach of his long memory, he has done as much research into
them as anyone I know.

To me, Paul Metzler is a tennis historian who brings past
players to life and adds stature to present-day champions.
I commend his book.

ADRIAN QUIST

Introduction

Styles of play have interested followers of lawn tennis from the first Wimbledon championship in 1877 to the present time. Throughout the game's history of almost a hundred years styles have been examined, compared, emulated, modified. But style by itself can make for dull reading—even though, for clarity, the appendix devoted to it may be welcome.

A more interesting way of discussing style is through stylists, and many champions whose names have become immortal in the history of lawn tennis are presented both for this purpose and as interesting figures in themselves. Sometimes they tend to take over the story, but it is all the better for it.

Our first style and stylist appear soon, but first we should glance at the beginnings of the game. Without more ado then, let us make the acquaintance of Major Walter Clopton Wingfield —officer, gentleman and sportsman in the reign of Her Gracious Majesty Queen Victoria of England.

P.M.

TO THE GAME OF LAWN TENNIS
AND ITS IMMORTALS

1 | Let There Be Light

WITHOUT becoming involved in stormy arguments of almost a hundred years ago, it's probably fair to say that lawn tennis began as a game called Sphairistike. It was patented in 1873 by Major Walter Clopton Wingfield, British Army (in which, in those days, one apparently had lots of leisure). The Major seems to have been of a romantic nature, for he was at pains to explain that Sphairistike was the gracious name by which the Game of Tennis was known in ancient Greece. He also seems to have had social mixed doubles foremost in mind. The game was clearly one in which young ladies and gentlemen could meet and mingle; the playing surface was aptly named "court"; the five-foot net would have induced gently arching strokes; and the court itself was of hourglass shape, matching the ladies' figures.

The Major achieved this seemingly improbable court shape by making the net narrower than the baselines, and by sloping the sidelines inwards towards it. Why? Surely to prevent short, angled shots—such as some cad might play, to make a lady run and show her ankles.

Other features of the game also suggest that the chivalrous Major was making allowances for the ladies. They were to serve from closer to the net than men, and the rules of play made no mention of double faults. There being no limit to the attempts a player could make at landing a service into play, one could presumably hit, miss, simper, and look attractively helpless for quite a time without losing the point and upsetting one's male partner. This was courtesy to ladies in one of its finest forms.

But whatever the inventor's original intentions may have been, the new outdoor tennis was soon taken over by the energetic young men of the day.

There had been earlier forms of outdoor tennis. In 1767 a small company of English gentlemen used to play a game of their own devising called Field Tennis, which provided noble exercise. Twice a week they met, to consume a large roast dinner and a good-sized pudding or pie before repairing at four o'clock to their sport. Play continued until the dusk of long summer evenings, and from time to time the players refreshed themselves with draughts from cool tankards.

Small wonder that these sportsmen fortified themselves a little both before and during the game, for the "field" was some sixteen acres in area. Nor, given the pleasant conditions, is it surprising that the game's adherents loyally and

Major Wingfield

The layout of a court as shown in the first edition of Major Wingfield's Rules.

roundly declared that "Field Tennis threatens ere long to bowl out cricket".

In 1837 there was talk of Open Tennis. But "open" in this case meant "open air", and the game was known also as Long Tennis, the length of the court being no less than 160 yards. Though up to six a side could take part, singles matches were also played. By the time Sphairistike made its bow, however, these earlier games had evidently exhausted both themselves and their participants.

Major Wingfield made several modifications to his game, and by the end of 1874 his hourglass court looked like this:

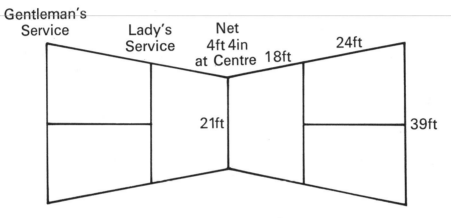

Gentleman's Service — Lady's Service — Net 4ft 4in at Centre — 18ft — 24ft — 21ft — 39ft

The server delivered the ball—underarm of course—into service courts abutting the baseline instead of the net. Only the serving side could score a point, and if they lost the rally the service changed sides. The game consisted of fifteen points, called "aces".

These simple rules were set out in a booklet that also contained instructions for setting up the court and explained the new outdoor game's connection with indoor tennis of old. It was noted that besides the ancient Greeks, later figures such as Henry V, Henry VII and Henry VIII had all been tennis-players. There was also an oval-shaped photograph of the inventor himself—in full beard and moustache, wearing a beret and a sporting waistcoat and carrying a long-handled racket draped negligently across one elbow. In addition, the Major provided a list of distinguished people who had bought his game. He began with royalty, proceeded to dukes, and, without descending much farther down the social scale, turned from the aristocracy

to the practicality of his price list. The whole game cost six guineas, extra balls five shillings a dozen, and an extra racket one pound, or—delightfully—fifteen shillings for ladies.

By this time the game was being played on former croquet lawns and other venues up and down the country. The would-be graceful name of Sphairistike was either ignored or shortened to "Sticky" by the soulless young men of the times, and the Major, yielding to the wind, eventually announced that "lawn tennis" could be an alternative name. A competitive spirit developed—the first Wimbledon championship was only three years away—and a new vigour entered the game. One imagines gentlemen discarding their blazers if not their neckties as well. At least one contemporary sporting writer wondered whether the game was not fast getting beyond a lady's ability to keep up with it "as it is very hard work for a man and a dress is such a drag".

Competition soon demanded that the Major's somewhat haphazard rules be made more specific. The allowable number of service attempts could not remain indefinite, and one needed to know if a ball landing on a line was in or out or simply a question for sportsmanship. There were also groups of people playing a game in which indoor tennis rackets were used on outdoor lawns. They had been playing before Wingfield's Sphairistike was patented, and were highly indignant at the Major's claim of invention; as far as they were concerned he had "invented" only one thing—the hourglass shape of his court. But none of these groups was co-ordinated with any other, and each had its own rules of play. Their

3

courts were rectangular, but of varying dimensions; nets were of different centre heights, while their sideline heights and the amount of resulting sag were purely circumstantial.

In 1875 the Tennis and Racquets Sub-committee of the Marylebone Cricket Club, after calling all interested parties together, issued its standardized version of the rules of lawn tennis. Wingfield's hourglass court was accepted, though its waisted ladylike form was thickened to some extent by widening the net to eight yards and shortening the baselines to ten. Net heights were fixed at 5 feet at the posts and 4 feet at the centre. Only one service fault was allowable and, most important of all, the service must now land between the net and the service-line instead of between the service-line and the baseline.

The game went from strength to strength, and in 1877 the first Gentlemen's Singles Championship was staged. The hourglass court was no longer practical and the All England Club rules, superseding those of the M.C.C., decreed a rectangular one (which no doubt the Major stubbornly chose to regard as a distended hourglass):

fault was allowable. A ball falling on the line was good, and so were all net-cords. Tennis scoring as we know it applied instead of the game consisting of fifteen aces, and players were to change ends after each set.

Lawn tennis was now set on a course of advancement that was eventually to make it a world-wide game. But alas, it was progressing without benefit of Major Wingfield. In the stormy arguments previously mentioned he was forced to the sidelines; the graceful hourglass and the Grecian Sphairistike were lost, and no one took up his unique suggestion for play all year round: "In a hard frost the nets may be erected on the ice, and the players being equipped with skates, the game assumes a new feature, and gives an opening for the exhibition of much grace and science."

He probably died bitter—but whether he invented lawn tennis or merely attempted to patent a passing version of it, we should at least recognize our Major as the man who got the game moving.

Meanwhile, there was great excitement over that first Wimbledon of long ago. There was

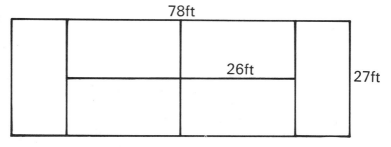

The net was to be 5 feet high at the posts and 3 feet 3 inches at its centre. The balls were to be covered in flannel cloth. The service was to be made with one foot behind the baseline, and one

keen technical interest, too—over nothing less than which of two styles of play would prove triumphant. From the very first Wimbledon there was interest in style.

2 | First Wimbledon

THE first Wimbledon entry consisted of twenty-two gentlemen. Most of them had already made their names in either Racquets or Tennis, and the question was which style, Racquets or Tennis, would prove superior in the new game, which had as yet no recognized style of its own. Such style as it did have was mainly underarm—to lift balls bouncing low from soft turf over a high net.

The ancient game of Tennis, sport of kings, was played in a roofed and walled court of 110 by 38 feet, across which was stretched a net 5 feet high at the posts. Along both back walls and one side wall, and somewhat less than halfway up, narrow roofs sloped inwards. The server hit the ball over the net and onto the sloping roof, along which it rolled until it fell off into the striker's court; the striker, taking the ball either on the full or on the first bounce, returned it across the net to any part of the court, provided it did not strike above a play-line marked on the side and rear walls. The method of scoring was similar to the one finally adopted in lawn tennis, and both server and receiver could score points.

This meagre outline is no more descriptive of the game's attractions than the bald statement that present-day lawn tennis consists of hitting a white ball back and forth over a band of netting. Shakespeare immortalized Tennis in a scene in *Henry V* where Charles, King of France, presents a cask of tennis balls to Henry on the eve of the battle of Agincourt—a scornful gesture implying that the young English king was more suited to sporting dalliance than to serious warfare. Many a schoolboy has since delighted in

A game of Real Tennis at St Petersburg before World War I

5

A Real Tennis player of the nineteenth century

Henry's thunderous reply about turning balls to gunstones.

Tennis lapsed during the Wars of the Roses, which followed soon after Henry V's reign—just as lawn tennis would later be suspended during the two World Wars—and returned strongly in the more peaceful reigns of Henry VII and Henry VIII in the first half of the 1500s. Over three hundred years later it waned because of the considerable expense associated with it and because of the rise of lawn tennis. Its name is now applied to the latter game, the original Tennis being described as Real, Court, or Royal Tennis. There are few Royal Tennis courts left in either England or America (where it was introduced as late as the 1870s) and no more than a couple in Australia.

Racquets, on the other hand, could hardly claim existence before the nineteenth century. It was played much as squash is today, but on a much larger area—60 by 30 feet, and sometimes even 80 by 40 feet for doubles (present court measurements are 32 by 21 feet). Also, a game consisted of fifteen aces instead of today's best of three or five games up to nine points.

For us, however, the main interest lies in the styles of play used in the two games, and this was what intrigued the supporters of that first Wimbledon championship of 1877. Great was the debate, we can believe, and the wagering too, in London's fashionable clubland.

The Racquets racket was much like a squash racket, though its head was pear-shaped rather than rounded. It was held with a grip that permitted forehands and backhands to be played with equal facility, and the Racquets supporters therefore argued that their men would be far too flexible and nippy for the Tennis chaps.

The Tennis racket was a queer implement. One edge of its frame being flattened to cope with low balls near the floor, and the other curved, the centre of its strings was not in line with its handle. It was heavy, too, and accepted form was to grasp it halfway up the handle and to play all strokes with undercut or slice. The Tennis clan contended that their men would be too strong for Racquets players in rough outdoor conditions, that their spin would bamboozle them, and that they could serve more powerfully ("Some of our chaps go up as much as shoulder-high, you know"). What was more, they were prepared to back their opinion with a few sovereigns.

In the event, all the theorists were confounded. The first Wimbledon was won by a Mr Spencer Gore, and it mattered not whether he had been Racquets or Tennis. Against all opponents he advanced to the net after a shot or two and volleyed them off the court. Anyone who thinks that net play in singles is something new, please note.

Spencer Gore, of course, was protected from passing shots by a net 5 feet high at the posts. But why, therefore, didn't all the competitors volley? Probably for the simple reason that no one had ever volleyed before. If a thing was not done, one didn't do it. But the winner did.

Spencer Gore's volleying tactics had an immediate effect on the rules of lawn tennis. The following year the net was lowered a little. Two years later, in 1880, it was lowered again, and the distance of the service-line from the net was shortened from 26 feet to its present distance of 21 feet. Two years later again, in 1882, the net height was finally fixed at 3 feet at the centre and 3 feet 6 inches at the posts, and there it has remained.

The first Wimbledon was a success and made

a profit of ten pounds. There were some complaints—perhaps from a few spectators who felt that a shilling a seat was excessive—but most of the game's supporters were well pleased with the championship. Its winner, as befitted an Old Harrovian and a Racquets player (Harrow in the 1820s had been the first school in England to play Racquets) took a shot at Tennis with the statement: "We detested the tennis scoring; it puzzled us pretty considerable." It's a pity that his portrait as well as his words has not been handed down to us.

Anyway, our question is answered. The technical style that won the first Wimbledon was almost certainly based on the grip used in Racquets and in present-day squash. Mr Spencer Gore would probably have shuddered to hear it, but, if we are to classify him under any style at all, he was what would now be called a Continental player (see Appendix I).

3 | Settling Down

SPENCER GORE did not retain his title in 1878, though he would have been forced to admit that practically everything was in his favour. As champion he did not have to tire himself by playing right through the tournament; instead, fit and rested, he awaited the challenge round.* Then his ultimate challenger, P. F. Hadow, arrived to play the match with a bad headache. Nevertheless Hadow won—7–5, 6–1, 9–7.

The net in 1878, although somewhat lowered as we have seen, was still a formidable barrier of 4 feet 9 inches at the posts, and once again Gore stormed it. Confronted by a tall, long-legged, long-armed man sprawling over the net and sometimes even reaching over it to volley (then legal), Hadow replied by lobbing the ball over his opponent's head. He must have done this by instinct, for he had not heard of the lob and, as he himself said, had certainly never tried it before.

Poor Spencer Gore! One year champion of England in dashing style, the next defeated setless by lobs. Wimbledon's motto, "If You Can Meet with Triumph and Disaster . . .", instead of coming from Rudyard Kipling might well have been born of its first two championships. But all was not gloom for Spencer Gore. Hadow, too, was an Old Harrovian, so it was not as if the championship had gone to some outsider or other.

As Wimbledon played, so played the nation. Gore's defeat cast doubt on the soundness of volleying tactics; determined baseline rallying took over. But since the net's centre was disproportionately low in relation to its height at the posts, nearly all drives were directed over the centre and the rallying lacked variety.

The 1879 Wimbledon was won by an unknown player from Yorkshire, a young cleric named J. T. Hartley, who thought so little of his chance of surviving more than a couple of rounds that he made no provision for his religious duties at home and in the middle of the tournament was forced to hurry back and forth over long stretches of the country.

Hartley successfully defended his title in 1880, when as champion he had only to make a one-day visit to Wimbledon. He defended again the following year, but by then he had taken his pitcher to the well once too often. Lawn tennis's first great star had arisen, and Hartley, somewhat ill and out of practice, was overwhelmed by a twenty-year-old named William Renshaw, to the

J. T. Hartley

*Until 1922 the holder of the Wimbledon title did not play through the rounds; instead the winner of the "All-Comers' Singles" met the holder or defending champion in the "Challenge Round". The Davis Cup competition is still played in this old-fashioned manner.

pitiless score of 6–0, 6–2, 6–1. Hartley may afterwards have wondered if his sole place should not after all be in the church, but his name appears again in 1882, as doubles champion with R. T. Richardson.

The years 1881 to 1889 were a halcyon period for William Renshaw and his twin brother Ernest. William won Wimbledon seven times—a record that still stands. He began with six straight wins from 1881 to 1886, defeating, in

P. F. Hadow with King George V and Queen Mary at the parade of champions held in 1926, fifty years after the first Wimbledon.

9

addition to Hartley, his brother Ernest twice in succession, and then a burly and hard-hitting player, H. F. Lawford, three times in succession. Then came a break; William developed tennis elbow (possibly the first occurrence of this now-familiar injury), Lawford won through to his fourth challenge round running and, there being no defending champion to oppose him, was champion himself. Although no one wished ill to Renshaw, it was a popular win.

In 1888, Renshaw, no longer champion, entered the All-Comers' Singles and was knocked out in an early round. This gave Ernest Renshaw his chance, and in the challenge round he beat the unfortunate Lawford, who seems to have been Renshaw fodder, in straight sets.

In 1889, William repeated his performance of 1881 by playing through to the challenge round and winning it. The defending champion, Ernest, thus (if one cares to work it out) became a triple Wimbledon runner-up. But the most appealing runner-up was Lawford. Second to one or other

W. J. Hamilton

of the Renshaw brothers four times, he had also been runner-up before they ever crossed his path—in 1880 to J. T. Hartley, clerical duties permitting.

William was finally beaten in 1890—by W. J. Hamilton of Ireland, in five sets.

The Wimbledon doubles championship was introduced in 1880, and for a time was almost a closed shop. The Renshaw twins won it seven times between its inception and 1889.*

The Renshaws' play completely changed the character of lawn tennis. William had a powerful

H. F. Lawford

*One can't help wondering which side of the court each twin occupied when receiving service, for it is difficult to visualize a doubles pair otherwise. Evidence is lacking, and one wonders if in the Renshaws' day the player who was next to serve went to the first or right-hand court for what was called the "take". Long since outlawed in competitive tennis, this old custom—somewhat similar to having the "honour" of hitting off first in golf—is still to be found in tea-party ladies' doubles in Australia. It gives an equal share in avoiding backhands without raising such a delicate matter.

William and Ernest Renshaw

overhead service and took the ball early with his ground strokes instead of on the drop. He also revived net tactics and made outstanding use of them. He developed a crushing overhead stroke as a counter to the lob—or at least a partial counter to it, for the lob has never been completely answered. Ernest Renshaw was said to have had a smoother, more graceful style than William, and a game without weakness. The twins disliked playing each other, and when they were forced to meet in tournaments Ernest seemed reluctant to try his hardest. Reports that most of the best players of the day would rather have played William than Ernest make us wonder if Ernest was not an even better player than his brother. On Wimbledon results he was not, even if you disregard his matches against his brother, and it seems pointless to question the supremacy of a man who won Wimbledon seven times. But the difference between the twins' play was far less than a glance at the championship roll might suggest.

The advent of the Renshaws also changed the general approach to the game. The days were past when Spencer Gore could be puzzled pretty considerable by tennis scoring, when Hadow's main concern and method of attack were respectively a headache and a lob, and when a Wimbledon championship could be won between sermons. The Renshaw twins played tournament tennis throughout the English summer, then went off to the Côte d'Azur to practise throughout the winter so that they would be in top form to play tournaments again in the summer. One can't help feeling that if the original idea behind banning professionals from amateur sport had nothing to do with class-consciousness but was entirely concerned with giving an amateur a fair chance, the rules might have gone further and banned gentlemen of leisure as well. But it would be worthier (though possibly less human) to admire the Renshaws' dedication rather than envy them their private means.

Inspiration having been provided, players increased in numbers; and equipment, especially rackets, improved correspondingly. A photograph of the Renshaws shows them holding rackets which, though still pearshaped, were a distinct advance over earlier models. The twins, with their flattened hair and drooping moustaches, are difficult to separate, though Ernest can generally be identified by his more retiring manner.

The Renshaws and the players of their era were products of the 1882 law that lowered the net-height at the posts to 3 feet 6 inches, its present height. This change permitted low strokes to be directed to all parts of the court; these in turn could be more effectively produced with a horizontal swing than with an underarm action, and so lawn tennis came to be played more or less in the form we know today. Something nearer to a balance between net and baseline tactics was struck. The Renshaws' volleying and smashing proved that in their competent hands the net position could pay handsome dividends; nevertheless the low net invited the development of skimming forehand and backhand drives—and woe betide an over-adventurous player who approached the net on a short ball. Eventually we find the driving technique showing the greater improvement and English tennis becoming based on ground-stroke play.

Lawn tennis's first recognizable style naturally became known as the English style (see Appendix I), and this at once poses the question whether all English players adopted what was an individual Renshaw style or whether the twins became outstanding examples of the English style. The latter is the more likely. It is not difficult to see how the typical English style of stroke-play developed. Lawn tennis emerged from Racquets and Tennis. Racquets being a game demanding flexibility before power, the racket was held so that little if any change was needed for forehand and backhand. In Tennis, the racket was wielded with a cut stroke, so that the same type of forehand grip was the natural one and the wrist was held low. Further, early lawn tennis was played exclusively on grass, the English sea-level air was heavy and often damp, and the balls were definitely on the soft side; clearly the task was to get the ball over the net rather than to keep it down.*

Here is a summary of the English grip and style in lawn tennis:

● Thumb and forefinger "V" somewhere on the left bevel of the racket handle, palm towards the top surface, and little or no change needed for the backhand;

*A present-day brand of ball, the English Slazenger, was first used at Wimbledon in 1901. Bounce and compression tests were not introduced till the 1920s. (Specifications of the size and weight of rackets are still to come!)

Wilfrid Baddeley

H. S. Mahony

Joshua Pim

- Strokes played with a low wrist, basically flat or with a little forward spin, but often, particularly on the backhand, slightly undersliced;
- Good reach on either side for wide balls; low balls handled with ease, and low volleying deft;
- Service sliced—to keep the bounce low, to force the receiver to hit up;
- Overall: flexible, but with no great power.

Later, when lawn tennis had spread to the Continent, this English grip and style of play came to be associated with the slow "hard-courts" of Europe and therefore to be more generally known as "Continental", even in England. Today it has no other name.

It is inconceivable that the Renshaws did not conform to this general style. So great was their dominance that if they had used any other style it would have been emulated and the typical English style would never have come into being. Lawford, not either of the Renshaws, was an exception. He had a powerful, rapidly topspinning forehand drive that was described as "unusual and ferocious". No doubt it sometimes put even the Renshaws on the defensive.

Before lowering our curtain on the attractive Renshaws, a closing anecdote seems fitting. William Renshaw figured in what must still rank

as one of Wimbledon's most exciting and nerve-racking matches. This was in 1889, during his second attempt to regain the title he had been obliged to forfeit in 1887. In the final of the All-Comers' Singles, the winner of which would play the defending champion, Ernest Renshaw, William encountered a fine player, H. S. Barlow, who won the first two sets from him at 6–3, 7–5, and then led for most of the third as well. William saved the vital third set at 8–6, but in the fourth set Barlow steadily advanced to a 5–2 lead. He held match point no fewer than six times, and William saved it no fewer than six times—once when he had fallen over and dropped his racket as well. His doggedness was finally rewarded and he won the set, 10–8. In the fifth set Barlow went to a seemingly unbeatable lead of 5–0, but William clung on, and eventually drew to 5–all. There was to be no anti-climax, and four games later William Renshaw was the winner at 8–6. It is dryly reported that the strain on the spectators must have shortened many lives. Barlow probably could have won the match when Renshaw fell and dropped his racket, but he sportingly returned the ball high and slow to give William a chance to recover. As for William, the match showed, as one would in any case expect of a seven-times Wimbledon winner, that he was no fair-weather champion who relied solely on his gifts.

These were great days for British lawn tennis, and it is with regret that we take leave of them. In doing so, a few minor disturbances of the times could be noted, such as a severe drop in Wimbledon attendances (because of the Renshaws' retirement and a simultaneous craze in London society for bicycling), an invasion by Irish players from 1890 to 1896, and, at the turn of the century, a distressing affair with the Boers in faraway South Africa.

The Irish invasion consisted of the frail-looking "Ghost" Hamilton, the brilliant and light-hearted Joshua Pim, who contended mightily against England's smooth Wilfrid Baddeley, and, finally, tall and volatile Harold Mahony. Baddeley was a twin, and he and his brother Herbert followed the Renshaw pattern and won the Wimbledon doubles, four times.

Passing years, however, dull the edge of detail, and in the broader perspective of tennis history the great days of the Renshaws seem to have merged peacefully and directly into the even greater days of the Doherty brothers.

4 | Immortal Dohertys

THE first National Singles Championship of the United States was held in 1881, only four years after the first Wimbledon. The winner was bespectacled Richard D. Sears, of Boston, who held the title for seven years running. As the first championship was played on grass, with the net, balls and rules imported from England, Sears probably held his racket with the English grip, and an old picture of him tends to support this view. Volleying tactics were also adopted, and were maintained longer than they had been in England; most of the leading U.S. players from the time of Sears until 1900 were essentially volleyers.

Amateurism, still a contentious issue today, reared its controversial head over Sears eighty-odd years ago. A picture of him in striped cap and blazer appeared on the box of a certain brand of cigars. It bore no name, but everyone knew it was Sears the lawn tennis champion and everyone agreed that he would hardly be allowing it to appear for nothing. U.S. administrators were outraged, but Sears retained his amateur status.

The French National championship began in 1891 and the German in 1893. Although, in the French list, the names of Vacherot and Aymé are prominent, it is to England that we return for our next outstanding champions, the Doherty brothers—Reggie ("R.F." or "Big Do") and Laurie ("H.L." or "Little Do")—who carried practically all before them in the years 1897 to 1906.

R.F., born in 1874, won Wimbledon four times from 1897 to 1900, was defeated in the challenge round of 1901—his final singles appearance at Wimbledon—and then handed over to his younger brother. Laurie, two years R.F.'s junior, was champion five times, from 1902 to 1906, and together the brothers won the doubles eight times. They won the Davis cup (introduced in 1900) for the British Isles on four occasions, from 1903 to 1906, and in this competition Lau-

rie, with a record of seven singles wins and five doubles wins, remains the only man to have played a substantial number of Davis Cup singles and doubles without being defeated in either department. Visiting America for the Cup challenge in 1903, Laurie won the U.S. National singles—the first British player to do so—and for good measure the brothers won the doubles as well.

The Dohertys brought off their wonderful performances with the English style, even though

Richard Sears

15

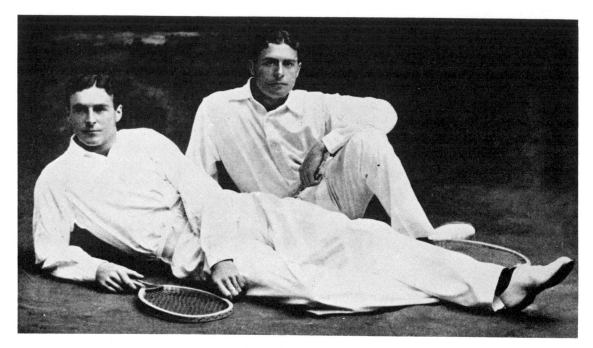

R. F. and H. L. Doherty

the later Eastern American style (see Appendix I) with its special grips for forehand and backhand was already well established. This style had been used by the American players in defeating the British Isles team in the first Davis Cup tie in 1900, and in the Dohertys' time it was being used by English as well as American players. The Dohertys did not favour the slight underspin characteristic of many other English players, but their style was nevertheless typically English and they stuck to the view that the less change of grip there was between forehand and backhand the better.

Both Dohertys were elegant stroke-makers and played excellent all-court tennis, but opinion differed as to which of them was the greater player. Laurie's record was longer, mainly because his elder brother's health was never good, even in the days of his best performances. Indeed, R.F. would probably never have been strong enough to win his four successive Wimbledons if he had had to play through the tournament instead of, after his 1897 victory, merely defending his title in one match. (What a boon such a system might have been to a man like Bunny Austin in the mid-1930s—a player with an outstanding Davis Cup singles record but one whose physical resources could not meet the demands of succeeding matches of tournament play.)

Laurie was faster about the court than his brother—but Big Do's anticipation was exceptional. Laurie was more severe overhead and on the volley, and his ground strokes were steadiness itself, but the elder Doherty's service and ground strokes were clearly stronger than his brother's and he was noted for a wonderful topspin backhand drive. R.F. once observed to his brother that if he but had his health he'd give him fifteen a game, but whether the remark was made wistfully or teasingly is not disclosed. Both were gifted players, R.F. possibly the more so; neither was robust, and R.F., as we have seen, lacked stamina to a marked degree.

Both brothers could handle any type of game or player they came up against; it mattered little whether consistency, guile, or power was the opposing keynote. Laurie, for example, was particularly noted for his ability to handle a cannonball service. Their matches were a delight to watch, creating box-office records at Wimbledon and a solid following that ensured the game's future.

Matches between these two champions were

"R.F."

already well known and that the brothers consistently followed their services to the net. Fully net-conscious, they introduced a new system of play when receiving. The non-striker was placed at the net and the receiver attacked strongly instead of concentrating on a safe return, then followed in to join his partner at the net. This, in more aggressive form, is the system in doubles today; but the Dohertys did not follow in as closely as the moderns do and their volleying was often from below net height. The non-striker's net positioning lapsed after the Doherty era, particularly in America, where it was considered superior for the two players to be in line formation for either attack or defence; it was revived in the 1930s, however, and has remained in favour ever since.

But, you may ask, how good were the Dohertys compared with today's champions? How good, really, was the play witnessed by men in high collars and ladies with wide picture hats, tight waists, and flowing ankle-length dresses? Did these people go into raptures over play that was, by present-day standards, only mild patball?

It has been argued by the old school that from the first Wimbledon to the Doherty era the main improvement was in players, and that since the end of the Doherty era the most noticeable improvements have been in rackets, balls, and court surfaces rather than in play. Modern tennis followers naturally refuse to countenance this. For a more satisfying comparison of standards of play let us examine as briefly as possible the line that goes back from the present time to that of the Dohertys.

The play of present-day Davis Cup stars and touring professionals would equal that of, say, Sedgman in his own era. Sedgman was a very good player before he could defeat such former masters as Crawford and Quist; Crawford and Perry as rising stars took defeats from Borotra and Cochet; Tilden defeated Borotra in every outdoor singles encounter, yet it once took Tilden, while holder of the Wimbledon and U.S. singles crowns, four closely contested sets to defeat a forty-three-year-old Brookes in a Davis Cup challenge round; Brookes, in his first Wimbledon attempt in 1905, lost in the challenge round to Laurie Doherty; and R.F., until it became the younger brother's day, used to beat Laurie. This does not mean that R.F., if returned

nevertheless disappointing. Like the Renshaws, the Dohertys disliked playing against each other, neither one being particularly keen to do his best. In the 1898 challenge round, which could have been a grand exhibition of the art of lawn tennis, R.F., the holder and the better player at the time, allowed his brother two sets in a colourless and uninspiring match.

Their doubles matches, with Little Do in the right-hand court and Big Do in the left, were graceful and exhilarating displays. And their attractive play was matched by their pleasing appearance. Both had dark wavy hair parted near the centre, and both wore white cricket shirts (Laurie's sleeves were buttoned at the wrist, R.F.'s were left flapping), long trousers, and white shoes. (Tennis dress had varied over the years, sometimes including striped football jerseys.)

In trying to picture the Dohertys' doubles play it must be realized that the art of volleying was

A. W. Gore

times, and in all he competed in the amazing number of twenty-nine consecutive Wimbledon championships. He was a veteran of forty-one years of age when he won the 1909 championship. He played in the first Davis Cup in 1900 and again as late as 1912. Playing in Wimbledon's Fifty Year Jubilee championships in 1926 at the age of fifty-eight, he had the honour of opposing and defeating royalty; the match was the first round of the men's doubles championship, the royal personage being the Duke of York, later King George VI.

J. C. Parke

to life and paid a suitably large professional fee, could seriously threaten a modern champion like Rod Laver, but it does suggest that many a good player of today, no matter how tight his racket strings or how short his shorts, could not have simply walked off with the Wimbledon championship in the Doherty period of 1897–1906.

In 1901, the break in what would have been a succession of ten Doherty singles championship wins, Wimbledon was won by Arthur W. Gore (probably a relative of our old friend Spencer Gore), who defeated a sick R.F., 4–6, 7–5, 6–4, 6–4 in the challenge round. Arthur Gore was a small, compact man with a heavy black moustache. Almost a one-stroke player, he had as his main weapons a strong Eastern American forehand, a fighting heart, and tremendous endurance. He was to win Wimbledon twice more, in 1908 and 1909—though it must be noted that Laurie Doherty had retired and Australia's Norman Brookes did not return to England to defend the title he had won in 1907.

Gore may not have been one of Wimbledon's most gifted champions, but he was certainly one of its most persistent. For his three Wimbledon crowns he contested the challenge round seven

Family names seem to have been established early at Wimbledon. The Gores won four Wimbledon singles between them, the Renshaws eight, the Baddeleys three, the Dohertys nine. The Renshaw and Baddeley twins won the doubles on seven and four occasions respectively and the Doherty brothers eight times. This gives a grand total of forty-three Wimbledon wins, to which could be added the Dohertys' successes in winning and holding the Davis Cup for the British Isles and their wins in the American championships. No Smiths, Browns, Joneses, or Robinsons have approached this Gore/Renshaw/Baddeley/Doherty performance.

The Dohertys were Britain's brightest stars. Except for Arthur Gore's two gallant wins in middle age and an isolated Davis Cup victory in 1912 (in which J. C. Parke, a dashing Irishman famous for his running forehand and backhand driving, unexpectedly defeated Norman Brookes of Australasia), it was not until the mid-1930s that Britons were again to be winners of the Davis Cup or of the Wimbledon or U.S. National Singles.

And what of the English style? Developed by the Renshaws and perfected by the Dohertys, it was not to win Wimbledon again until 1925. In the intervening period British tennis writers, contrasting the play of successful American champions, painted a dreadful picture of a cramped English style and of super-cautious English tennis. The service was patted. The forehand was almost powerless; with a bunched-fingers grip and low, stiff wrist inducing under-spin, the ball was allowed to drop instead of being attacked and was struck from nearer the right leg than the left. The backhand was a similar stroke, made from the other side. What volleying was attempted was from too far back and was essentially defensive.

This is the only picture that many people have of the English style, though it is obviously impossible that the Dohertys or even the Renshaws played in such an inhibited manner. Nevertheless, English tennis was certainly in decline; even when the English style next won Wimbledon (1925) it was in the hands of a Frenchman, René Lacoste.

With English tennis in this state it is clearly time to turn elsewhere—to America—for both style and stylists.

5 | America and the Davis Cup

AMERICANS may have used the English style in their early days of lawn tennis, but they certainly did not retain it. Impatient for more power, for the forehand drive they moved the wrist and the palm of the hand solidly behind the handle of the racket and met the ball ahead of the left hip.

Such a forehand grip would not do for the backhand, and so a distinct change of grip was made. Sometimes the change was as large as ninety degrees, bringing the thumb and forefinger "V" to the rear surface of the handle and directing the knuckles of all four fingers forward. Considering the open "V" a weakness on the backhand, Americans ran the thumb straight up the back of the handle for support. In the English backhand the thumb was often placed diagonally across the back of the handle, it being a matter of personal preference whether the thumb were thus advanced for support or wrapped round the handle for greater firmness of grip.

Nor were the Americans satisfied that the English discipline of keeping the wrist low for forehand and backhand driving was necessary, or even desirable. What the English described as a low wrist the Americans, seeing an over-stiff version, called a cocked wrist; what the English saw as a beautifully held low wrist the Americans came to regard more as a break in the straight line between arm and racket. Where the English bent their knees to balls of lower bounce the Americans preferred to drop the racket head somewhat. If the English style was crisp, the American was sweeping; if the English could be flexible, the American was powerful. This power needed controlling, and the Americans, with their more suitable grip, used topspin to a greater degree on the forehand than did the average English player; topspin was also normal with the American backhand, whereas the English backhand was often a little undersliced. Americans regarded English groundstroking as predominantly safe, their own as adventurous.

The Americans also volleyed more severely and, as we have seen, the volleying game lasted longer in America than it did in Britain. Here again, however, there was greater development in driving technique than there was in volleying, and eventually the volleying game was forced to give way in America as well.

A nation of natural throwers—from a long association with baseball—the Americans were soon strong servers. Pace had the advantage of putting the ball out of the receiver's reach or of causing him to hurry and mis-hit, but it must be remembered that one of the objects of the English sliced service was to keep the ball low and thus force the receiver to hit up. Pace does not give such a result; rather, it tends to make a sliced service bounce between waist and shoulder height—the most suitable height from which to drive hardest. To overcome this the Americans proceeded in the opposite direction, namely, to make the ball bounce too high for comfort—in practice, with a disconcerting swerve in the air and a sharp break after the bounce. In short, they developed what became known as the American Twist service, referred to in modern times as the kick service.

For the sliced service the ball is thrown between the head and right shoulder, the racket hitting the right side of the ball in a curving swing and finishing to the left of the server's left leg. The ball, spinning round a more or less vertical axis, swerves in the air from the server's right to his left and on bouncing breaks slightly in the same direction, the bounce being somewhat lower than that from a flat-hit ball.

For the American Twist service the throw is between the head and left shoulder, the back is arched, and the racket head is whipped upwards and across the ball from left to right, finishing to the right of the server's right leg. The ball receives a powerful diagonal combination of topspin and sidespin. Looked at from the back of the ball, the direction of the spin is from the bottom left corner to the top right corner, or

20

The U.S. team of 1900
M. D. Whitman, Dwight F. Davis, H. Ward

south-west to north-east. The topspin makes the ball arc high over the net, drop sharply, and bounce high. The sidespin causes it to swerve from the server's right to his left like a sliced delivery, but because the axis of the ball's spin is tilted instead of vertical, the bounce breaks back against the swerve. The combined result of the American Twist service is an arcing ball that swerves towards the receiver's forehand and kicks towards his backhand.*

All of this—forehand grip farther behind the racket and a large change of grip for the backhand, lower racket head, greater speed with more topspin, and kicking service—became known as the American Style (see Appendix I). We should now meet some of its exponents—and who better than the three young Harvard men who opposed the British Isles team in the first match of the Davis Cup, in 1900.

---

*The Americans also introduced a Reverse American Twist service. This belongs more properly to the Western American style of play discussed later. It is only mentioned here to avoid confusion of terms and also because it happened to be used by one of the three American players in the first Davis Cup.

The Americans were a formidable and interesting trio: Malcolm Whitman, winner of the U.S. singles title from 1898 to 1900, was the current champion. Holcombe Ward, famous for his American Twist serve, became champion in 1904. Dwight Davis, donor of the Cup, who was to become America's Secretary of War and later Governor of the Philippines, was at that time a tall, aggressive left-hander somewhat below Whitman in singles but a powerful doubles player. He had been runner-up in the U.S. All-Comers' singles in 1898 and 1899, and with Ward he won the U.S. doubles title three years in succession from 1899 to 1901.

The British Isles team consisted of A. W. Gore, H. Roper Barrett, who later won the Wimbledon doubles three times (and who, later again, joined forces with Gore to defeat their future King and his partner) and E. D. Black, a Scottish champion and a dark horse whose name does not appear on any Wimbledon roll. The match was played at Longwood Cricket Club, Boston. Court surfaces and equipment were evidently well below English standards and the temperature was 136 degrees Fahrenheit in the sun.

Whitman beat Gore, Davis beat Black, and Davis and Ward beat Black and Roper Barrett—all with the loss of only one set. The rest of the match was washed out by rain with the score between Davis and Gore standing at 9–7, 9–all.

For a first-hand account of it we turn to an offended Roper Barrett:

The ground was abominable. The grass was long. Picture to yourself a court in England where the grass has been the longest you ever encountered; double the length of that grass and you have the courts as they were at Longwood at that time. The net was a disgrace to civilized Lawn Tennis, held up by guy ropes which were continually sagging, giving way as much as 2 or 3 inches every few games and frequently requiring adjustment. As for the balls, I hardly like to mention them. They were awful—soft and "motherly looking"—and when served with the American Twist came at you like an animated egg-plum.... They not only swerved in the air, but in hitting the ground broke surely from four to five feet.... We had never experienced this service before and it quite nonplussed us. The spectators

21

were most impartial and the female portion thereof not at all unpleasant to gaze upon.

The first part of this account we naturally deplore, but must pardon; a gentleman accustomed to conditions at Wimbledon by 1900 must be allowed his standards. The last part we applaud as most gallantly said. It is the middle part, about the effects of the Americans' services, that really interests us, and it's a pity it's not complete. Let's examine what happened.

Ward served the American Twist with its swing to the forehand and kick to the backhand. Davis delivered a left-hander's American Twist, swerving to the backhand and kicking to the forehand. Whitman had a Reverse American Twist, swinging to the backhand and kicking to the forehand. Players of a later period, well accustomed to these three services, would have had no difficulty in knowing what was coming, but to the British players of 1900 it was all a complete muddle. The American Twist from Ward swung, like an English sliced service, to the forehand, so the British players would have expected its bounce to continue in the same direction. Then came Davis, an accursed left-hander, of whom there were so few about in the early days that one was not used to them and never knew what they were up to. And then there was another right-hander, only he was in reverse. Add to this the innumerable bad bounces from a grass court in poor condition—perhaps some of them even kicked a few of the baffling American Twists the wrong way, so that one couldn't be sure of anything—and you can see that the British players were, as Spencer Gore would have put it, confused pretty considerable.

True, the Americans were not serving all the

Ward, Davis, and Whitman in the 1930s

time, but if a man's service cannot be broken it becomes impossible to beat him. Apart from their services, the Americans held some other good cards in the prevailing conditions. They played their ground strokes with a lot more top-spin than their opponents did, and Davis and Ward, at least, based their game on the volley. Volleyers and topspin players do not play better on rough courts than they do on smooth, or even as well, but they are less affected by them than any baseliner whose game happens to be founded on accuracy and flat driving. Making every possible allowance for poor conditions and home-ground advantage, the best we can say for the British side is that the scores could have been closer. A fair summing-up is that the Americans were the better team, for experience shows that if one man can beat another in poor conditions he is more likely than not to beat him in good conditions. One thing, however, was certain: the American style had resoundingly defeated the English style.

The Boer War bothering them a little, the British Isles did not challenge for the Davis Cup in 1901. Instead Dwight Davis and Holcombe Ward visited Wimbledon, and we read that they "were a pair very much to be reckoned with. With their black shoes and sinister 'American' twist services, at that time unknown in England, they seemed almost to mesmerize the home players." In the challenge round of the doubles they met R.F. and Laurie Doherty. Amid great excitement Davis and Ward—or was it the American style?—won the first set, but from there on the Doherty machine was too sound and the result was not in doubt.

In 1902 the British Isles renewed their challenge for the Davis Cup, sending to America a strong team consisting of Dr J. Pim, Wimbledon champion of 1893 and 1894, R. F. Doherty, champion from 1897 to 1900, and H. L. Doherty, champion of Wimbledon for the first time only a month earlier. The United States chose Whitman, Davis, and Ward once again, but this time added William Larned, a player destined to rise to greater heights than any of his team-mates. Larned had supplanted Whitman as National champion in 1901 and was to retain his title in 1902 despite the Doherty invasion. He was again champion from 1907 to 1911, making a total of seven National championships, a record set by Sears and, since Larned, equalled only by Bill

Tilden. Larned's game, though he could volley with the best, was built on strong baseline driving. It was he who really ended the volleying reign in America, and his play set the basic pattern of American and world tennis for many years to come. Though he often varied his top-spin driving with fast and almost flat strokes, he was a typical American stylist with palm and wrist well behind the racket handle and a large change of grip for the backhand, giving him plenty of power on either wing.

With such players as Larned and Whitman in the singles and the aggressive Davis and Ward in the doubles, the match against the famous Dohertys was expected to be a battle of giants.

William A. Larned

It is thus disappointing to record that two factors intervened—selection and weather—and reduced the standard of a potentially great Davis Cup tie. The British Isles' captain chose to play Dr Pim rather than young Laurie Doherty in the singles, thus confining the appearance of at least one Doherty to the doubles match alone, which in 1902 was played on the third and last day. He may have reasoned that this tie was likely to be a rugged one, and Pim was certainly a strong and aggressive player. His method was to crush his opponent without paying the slightest attention to the type of game he played. "I don't care what he does, it's what I do that counts," Pim once said.

It may have worked at Wimbledon in 1893 and 1894, when Pim won his two championships, and probably it had on many other occasions, but it did not work in the Davis Cup singles of 1902. Pim was well beaten by both Larned and Whitman. R.F. defeated Larned, but it was a Pyrrhic victory. Play was ended by rain on the first afternoon with the Doherty-Larned match unfinished. The following morning R.F. defeated Larned after trailing him by two sets, but was then beaten setless by Whitman. The tie was over before the Wimbledom champion, Laurie Doherty, had stepped on the court. Partnering his brother in the doubles, Laurie showed what might have been; he and R.F. repeated their 1901 Wimbledon doubles win over Davis and Ward before a record crowd of some ten thousand enthusiastic spectators. And they then went on to take the 1902 U.S. National doubles title.

As for R.F.'s unfortunate two matches in one day with Larned and Whitman, it was almost the same story in the National singles championship, where it possibly cost R.F. the title. In the final of the All-Comers' singles he again met Whitman, and again his match had to be carried over to the following morning. He won, but in the intense heat of the afternoon he lost the challenge round to Larned, whom he had defeated in the Davis Cup. On the other hand, perhaps R.F. had been fortunate in his two interrupted matches—he may not have been strong enough to win either of them otherwise.

Few would dispute that in the 1902 Davis Cup the American and English styles had broken about even. From 1903 to 1906, as we know, there was no holding the Dohertys, either in England or out of it. The British Isles took the Cup from America in 1903, Laurie Doherty defeating Larned in the Cup singles and also in the challenge round of the National singles, and the brothers retaining their 1902 National doubles title. The British team retained the Cup —the competitors for which now included Belgium, France, Austria, and Australasia—for three more years until the Dohertys retired at the end of 1906. There were some rousing battles and some famous names appeared, but no team could get past the Dohertys. Perhaps this period was really a triumph for the Dohertys rather than for the English style, for when the brothers retired the American style became indisputable master.

It was not long, however, before the American style in turn had a healthy rival of its own—the Western American style (see Appendix I).

It seems that anything America can do, Californians feel sure they can do better, and the American style soon became simply the Eastern American style. Over in the Golden West they refused to be bothered with grass courts that were useless after a drop of rain. They laid down concrete courts—on which the ball bounced higher, so that more topspin was needed. The balls soon wore thin on the concrete surfaces and became lighter and more difficult to keep in court, so yet more topspin was needed. To apply this topspin—by now excessive—for the fore-

Japan's Harada

24

hand, the Californians eventually gripped their rackets behind the handle with the palm practically under it and met the ball well in front of the left hip. The change back to the backhand was then unacceptably large, so the Westerners changed in the opposite direction: moving a little beyond the forehand grip, they turned the racket head over the top and played their backhands with the same face of the racket as they used for the forehand. Like its forehand, the Western backhand grip permitted heavy topspin.

The Western grip also played a large part in introducing two types of reverse service—the Reverse Spin and the Reverse Twist. The reverse spin was relatively mild, its main effect being to swing the ball wide of an opponent's backhand; it amounted to the slice serve in reverse. The reverse twist service could be spun so viciously that the ball was often flattened to an egg shape as it hummed through the air, the bounce being a sharp kick and break to the opponent's forehand side. Both types of service were generally called reverse serves.

The effect of almost tearingly topspinning a ball with forehand, backhand, and Reverse Twist service—was to wear out its cover before its compression was softened to any degree. Thus, aside from the wear from the concrete surfaces, the more the Westerners spun the ball the more they lightened it and the more, therefore, they needed to spin it. Mercifully this cycle was ended by the greater durability of later tennis-ball covers.

The true Western American style was characterized by a forehand and backhand played with the same face of the racket, and by a reverse service. However, it is the forehand grip that basically defines a style, so that even if the reverse serve is discarded and the backhand played with the opposite face of the racket from the Western forehand, the style is still Western.

We have seen that in both of the American styles, Eastern and Western, powerful topspin driving developed. Topspin play is the most difficult for a net player to oppose; threatened with wide angles on crosscourt passing shots and with attacking topspin lobs, the net man knows little peace, for he must always give first thought to covering down-the-line passing shots. And such balls, even when they are well within reach, are far from easy to volley if they have been hit with heavy topspin.

In both East and West this onslaught ended the earlier American trend of basing the game on net attack alone. Many fine volleyers were yet to make their appearance, but groundstroke effectiveness was no longer to be discounted.

The Western style was not confined to the Pacific coast of America. It was used in Australian hardcourt tennis, where it was once known as the Hardcourt or Topspin style, and also in Japan, where it developed from the lightness of the balls used in the early days of tennis in that country. The Englishman used to take his tennis racket with him wherever he went, and all over Asia tennis was originally played in the English style, except in Japan. To this day, in Singapore for instance, the Western style is known as the Japanese style.

We shall come in due course to the two greatest exponents of the Western style—Maurice McLoughlin and William Johnston. Meanwhile two wonderful but contrasting players await us— Norman Brookes of Australia and Anthony Wilding of New Zealand, or Brookes and Wilding of Australasia.

6 | Brookes and Wilding

"You never saw Norman Brookes play?" said the old gentleman in his soft voice. "Of course you didn't. Too young. Marvellous to watch. . . . He was left-handed, and he played like a wizard. That was his nickname, too—the Wizard. Always at the net—sometimes behind that perplexing service of his that swerved and broke in all directions, and sometimes from behind a swift return—but he always seemed to be there. And try as they may, and hit as they liked, his opponents could never put the ball beyond him. He seemed to be waiting for it, and would volley it away well beyond their reach, or sometimes he would drop it over the net a fraction.

"It was before the First War that I first saw him play—1913 or 1914 I suppose it was. I can picture him as though it were yesterday. A small figure of a man. Wiry build. Thin, brown face, rather lantern-jawed, and grey tweed cap. Didn't appear to move particularly quickly, but he was always there. Marvellous anticipation. Made it look as though he were merely waiting for the ball to come to his racket.

"He used a flat-topped racket, even when the new ones had been in for years; and slacker strings, too—for his touch, no doubt. There was a keen mind behind that poker-face of his; he could tell to a fraction of a second when his opponent was going to make a certain shot, and then he would move into position to take it. And he seemed to know what was most awkward for all his opponents, and that was the sort of ball he always sent over.

"No, apart from those wonderful volleys and that unexpected service of his, I can hardly remember his strokes. There were certainly no graceful swinging forehand drives, no backhands hit with a flourish. But the service was remarkable—kicking up at his opponent one moment, and curving and slithering the next. And, by Jove, sometimes no break at all when the other fellow was expecting one, and the ball would slip straight through and almost hit him

Norman Brookes

26

in the ribs. Of course he got some very easy volleys in return; I felt I could have put half of them away myself. But on the whole his game seemed to be more the man, if you know what I mean, than his strokes.

"His grip? My dear lad, I haven't the slightest idea. I wasn't playing him, you know. I was in the stand, at least twenty yards away. It was a warm sunny day . . . rather like today . . . I remember. . . ."

People who played Brookes were left with similar impressions: awkward serve, marvellous volleying touch, uncanny anticipation, the ball coming swiftly from anywhere and everywhere, and you could scarcely say how the whole thing was done. The great Bill Tilden himself, past-master of footwork and staunch believer in free stroking, admitted that wherever he stood and whatever he did, Brookes's serve seemed to come up under one or the other of his arms, cramping his play.

Photographs show that Brookes played with an Eastern American grip, and there can be no doubt that he used little backswing and took the ball early. Never using more action than was strictly necessary, he had few off days; and being a man who didn't give anything away without good reason, he probably never missed an easy ball in his adult lifetime. His service was a bewildering mixture of left-handed American Twist, sliced and flat balls that effectively paved the way for his persistent net attack; and once ensconced at the net he was a hard man to pass and his volleying was deadly.

He volleyed with his hand an inch or so short from the end of the racket handle. His marvellous touch was attributed to this (erroneously, we now know), and for years afterwards many Australian coaches and leading players advocated a shortened grip for the volley. Early players were less governed by proven methods and were less moulded to an accepted style than more recent champions have been; they were more given to experiment. Brookes and others often played a high backhand volley or a backhand volley near the net as a special type of stroke and used a Western grip for it. This method, too, was taught by some coaches. Seeing a photograph of such a stroke—played, of course, by a man in old-fashioned clothes and wielding an odd-shaped racket—a modern player might get the false impression that early players' strokes were in general no better than this strong but awkward-looking backhand prod. On occasion Brookes also blocked ground strokes over with this back-to-front grip, but not even his closest student, Tilden, described him as a Western player.

We are told that Brookes had four different types of service delivery. Allowing for the three modern ones—kick, slice, and flat—we can only account for a fourth by assuming that a master of curve and break like Brookes would have flung in a Reverse Twist every now and then—something no modern champion would dream of doing in an important match.

A Brookes service

Brookes was not regarded by his contemporaries as a leading stroke-maker; as the old gentleman has said, it was the man behind the strokes that Brookes's opponents most respected. A shrewd tactician, he was quick to seize the initiative from the outset and to capitalize on any advantage he got. A natural player and a master strategist, he gave more consideration to his opponent's game than he did to his own.

There's no doubt that Brookes's left-handedness gave him a tremendous advantage. Nowadays when two teams meet there is a left-hander among them almost as often as not, indicating that there is one left-hander in about every dozen or so players. In Brookes's day they were rare—rare enough to suggest that most of them must have been broken from left-handedness in their tender years—that they had probably been induced to follow their parents' chosen way (a glove put on the left hand, and so forth).

Brookes was born in 1877—the year Wimbledon began—and was twenty-eight when he made his first Wimbledon attempt in 1905. Since he had already made his mark as Australia's leading player, his matches in the All-Comers' Singles were watched with keen interest. He disappointed no one, and eventually faced Laurie Doherty in the challenge round. Brookes had been so impressive in the earlier rounds that this match became regarded as H.L.'s supreme test. He met it successfully, defeating Brookes in straight sets for his fourth Wimbledon crown in succession. There were many who were not entirely satisfied with the result, for once again the challenger had almost exhausted himself in a terrific struggle in the final of the All-Comers' singles on the preceding day.

Probably Brookes's only weakness was a certain lack of stamina in long matches (during which he sometimes drank champagne) and during a series of matches. In view of his astounding durability as a champion, this lack of short-range stamina is surprising. It will be recalled that at the age of forty-three he was able to extend Tilden to the limit, and he later capped this with an even greater performance. Visiting England in 1924 on what was primarily a business trip, he again entered the Wimbledon singles —and brought the number-one court to its feet with an amazing five-set victory over the American player Francis T. Hunter. Hunter, a renowned fighter, was Tilden's favourite doubles partner, he had been the Wimbledon runner-up the previous year, and at the time the forty-seven-year-old Brookes defeated him he was rated fifth-best player in the world.

Nevertheless, in 1905 Laurie Doherty was deservedly world champion. But Brookes had yet to attain his peak. Returning to Wimbledon in 1907 a noticeably better player, he defeated Arthur Gore in the final of the All-Comers' singles and, as Doherty had retired and was no longer defending his title, automatically became champion. Although British, Brookes was the first man from outside the British Isles to win the Wimbledon singles. He was the first left-handed winner, too—and the only one of his kind until Jaroslav Drobny won in 1954.

Thus, though there was a difference of only a year in their ages, Brookes and Doherty never met when each was at his best. If it is difficult to compare two such players of the same era, how much more difficult it is to compare either of them with later champions, and how impossible to decide who was the greatest player of all time.

Anthony Wilding, as already indicated, contrasted strongly with his friend and Davis Cup teammate. A handsome man, he stood several inches over six feet and was so beautifully muscled that his physique was often copied for statuettes. He trained hard, practised hard, and would never let anyone down. His play was long-swinging, powerful, and sound. Mainly a baseliner, he hit his service almost flat, his forehand with strong topspin, and his backhand with a slight roll. He won his matches from his own power; as with Dr Pim of earlier years, it was what he did, rather than what his opponents did, that counted.

Wilding's style was certainly not that of the low-wristed classical Dohertys, nor did he hold his racket with the wrist and palm of the hand as far behind the handle for either forehand or backhand as did the American players of the period, and Brookes. His style did, however, involve a distinct change of grip between forehand and backhand, and so must be classed— though only just—as Eastern American. Similarly, his service was neither the American Twist nor the flat cannonball then being developed in America, nor did it bear any relation to the earlier curving and low-bounding slice. He hit it with the full force of his perfectly conditioned body, but used a little sidespin for control.

28

It could be noted here that even though Brookes and Wilding played in an Eastern style, each interpreted it in a widely different way from the other. Brookes's style approached Western and even contained some elements of it; Wilding's was almost English.

A wonderful sportsman and immensely popular, Wilding was a New Zealander who became captain of Cambridge University and whose life in England gave him ample opportunity for appearances at Wimbledon. Seven years Brookes's junior, he was twenty when he first entered for the Wimbledon championship in 1904. He competed again in the following four years to 1908, his most notable performance being in a second-round match in 1907 when he forced the eventual winner, Norman Brookes, to five well-contested sets. In 1906 he won the Australian championship, established only a year earlier. In 1909 he again won the Australian championship, and also the Victorian State championship, in which he defeated Brookes. Perhaps this win, over a man he considered an even greater player than the Dohertys, set the seal of confidence on him, for he returned to England to become Wimbledon champion four times running from 1910 to 1913.

Though he won the 1910 title from a field of over ninety entrants, the 1913 title was Wilding's most spectacular success.

The west coast of America had just produced its first great champion in the form of Maurice McLoughlin, a truly terrific player, colloquially known as the Californian Comet. McLoughlin played in the heavy topspin Western style, and was the first of the only two really great singles champions to have done so. He was tall and strong, and his first service was a flat "railroad" delivery and his second a vicious American Twist.* Tilden described him as a hurricane hitter and as the player who introduced the cannonball service and the modern net attack. With his shock of fiery red hair and his cheery grin, the Californian Comet was a great drawcard wherever he went. In 1912 he had taken the U.S.

*The Reverse American Twist did not last long in championship tennis as part of the Western style. Its initial advantage of being unusual gave way to its disadvantages of being both tiring and inaccurate. For a number of years players sometimes used it every now and then to surprise an opponent. This was later discontinued; used sporadically, a service is likely to miss and thus amount to a wasted delivery.

National singles crown from William Larned. At Wimbledon in 1913, having won the All-Comers' singles with his devastating service and net attack, he was favoured to take the title from Wilding and become the first non-British winner.

Standing in fearlessly against his opponent's terrific services, Tony Wilding played his greatest match, and McLoughlin did not take a set. The score was 8–6, 6–3, 10–8, and throughout the match it seemed that the courageous McLoughlin put everything he had into every point. Never had there been a more fighting loser.

The Western style had not won Wimbledon; indeed, in the whole of Wimbledon's history it has been successful in the hands of only one man

A. F. Wilding with Brookes in 1907

Maurice McLoughlin

—W. M. Johnston, the famous "Little Bill", in 1923.

McLoughlin's 1913 Wimbledon attempt was his only one, but this was due to the outbreak of the Great War and not to any fading of the Comet. Returning to the States he retained his National title; he was the main force in bringing the Davis Cup back to America in 1913, after a break of ten years; and in 1914, although the Cup was won by Australasia, the Comet beat both Brookes and Wilding, allowing them only one set between them.

The 1914 Wimbledon was an anticlimax for Wilding. A player who needed hard work, he was clearly not as fit as usual, and asked permission to play through the tournament instead of only in the challenge round. Permission was refused, and so he missed the match practice he badly needed. On the other hand, everything went well for Norman Brookes, who was appear-

ing again after an absence of seven years. He had little trouble in reaching the final of the All-Comers', where he met Otto Froitzheim, already three times champion of Germany and destined to be so twice more, the last time as late as 1925. A graceful stylist of the Doherty type, Froitzheim was a fine player with knifelike passing shots, and only after an exhausting match in which both players took a long rest before starting the fifth set did Brookes, with a mixture of doggedness, luck, champagne, and perhaps even a couple of doubtful calls, manage to win at 8–6.

An exhausted Brookes would probably have fallen easy prey to Wilding, but Brookes's luck held. Heavy rain fell and he was blessed with two days' rest. He won the challenge round in straight sets. The magnificent Wilding, champion for the last four years, was dethroned.

Even though Brookes was his friend of long standing, it must have been a bitter defeat for Wilding. Brookes had been the senior player, Wilding had replaced him and was heading for five straight Wimbledon championships and honoured retirement in the manner of Laurie Doherty, and now Brookes had returned and defeated him. Brookes's age, then thirty-seven, must have been the last drop of gall for Wilding. He took it all, however, with perfect sportsmanship and composure.

Wilding was never to have the consolation, ten years later, of seeing a forty-seven-year old Brookes topple American champion Frank Hunter. In 1915 Captain Anthony Wilding was killed in action in Flanders, and the tennis world seemed suddenly empty.

No account of Brookes and Wilding would be complete without mention of their Davis Cup partnership. Combining under the banner of Australasia, they won the Cup from 1907 to 1910, and regained it in 1914.

Summarizing this era—which the war was soon to close most effectively in any case—one recalls that the advent of the Dohertys and the vigour of the Americans had brought to the game a new concept of speed of shot and speed about the court. It is therefore with considerable interest that one reads in the *Encyclopedia Britannica* a description of the 1914 Davis Cup doubles match contested on the very eve of the war, between Brookes and Wilding of Australasia and Mc-Loughlin and T. C. Bundy of the U.S.A.: "There have perhaps been greater matches in tennis history; but few so dramatic, so grim or so spectacular. The speed of shot on both sides was tremendous. The rallies were few. It was a different game from the poised, accurate, garden-party tennis of the Dohertys. Tennis had changed as the world was changing."

Exit the Dohertys, eclipsed. Not enough power. And so it has gone on: decade by decade the champions of the day have been regarded as having more power than earlier players could have dreamt of; except in the Cochet and Crawford eras, when the moderns were thought to have become much more dextrous and flexible than their predecessors.

We should not decry progress, but we can hardly blame an older player when, with tongue prominently in cheek, he observes: "Oh yes, that was the trouble with us old-timers—if we weren't as weak as water, we were as clumsy as cart-horses."

7 | Australian Scene

THERE had been some good players in Australia besides Brookes and Wilding. Official tournaments had begun with the Victorian and New South Wales championships in 1880 and 1885 respectively, and tennis was not so new to the country as the date of the first Australian championships, 1905, might suggest.

Many well-known names, such as Alf Dunlop (originally from New Zealand), Drs Poidevin and Sharp, Rodney Heath, Horace Rice, A. B. Jones, and S. N. Doust appear in the lists of the Davis Cup and the Australian or State championships. Of all these players, the left-handed Horrie Rice, small, stocky, ebullient, and wearing distinctive white knickerbockers and long black socks—is perhaps best remembered. With a heavily sliced service and a rocklike backhand (unusual for a left-hander, but developed from his boyhood sport of singlesticks fencing), Horrie Rice won championships from the 1890s to the mid-1920s, from New Zealand to Scotland. There are many tales associated with his name and long career. It was said that no one could be sure that a point against him was won until the ball had bounced at least three times. He won the Queensland State singles in 1901, 1911, 1912, and again in 1922. After his last win an enthusiastic senior citizen slapped Horrie's back and said: "That's the stuff, son. Following in Dad's footsteps. I can remember the day old Horrie won this twenty-one years ago." Rice played his first interstate match for New South Wales in 1894 when he was twenty-two, his first Davis Cup match in 1911 at thirty-nine, and his last interstate match in 1925 at fifty-three.

Fine players though some of these early Australians were, there was yet only one Norman Brookes. Rice said that he always enjoyed playing Brookes: "He makes the game extremely restful, by playing so many shots right out of reach."

But even a man as durable as Brookes must come to the end of his road. Although he be-longed essentially to the pre-war period, for the good of the game he reappeared as soon as tennis restarted in 1919, in which year he defended his Wimbledon title (unsuccessfully), won the United States doubles title, and represented Australasia in a winning Davis Cup team. He again played Davis Cup in 1920 and, though not called upon to play, was in the team of 1924.

After Brookes, four other great Australian players came to the fore—Patterson, Anderson, O'Hara Wood, and Hawkes. But before describing these players we should look at the style of play that had developed in Australia by the early 1920s.

There were two parallel developments—grass-court and hardcourt, the surfaces of the latter being determined mainly by local availability of materials. Grass and hardcourt competitions

Horrie Rice

were conducted separately, and two different styles evolved—driving on grass, and cutting, slicing and chopping on hard surfaces. There was, however, this much similarity between the two styles—the forehand was the dominant stroke, and though there were a number of volleyers about, the singles game was by and large founded on ground strokes. Among the champions, one backhand player stands out—"Sos" Wertheim, a big personality in Australian tennis in the 1920s and a Davis Cup representative in 1922.

Australian grasscourts give a somewhat higher bounce than those of England, so it is not surprising that Australians played in the Eastern American style rather than the English, and drove the ball with plenty of topspin. A large change of grip was made for the backhand, orthodox form being to advance the thumb along the back of the handle for support. Because the balls retained their weight (on grasscourts, whatever weight is knocked off the cover of the balls is more than compensated for by moisture and green smudges from the grass), the 1920s grasscourt players based their game on solid driving.

The hardcourts—loam, antbed, gravel, asphalt—lived up to their name. They were hard on the feet and hard on the less durable tennis balls of the time. To control the rapidly lightening balls, most hardcourt players used some degree of underspin. The backhand was largely defensive, and players ran round it far more often than they do today. Some were most adept at this—as witness one young man's experience when opposing such a player. Asked the score by a newly arrived supporter, he replied that he was love-four down. "Well, for Heaven's sake, play his backhand." "I can't. This chap hasn't got a blasted backhand."

There were also some hardcourt players who employed the Western American style, called in Australia the Topspin style. Thrashing the ball with reverse-twist services and heavily topspun drives on both wings, they were awkward players to handle on their day. But a heavy Topspin style is also heavily demanding on its user. Its action is up-and-over rather than in line with the intended path of the ball, and any loss of confidence leads to erratic play. On their off days some Topspin players would recklessly hit their way to defeat; others would forgo their driving game and resort to safer cut strokes.

The courts of grasscourt clubs were well watered and well grown, and there was a good sprinkling of private grasscourts, often tree-shaded. By contrast, the criterion of a good hardcourt seemed to be sheer hardness, and heavy rolling was probably the main element in its preparation. The later concept of fast grasscourts and slow, soft "hardcourts" would have sounded incomprehensible to Australian players of earlier days.*

Styles and methods being less stereotyped than they are today, it comes as no surprise to find four different types of player in Patterson, Anderson, O'Hara Wood, and Hawkes, even though all of them could be grouped as Eastern American.

To many of his legion of admirers, Gerald Patterson, born in 1895, was of heroic stature. A big man, strong of jaw and shoulder, he had a grand fighting temperament and his manner and game were formidable. Winner of a Military Cross in the Great War, he was a popular and impressive winner of the first Wimbledon to be held after it, in 1919—a win he repeated in 1922. He won the Australian championship (played in a different State each year) only once, in 1927, but the singles championships of his own State, Victoria, became virtually a Patterson preserve; in the nine years from 1919 to 1927 he won it no fewer than eight times before being overtaken by time and a young Jack Crawford. The missing year was 1925, when Patterson was trying to popularize a steel-framed racket with wire strings. His failure was presumably disastrous for the racket's sales, but it had its happier side, for the winner that year was one R. E. Schlesinger. Modest, popular, and a fine sportsman, Schlesinger, a Davis Cup player in 1923 and 1924, was so well known throughout the 1920s that one is amazed to find that he won the Victorian singles championship only once.

Patterson had a pile-driving smash that Sir Norman Brookes, as late as 1956, considered the greatest tennis had seen. But while a smash, like a rook or castle in chess, has great potential, it is

*We find a similar thought in Norman Brookes's mind during his 1914 quest for the Wimbledon singles. He played as many tournaments as possible on hardcourts in the south of France rather than on the average grasscourt, "finding them a good medium for speed in preparation for the swift and true Wimbledon turf".

33

often out of the game for much of the play. It is for his thundering service that Gerald Patterson is best remembered. On other courts of world renown an outstanding display of serving is sometimes accorded the honour of being among the best ever seen; at Kooyong its highest praise can only be that it is the best since Gerald Patterson's.

Patterson's service action, described as perfect, was based on the American Twist. For the first service he threw the ball straight up above his head and hit it with great strength from his muscular back and shoulders, sometimes as a flat cannonball, but mostly with a little controlling topspin. Action-strip photographs show that in making full use of his height of almost six feet he reached higher with his right shoulder than other players as he pounded the ball over at full power. With excellent control of curve and placement, his acing became legendary.

His second service was the American Twist.

Throwing the ball up between head and left shoulder, bending his knees, arching his back, and taking the racket head round in a deep swing below his back, he struck upwards, delivering severely with speed and kick.

Since his game was based on service and net attack, Patterson's volleying, as would be expected, was powerful. Just how powerful was once demonstrated in a doubles match when he partnered Hawkes against Borotra and Lacoste during Australia's 1925 Davis Cup tie with France. Intercepting a service return from Lacoste, Patterson unintentionally volleyed the ball onto Borotra's temple with such force that the Bounding Basque was knocked unconscious. Thinking that the inert Borotra might be up to another of his pranks that delighted crowds and broke his opponent's concentration, Patterson leant over the net and prodded him with his racket. But there was no fooling this time: Borotra was out.

Borotra knocked unconscious

Patterson's forehand, though on occasion he made generous use of chopped strokes, was strong and well produced in the Eastern style. His Achilles' heel was his backhand. Harry Hopman has said that Patterson had two backhands, a defensive one that was heavily undersliced and an attacking one made with swishing topspin and played in the Western style with the same face of the racket as the forehand. Once, playing on the Wimbledon centre court in a doubles match with Jack Hawkes in 1928, Patterson struck upwards for an intended Western looping backhand winner, mistimed it, and hit the ball with the top side-frame of his racket; it went clean over the centre court stand.

Hopman's remarks were made in recollection, not analysis. A critic like Tilden would have said that Patterson was master of neither type of backhand; a lover of tennis and its strokes, and at times highly dramatic in his phraseology, Tilden regarded Patterson's backhand as the tennis tragedy of the 1920s.

Patterson was never able to overcome the two technical weaknesses—faulty footwork and cramped swing—that beset him on this stroke. He did, however, cover his weakness to some extent by playing from the net as much as possible. At times he seemed to employ force of character more than anything else; when his back was to the wall he scorned weakness and let fly with his Western backhand, sometimes turning defeat into victory with one stroke. He was a great singles player and, because of the cover available for his backhand, an even greater doubles player. Here, with wonderful support from each of his two famous left-court partners, Pat O'Hara Wood and Jack Hawkes, he achieved spectacular success.

Gerald Patterson

Anderson, always J.O. and never James, was taller again than Patterson. If Patterson suggested a mastiff, J.O.—long, lean, and spare—was clearly a greyhound. His service was only fair—lacking in wrist snap, his first delivery was fast mainly because he was tall enough to hit it flat—and his backhand was often defensive; but with a forehand drive like the crack of a stockwhip his game never lacked speed. It was difficult for any of his opponents to shut his forehand out of the game, and against most of them he seemed to have it constantly in play. His forehand grip was what may be called an extreme Eastern (see Appendix I). Unlike most players who use such a grip, however, he did not base his drive on topspin but was a master of the flat, rising-ball stroke. His most devastating shot was made from shoulder height, and a kicking service he could take on the forehand was his favourite meat and drink.

The extreme Eastern grip, though it allows great forehand power, leads to difficulties with the backhand, the change for an adequate backhand grip being larger than that required by any other type of forehand grip. If this large change is not made, the backhand is likely to be weak,

35

J. O. Anderson

particularly against high balls; if it is made, the process is often too slow against fast services, especially if the player likes to stand in and make his forehand service returns on the rise. Anderson avoided both these pitfalls by using a Western backhand.

The Western backhand has disadvantages against balls that get behind the player and those that are wide or low. Anderson was a confirmed baseliner in singles, so not many balls got behind him; as for the wide ones, at least he was tall and had a long reach. True, his arch-enemy, Patterson, and others as well, sliced or chopped many low-bouncing balls at his backhand, but all told, Anderson was secure enough and his backhand could stand up to strong serving, Patterson's included.

Anderson played tennis seriously and gave his opponents little quarter. Having sound ground strokes, exceptionally powerful on the forehand, he saw no need to leave the baseline. If an opponent also preferred the baseline, Anderson

overpowered him with crushing drives; if he preferred the net, Anderson took grim pleasure in cleanly passing him or in almost drilling clean through him. The tall frame, the long arm with the racket held straight in line, and the determined mind all combined to allow Anderson to hit the ball very hard. In later years, Anderson used to call his successors a lot of ball-pushers.

Clashes between Patterson and Anderson were always electric. Powerful services were met as often as not with stinging returns. Patterson had a fine forehand, but Anderson's was greater. Anderson had a sounder backhand, but Patterson had a greater variety of strokes and played an all-court game. Patterson was tigerish; Anderson was a cold player who refused to give an inch. It was said that the two men had little in common and did not particularly care for each other. To Victorians there was only one Gerald Patterson; New South Welshmen, though prepared to grant Patterson everything, maintained that J.O. was the better singles player.

Anderson won the Australian singles championship three times—in 1922, 1924, and 1925. He won the New South Wales singles in 1914 (the year Patterson began his triumphs by winning the Victorian, New South Wales, and Australian doubles championships, all with A. Campbell) and again in 1919 and 1923. He did not win the Wimbledon singles, though he won the doubles in 1922; nor did he ever take the Victorian singles crown from Patterson. J.O.'s tournament wins (particularly those over Patterson) must have pleased him greatly, but he has said that his greatest satisfaction came in the 1922 and 1923 Davis Cup matches in which he forced Tilden to five sets and defeated Johnson —feats no other Australian performed against these players.

World ranking lists for the seven years from 1919 to 1925 favour Patterson as the better player. He was unranked once and was placed higher than Anderson twice. Anderson was unranked three times and was placed higher than Patterson once. At Wimbledon in 1922 Patterson, en route to his championship, defeated Anderson in five rousing sets, but Anderson and R. Lycett (Great Britain) won the doubles final from Patterson and O'Hara Wood at 11–9 in the fifth set.

Between them from 1919 to 1928 these two protagonists represented Australasia and Australia in the Davis Cup eleven times. In the Sydney harbourside suburb of Double Bay is the spot where the 1919 Patterson and Anderson Davis Cup was played and won.* It is built upon now, and two main streets cross it; at their intersection are signs reading "Patterson Street" and "Anderson Street".

Pat O'Hara Wood, (younger brother of Alf O'Hara Wood, Australian champion in 1914) was short and springy, with tanned face and light hair. Of firm character, he was not to be taken lightly by anyone—but O'Hara Wood was a lilting name and it does seem that all the world loves a man called Pat. He was the top Australian and world stylist—in the Eastern American style that dominated the early 1920s. His strokes were smooth and his footwork impeccable.

Orthodoxy in the Eastern American style has varied from the twenties to the present time. Nowadays the standard Eastern forehand grip is probably that which places the thumb and forefinger "V" directly on the centre of the top surface of the racket handle, the backhand grip being about an eighth of a circle, or forty-five degrees, anti-clockwise from it. A somewhat circular backswing is acceptable for the forehand (some purists say it should be straight), but for the backhand at least, a straight backswing is recognized form. For both forehand and backhand the racket head does not go much behind the line of the shoulders for the backswing, and the end of the follow-through is intended to be approximately in the direction of the ball's flight, thus carrying the racket across the line of flight as little as possible. The whole accent of today's style is on balance, mobility, and preparedness for the next shot.

In the 1920s the Eastern style, while not neglecting balance, was essentially directed at achieving power. Most players used a forehand grip a little farther round, or behind, the handle —which placed the "V" somewhat to the right of centre. For the backhand the thumb went up the back of the handle as the player changed grip a good ninety degrees, anything less being regarded as shirking the issue. For the forehand swing (and here we are speaking of champions'

usage, not what was taught to beginners) the racket was taken back in a full circular swing well behind the back and, with the wrist and racket head laid back as far as possible, the ball was met in front of the left hip and at full arm's length. The follow-through was not checked, it being considered a fine feature if the racket head wrapped itself around the neck. For the backhand, a circular swing to build up maximum power was correct form. For both forehand and backhand a wide stance, with front leg well advanced, was advocated, and definite topspin was applied for control. All told, a champion was not there to pat the ball, he was there to hit it.

O'Hara Wood did all this with almost perfect smoothness and neatness. His foot placement was meticulous; if he were ever in danger of arriving with the wrong foot outstretched for a wide ball he made a short change of step and brought the correct foot to earth before the stroke was made. Mechanical? Never.

A sound stroke-maker, O'Hara Wood kept his racket in line with the ball and in contact with it for as long as possible. He had few off

Pat O'Hara Wood

*Brookes—though he played in the doubles with Patterson and allowed his opponents only two games in three sets—would hardly mind our handing the palm to the two younger singles players.

days, and was rarely beaten by an inferior player. His lack of height precluding a flat service, his delivery was based on the American Twist, with variations of twist and pace.

O'Hara Wood won the Australian singles in 1920 and 1923, and the doubles four times between 1919 and 1925. At Wimbledon in 1919 he won the doubles title with R. V. Thomas of South Australia, and in 1922 the mixed doubles with Suzanne Lenglen (he was also runner-up with Patterson in the men's doubles). In Australian Davis Cup teams he was third string to Brookes and Patterson in 1920, mainly a doubles player (with Patterson) in 1922, and in 1924 he and Patterson were a two-man team. World famous in his own right as a player and stylist, he is perhaps best remembered by men of his own generation as the wonderfully sound left-court partner of Gerald Patterson.

Patterson's other famous left-court partner, Jack Hawkes, was also a Victorian. Of medium height, trimly built, and fair skinned, he too swung his racket freely, but if Brookes and others had been awkward left-handers to handle, Hawkes, like a left-handed knight of old, should have been branded with the Bar Sinister. His shots seemed to come from anywhere and go everywhere, and some of his opponents protested that Hawkes surely had no more idea of where the ball was going than they had. As a middle-aged Victorian interstate player of the period once put it: "... absolutely square-on to the net, more often than not. Hasn't got a decent shot in his locker. He's got a curving and kicking Twist serve that is good; it needs to be—he finishes it with his head behind his back and until he's run in several paces he doesn't even see the ball!"

Hawkes was most unpredictable, but this was no doubt exaggerated by the scarcity of left-handers in his time. He had yet another un-

J. B. Hawkes

expected trait: though unpredictable, his strokes were unusually safe. He was a fine sportsman and a popular player, and a great volleyer with outstandingly quick reflexes. He won the Australian singles in 1926 (between Anderson and Patterson wins), the doubles, with Patterson, three times, and the Victorian doubles, again with Patterson, five times. At Wimbledon in 1925 he and Patterson were runners-up in the doubles. In the Davis Cup he alternated with O'Hara Wood, Wood playing in 1920, 1922, and 1924, Hawkes in 1921, 1923, and 1925. There seems little doubt that the greatest doubles match Australians in the 1920s could have wished to see would have been Patterson and O'Hara Wood versus Patterson and Hawkes.

There were other fine players about in all States of the Australia of the 1920s. R. H. Gemmell, of West Australia, with his powerful Western-style topspin driving won the Australian singles and doubles championship in 1921 and his own State title six times. R. V. Thomas, of South Australia, New South Welshmen Norman Peach, C. V. Todd, and country champion Fred Kalms, and Victorians "Sos" Wertheim, Bob Schlesinger, and Ian McInnes, all played in Davis Cup teams. Little below them were Les Baker of New South Wales, R. O. Cummings of Queensland, E. T. Rowe and the six-foot-four Gar Hone of South Australia, while J. L. McGough, Bill Sheehan, Pic and Tommy Newton, and V. E. Page, of Tasmania, made names for themselves in the island State. From these ranks emerged Davis Cup players of the early 1930s, Jim Willard, Gar Moon, Jack Clemenger, and Cliff Sproule, Australian doubles champions Ray Dunlop and Charlie Donohoe, and Tasmania's outstanding Alan Knight. Finally, it was from among the players of the 1920s that two of Australia's most famous players, Jack Crawford and Harry Hopman, received their baptism of fire as rising juniors.

The play was powerful. Rackets were of modern design and tightly strung with fine gut for grasscourt championship play, and the players —it was before the days of national tennis popularity—were generally adult.

Australia also had its tennis sweetheart in the attractive person of Daphne Akhurst, who was five times woman champion of Australia between 1925 and 1930, and whose photograph still hangs

near the staircase in Sydney's White City clubhouse.

Over the whole scene presided the spare, austere figure of Norman Brookes as president of the Lawn Tennis Association of Australia, and sometimes even as sole Davis Cup selector. From time to time throughout his presidency of the L.T.A.A. from 1926 to 1955, Sir Norman (as he became in 1939) was referred to by the Press as a despot. In fact, however, Australian

Daphne Akhurst

tennis was being guided by a man of high integrity who had more experience of championship play than any of those whose destinies he was directing.

Patterson and Anderson, O'Hara Wood and Hawkes, strong reserve players, coming champions, and a world-minded L.T.A.A.—yet between the 1919 Davis Cup challenge round (played at Double Bay in January 1920) and the 1930s, not one challenge-round win graced the records of Australian tennis. Patterson and the rest had the misfortune to run into the greatest Davis Cup years of both America and France—the period of America's Tilden and Johnston, and of France's romantic "Four Musketeers".

8 | Grand Master and Company

AMERICA produced many of her greatest names in sport in the 1920s—Babe Ruth in baseball, Bobby Jones in golf, Jack Dempsey in boxing. Lawn tennis, for its part, offered two Bills, Big Bill Tilden from the east coast and Little Bill Johnston from the West.

America's tennis of the 1920s resembled Australia's in that among a large number of very good players four were outstanding. These were the two Bills, Vincent Richards, and R. N. Williams, and as a Davis Cup team they make an interesting comparison with their Australian contemporaries.

Tilden, like Patterson, played singles and doubles; Johnston, like Anderson, was chosen mostly to play singles. Richards and Williams took turns in partnering Tilden, as O'Hara Wood and Hawkes did with Patterson; and in one year, 1924, Richards was chosen as a singles player too, as O'Hara Wood and Hawkes had been. Unlike O'Hara Wood and Hawkes, however, Richards and Williams also joined forces, playing doubles matches for the United States in 1925 and 1926.

No team containing Tilden, Johnston, and either Richards or Williams was even beaten, and one combination or another of these players won the Davis Cup for the United States from 1920 to 1926—a stretch of dominance which, despite Australia's long list of successes since World War II, has never been equalled.

R. Norris Williams—"Dick" to his many friends—was a type of player who could only have existed in the period of the Great War and the roaring twenties (he was, incidentally, a survivor of the *Titanic* disaster). He sometimes based his game on daring alone, standing in close against any type of play—even against Patterson's service—taking the ball well on the rise and hitting hard for the lines. He was often pigheaded in his use of these dangerous tactics and of course went through patches of both purple and the deepest grey. Once, in a match against

Tilden, he won one set to love with the loss of only three points, lost the next in no more than eight minutes, and later, from a commanding lead of 4–1 in the fifth, lost the match in a deluge of errors.

"Why do you do it?" asked Tilden. "Why not have some safety margin?"

R. N. Williams

"Once in a while I get my great day," Williams replied. "I'd rather have one great day than sacrifice it to safety."

Tilden admired Williams's spirit, but deplored his attitude—particularly, one feels, because Williams's footwork on the forehand side was unsound and because Tilden was a man of uncompromising views on tennis, and especially on foot placement. Williams stood rather square-on to the net for his forehand, and from such a stance tended to hit across the ball instead of straight through it for as long as possible. To play the basic shot of tennis in unsound fashion and then to stand right in on the ball and try to skin the net and hit the lines. . . . Tilden could only shake his head sorrowfully whenever his friend Dick aspired to one of his great days.

It would be reasonable to expect that Williams had a short championship life and a gay one. But his tennis life was long, its foundation being accuracy rather than great-day tactics. In 1913, at the age of twenty-two, he was a Davis Cup player, and he was still representing his country thirteen years later in 1926. He played in six Davis Cup teams in all, five of which were winning ones, the losing year being 1914, when Brookes and Wilding triumphed. In tournament play he won the U S. singles in 1914 and 1916, and the doubles, with Richards, in 1925 and 1926.

Vincent Richards was born in 1903. Twelve years younger than Dick Williams, ten years younger than Tilden, and nine years younger than Johnston, he was very much the shining youth of American tennis—and not only in relation to his team-mates, either, for he was indeed a prodigy. At the age of sixteen he defeated Tilden to become the 1919 American Indoor Champion—a title he won again in 1923 and 1924. A cheerful looking fellow with a mind of his own, he was once described by the downright Tilden as "a youngster with a grin like Skippy and a confidence like Mussolini".

Both Tilden, in 1927, and Sir Norman Brookes, in 1954, had no hesitation in calling Vincent Richards the finest volleyer of all time. In the 1960s, after two decades of Big Game serve-and-volley tennis, this judgment might sound provocative. We can point to taller players who must have had a greater reach than Richards, and to better-trained champions who must have been

stronger than Richards in any fifth set and whose reflexes were probably at least as quick. We also know that many later players have volleyed more aggressively than Richards. But since we shall never be able to resolve the matter, let us instead regard volleying as meaning the volleying strokes themselves; then, for low or defensive volleys at least, we can accept the opinion of two of tennis's shrewdest judges that Richards's volleying was masterly by the standard of any period. At all events it was impressive enough to make Tilden —high priest of the Eastern American style— recognize that there was, after all, some use for the outmoded English grip. Richards volleyed with his wrist low in the English style, and Tilden came to write that the Eastern style could—and, later again, that it should—include volleying made with the English or Continental grip.

Richards founded his game on his service, on his magnificent volleying and half-volleying, and on his confidence. When Tilden begged him to take six months or a year off from tournaments and learn some decent driving (and stand sideways to the net while he was at it), Richards replied that he preferred to win now rather than worry about the future.

The future did not take care of Vincent Richards. Prodigy and doubles champion though he was, the ground strokes of Johnston, Tilden,

Vincent Richards

42

Lacoste, and Cochet were to prove too good for him and he was not rewarded with the singles championship of America, England, or France. At twenty-three he turned to professional tennis.

"Little Bill" Johnston was loved as much as he was respected—and the respect in which he was held was enormous. Perhaps his greatest admirer was Tilden. Granting Johnston the finest forehand he had ever seen, Tilden wrote that until the courtly Baron Gottfried von Cramm appeared in the top rank Johnston stood out as the game's greatest sportsman and that even von Cramm, sportsman *par excellence*, could but equal him.

Johnston weighed only about 130 pounds, but in forehand and volley he had a merciless attack, and was always ready to play till he dropped. He attained astounding power from his forehand despite his small build and the heavy topspin he often employed; holding his racket with a Western grip, he gained flowing momentum from an exceptionally large swing and full body rotation backed by wonderful timing and weight control. He lifted the racket above his head, took it well round behind his back, rotated his hips, swung forward and round with the somewhat bent elbow induced by a Western grip, and in his follow-through carried the racket right round his neck. It was the most circular path ever travelled by a tennis racket in the forehand drive of a champion.*

Unlike most players with an exceptionally powerful forehand drive, Johnston constantly sought the net, where his high volleying was homicidal. His backhand, also Western, was not of the tearing topspin variety but was essentially sound. Similarly, his service, though not particularly well produced for a champion, was sound rather than attacking. It was basically a slice, and he used it mainly to obtain depth, relying on his forehand to clear the way for a net attack.

He first came to fame with a National singles over McLoughlin in 1915. He won the National doubles, with C. J. Griffin in 1915, and again in 1920, and regained the singles title in 1919 by defeating Tilden. It was this match, in which Tilden's backhand was badly mauled, that made him retire from tournament play for six months

*Johnston also took a long grip on the handle. When playing well, he liked nothing better than "to feel the leather in his palm".

(hence his later advice to young Vincent Richards) to perfect a rolled backhand sound enough to pass Johnston's net attack. At Wimbledon in 1923 Johnston crushed all opposition, losing only one set and winning the final 6–0, 6–3, 6–1. However, world ranking lists, which omit the years 1915–18, show that except for 1924, when he was ranked fourth, Johnston was in second position from 1919 to 1925. It was his fate to play in the Tilden era.

It is arguable whether the two Bills in their heyday were better known for their unequalled run of Davis Cup successes or for their Homeric meetings in the National singles, which they contested no less than six times. Records show Tilden to have been the winner of the last five encounters, and this could give the impression that Johnston was regarded as number-two in America and that the outcome of each successive

Bill Johnston's Western forehand

final was taken for granted. On the contrary, Johnston was favoured to win on several occasions, partisanship for him ran high, and although the Wimbledon championship was a more international affair, the Tilden–Johnston National finals were recognized as providing the greatest tennis to be seen anywhere in the world. Though they held each other in high regard, neither Bill showed any Renshaw or Doherty reluctance. There is little doubt that Tilden's finest tennis was played against Johnston, and that Johnston was capable of forcing him to play it. In Tilden's own words, every time he met Johnston it was a knock-down, drag-out battle, for each knew that nothing but his best could win. Typical of this was their 1922 meeting, perhaps their greatest match. Both had won the U.S. National singles challenge cup twice, and now it was to become the personal property of the man who won it. A famous trophy, it bore the names of such men as William Larned, Maurice McLoughlin, R. N. Williams, and R. L. Murray (the 1918 winner) besides those of Johnston and Tilden. Johnston, who wanted it more than any trophy in the world, planned to retire if he won it. Tilden, the winner for the last two years, also wanted it with his heart and soul.

It was always Johnston's plan to overwhelm his opponents before the effects of his demanding game could cause his strength to run out. Tilden's strategy against Johnston was to weather the opening storm and to rely on his greater stamina and all-round stroke equipment to bring him victory; nevertheless, he had not the slightest intention of yielding the opening sets easily, if at all. Both men were in great form from the start, but do what he might, Tilden could not withstand Johnston's attack; the first two sets went to Johnston, 6–3, 6–4. Tilden got an early break in the third set, and Johnston let it go, saving his energies for the next. He came back like a tiger after the rest period, and went to a commanding lead of 3–0. Then two incidents occurred, both of them inspired by Johnston's supporters, and, ironically, neither of them helping his cause.

As Tilden was changing ends to serve at 0–3, a senior official with whom he had been at odds observed to him that it had been a good match. According to Tilden, the loathed official made his remark with a cold smile and emphasized the word "been". In a rage, Tilden walked out to serve swearing to himself that he would win the match if he died doing it. Johnston, however, was in such a fine lode of play that he forced the score to thirty-forty and held game point for a 4–0 lead with his own service to follow. Taking the net, he smashed a ball at Tilden's feet for an apparent winner—only to be beaten by a miraculous backhand half-volley lob that scraped over the edge of his groping racket and landed in court. There is no way of knowing if this amazing shot in itself demoralized Johnston, but the incident that followed it certainly did. An overwrought spectator suffered an attack of near-hysterics and yelled a string of remarks such as "He didn't make it! I tell you Tilden didn't make it! No man ever made that shot! He's a liar!" until he was either placated or led away. This badly upset Johnston, and acted as yet another spur to Tilden's determination. Tilden won the next six games and the set.

Such was the change of fortune that Tilden established a 4–1 lead in the fifth. Johnston, almost on the point of collapse, forced his way to 4–5, but it was his dying effort. Tilden held the last game for the match.

Later, showered, changed, and ready to leave the courts, Tilden looked in on Johnston at his locker. Too weary to change, Little Bill was sitting on a bench, still in his tennis clothes.

"I was lucky to win, Bill," said Tilden.

"No, you weren't," Johnston replied. "I played the best tennis of my life today and you beat it; you deserved to win." He held out his hand. "Look out for me next year, you big stiff," he said.

Such was Little Bill, and such, too, was the pattern of matches between the two rivals. For most followers of tennis the eventual and reluctant verdict was that a good big man always beat a good little man, that a tall man with long legs needs to run less, and so, at the end of a long match, his stamina will be superior.

But there was more to it than that. Even if you disregard Tilden's natural advantages, what his five successive victories over Johnston really demonstrated was the superiority of the Eastern style over the Western. It was mostly Johnston's Western style, with its restricted reach and exacting topspin action, that tired him out. Tilden was well aware of this, and part of his strategy of weathering the Johnston storm included the tactic of playing as much as he dared to Little Bill's fierce but tiring forehand to drain his energy. Another Tilden tactic was to slice the ball to this forehand, with the double purpose of keeping its bounce low and of giving Johnston no prior topspin to bite into. Against an under-spun ball a topspin player must use more spin of his own making to achieve the same degree of control—and this, again, can be exacting.

In Australia the Western is generally regarded as an ugly style.* Hearing that Little Bill Johnston's forehand drive—complicated and often heavily topspun—was once described as the poetry of motion, one can't help thinking that tennis followers of the 1920s could not have understood the game too well. But this is clearly impossible to justify; we must instead pay tribute to Johnston's marvellous timing and weight control for creating such a pleasing overall effect.

It was the end of an era. The crashing Western style, as far as championship singles is concerned, was brought to fame by the colourful McLoughlin and died in virtually the same generation with the unassuming Johnston. It has, however, been used by Americans whose names became famous as doubles players—Harold Hackett, Davis Cup player of 1908 and 1909 and winner of the National doubles title with F. B. Alexander from 1907 to 1910; the Kinsey brothers, Robert and Howard, winners of the National doubles in 1924, who used the Western style in its most exaggerated and looped form; and later, George Lott, a masterly doubles player who used it with rare touch and finesse, and who represented the U.S.A. from 1928 to 1934 (during which time he also won seven National and Wimbledon doubles titles—three with Lester Stoefen, two with John Doeg, and one each with John Hennessy and John Van Ryn). Probably the nearest forehand users of the genuine Western style in the more recent years of the 1950s have been Gardnar Mulloy and Victor Seixas, though both of them played Eastern-type backhands

*Not always, though. Dr L. O. S. Poidevin, playing Davis Cup for Australia in 1906, used a Western grip and played forehand and backhand with the same face of the racket, his grip becoming known, in Sydney at least, as the Poidevin grip. About twenty-five years later his son, another L. O. S. Poidevin and later a doctor, won the New South Wales Schoolboys' Championship using the same grip. The younger Poidevin, presumably in the same style as his father, hit his shots flat and cleanly from a short swing and was a most attractive stroke-maker.

George Lott: Western player, though this fore-hand volley is Eastern

using the opposite side of the racket face.

California has since provided America and the world with many champions, but though they have been Westerners geographically, they have not been Western stylists. Most books of tennis instruction now mention the Western merely for the sake of completeness, and one reads such obituary-like references to it as "The Western grip was last used with success by W. M. ('Little Bill') Johnston of California, U.S.A., who was

John Doeg

a world champion in the 1920s. It is now of academic interest only."

Exit the colourful Western, and enter—for the first time in his own right—William Tatem Tilden, tennis colossus. Lean, 6 feet 2 inches tall, with high-set shoulders, "Big Bill" was a flamboyant showman. He dramatized or burlesqued his way through many a match, and his long, loose and furry sweaters gained him the subsidiary nickname of "The Grizzly". Dynamic and uncompromising, he tried to dominate everyone in the game, even if mostly for their own good. As a result, he feuded almost constantly with U.S. lawn tennis officials and was not popular on his own courts. With his high intelligence and his sardonic humour, he could be a strong friend or a stern enemy.

Tennis has always been an art, but to Tilden it became a theoretical science as well. There was no stroke in the game, and scarcely an aspect of any stroke, that he did not analyse, practise, and master—though at times his contemporaries wondered whether the main result of this mastery was his use of it in match play or his verbal justification of the many theories he developed on practically everything to do with the game. But despite his remarkable and overpowering personality both this and his theorizing have faded in the glow of his deeds on the court. Born in 1893, he was ranked first in the world from 1920 to 1925, and as late as 1930 was still ranked second only to Cochet. He did not lose a Davis Cup singles for six years. He won the U.S. National singles seven times and Wimbledon three times; his first Wimbledon win, in 1920, made him the first non-British winner, even though giants like Larned, Beals Wright, and McLoughlin had competed before him, and his last, ten years later, came when he was thirty-seven. In all, counting singles, doubles, and mixed doubles in America and abroad, Tilden won the almost incredible number of sixty-five national championships.

Bill Tilden was only six years old when he happened to see his brother's tennis racket lying about unguarded. It was an old Pim, heavy and thick-handled, discarded by the thirteen-year-old elder Tilden who had gone off to play with his brand-new Hackett and Alexander. Young Bill took it, and began his lifelong and never-to-be-satisfied desire to know everything there was to be known about the game of tennis.

At the age of seven he won his first cup, in a tournament for boys under ten years. Details of the final match are not altogether surprising. Tilden defeated a "hated rival" 6–0, 0–6, 19–17. For the next few years, as he himself confesses, he was a swollen-headed player who hit the ball far too hard for control. It was not until he was twenty that he gained any prominence; this was in 1913, when he partnered Miss Mary K. Browne in the National mixed doubles championship. In the mellowness of later years Tilden admitted that in every round including the final Miss Browne overcame all efforts made by the other three players on the court to deprive her of victory.

The 1914–18 war did not halt tennis in the United States to the same extent as it did in other countries; nor did Tilden's army service prevent him from competing in a number of tournaments. Although in 1918 he was runner-up to R. L. Murray in the U.S. National singles and won the doubles with a sixteen-year-old Vincent Richards, his play was not outstanding and he gave few glimpses of the world champion he was soon to become. In these years he was striving to build up an all-court, all-stroke game, one of his theories being that such a game must overcome all others.

He met with discouragement on all sides. Some players conceded that there was nothing wrong with an all-court game, but insisted that the all-stroke concept was ridiculous—that Tilden should be satisfied to develop a few good strokes and to build varying tactics around them. Others maintained that the all-court game itself was suspect—that more often than not it was only a compromise, not an improvement on a game that was either volleying or essentially baseline. The more forthright of Tilden's friends told him plainly that he was a darn fool to be frittering away his tennis gifts and that he would end up with scarcely a shot to call his own.

But Tilden's imagination was fired. If a service could be mastered flat, topspun or sliced, then why not every other stroke as well? And why not "all-speed" as well? Disdaining even to run before he could walk, Tilden was a young man who preferred to bolt; in his early days he played beyond his powers and took many defeats for his pains. It was typical of him, for example, to regard his heavy defeat by Johnston in the final of the U S. National singles in 1919 as supporting his theories rather than contradicting them. Others might decide that Johnston's slaughter of Tilden's backhand showed that Tilden's experiments had left him with nothing; Tilden decided that all he needed was one more shot—a powerful rolled backhand drive that could stand up against a combination of speed and heavy topspin. This was the shot he was striving to perfect when he took his famous six months off from tournament play. One cannot believe that Tilden didn't already have a rolled backhand of sorts; the specialist shot he was after was an anti-Johnston backhand.

The natural way for most people to meet a fast, topspinning, high-bouncing ball to the backhand is to slice downwards at it. To attempt a high topspin backhand instead seems chancy—more the sort of neck-or-nothing shot you would be forced to play in order to pass an opponent well positioned at the net. Tilden refused to look at it that way; to him a slice was the easy way out, not the most effective. He decided that against a Johnston forehand a topspin backhand drive was not only a more attacking and flexible passing shot (as everyone already well knew) but that it could also be a better-controlled shot. The basis of his theory has already been mentioned in describing how he played underspin shots to make it difficult for Johnston to control his topped forehand. The answer to Johnston's topspin forehand to his opponent's backhand side, Tilden was certain, lay in using topspin himself, to bite *into* the spin of the oncoming ball. All he had to do was perfect his timing, and it is more difficult to time a topspin backhand drive than it is to time a slice.

The determined Tilden attained the required timing. He developed a rolled backhand drive that was both attacking and solid under pressure. This shot gave him the last push to the top rung of the ladder; and from then on—i.e., from 1920 —his range of strokes gave him possession of the world tennis stage.

It is interesting to examine this range. Tilden could hit his ground strokes, forehand or backhand, flat and deep to the baseline; he could also slice them to give a low bounce on stroke after stroke against a Western-grip player; and he could topspin them sharply across a volleyer's body. A close student of all his opponents' styles, he delighted in winning a match by playing shots an opponent liked least, even when his own strokes were far superior.

He served his cannonball at 124 m.p.h.,* kicked his American Twist sharply, and could curve a sliced service wide and low away from Western players. His mixing of these services, and indeed of all his shots, was judicious, but we must not imagine that his wonderful ball control took the place of speed. Against Johnston he

*The exact speed does not matter; the point is that it was in the bracket of speedsters forty years later who served with a ball of possibly higher compression.

was sometimes forced into restraint and against the Topspin Japanese players Shimizu, Kumagae, and Harada he chose to win with slices, but he loved speed. He sometimes held four balls in his hand to serve, and it is said that from such a bunch he once banged down four aces to finish off a tournament; and when he and his opponent were both at the baseline he often hit his swinging forehand and backhand drives for clean winners.

The speed of one particular Tilden forehand recalls the incident in which Jean Borotra was knocked unconscious by a Patterson volley, and

Bill Tilden

48

by coincidence Patterson was again one of the players involved. The occasion was the U.S. National doubles final of 1919. Brookes and Patterson were playing the holders, Tilden and Richards. At 3–4 and thirty-forty in the first set, Patterson sent a thundering service down the centre. With the chance of a vital break-through, Tilden hauled off and hit a terrific forehand. Richards, always ready to intercept, moved across; he moved just too early for a shot of the combined speed of Patterson's serve and Tilden's forehand, and the ball took him almost on the left temple and knocked him off his feet. He played in a daze for the rest of the set and with his eyesight affected for the rest of the match.

Tilden has gone down in history as the master of controlled speed. His wilder years were more or less concealed by the 1914–18 war and his game matured fairly late. He was twenty-seven in 1920, the first year of his greatness and the year of his first Wimbledon, U.S. National, and Davis Cup singles wins. There was no doubt about his control; apart from his consistent championship and Cup wins from 1920 to 1925, in one American tournament he once won fifty-seven consecutive games. It was once said of him that he could almost make the ball talk.

Tilden used an Eastern forehand grip and changed it somewhat less than ninety degrees for the backhand; here he also flouted American tradition and wrapped his thumb round the handle for strength of grip rather than advance it along the back for support. He served with the Continental grip, used any grip he fancied (depending upon the height of the ball) for his slices, and volleyed (at any rate after the impression young Vincent Richards made on him) with a Continental grip. He described his forehand grip as the "shake-hands" grip—obtained by holding the racket straight out in front in the left hand with the short strings pointing downwards and then taking hold of the handle as though shaking hands with an old friend. The handle lay so diagonally across the palm that the racket could virtually be called an extension of the arm. Here Tilden's theory, a somewhat confused one, was that under stress a straight line was always stronger than a broken one.* This "shake-hands" grip of Tilden's is today referred to as the Full Eastern.

In 1923 Tilden lost the top joint of the middle finger of his right hand in an accident and was forced to modify his grip. As a result his Full Eastern became, if the term is permissible, even fuller. He placed the racket handle even more diagonally across his palm than he had before, and this in turn forced him to move the palm of his hand a little farther behind the handle. When viewed from the front the forehand grip of practically every player shows the thumb lying somewhere between the tips of the index and middle fingers; Tilden's new elongated grip showed the thumb practically in line with the stump of the maimed middle finger.

We are told that Tilden played all the better for his new grip, but this is surely a distortion of the facts. It is more likely that if his play improved it was because he had not reached his peak at the time of his accident. One does not obtain a better grip from a maimed hand; and as for the possibility that the hand's new position on the racket handle was a better one than the old, one can hardly imagine that an inveterate experimenter like Tilden would not have discovered this before. The episode was, however, a measure of Tilden's courage and determination.

All-court, all-stroke, all-speed . . . one wonders whether Tilden was "all-style" as well. Did he play his ground strokes in all the different styles so that he could have the advantages of each without its attendant disadvantages? Did he use a Western grip for high balls, an Eastern for waist-high, and an English or Continental for low or wide ones? He did not. It has been said that he could hit a Western or Continental forehand with the same facility as his basic Eastern, but the claim is exaggerated. No doubt he could have beaten many an opponent using any grip he liked, but he played all his matches with an Eastern style.

No matter how great a player's stroke range, he has his basic style (Tilden's was Eastern); and no matter how varied his tactics he also has his basic method of play. Tilden's basic method of play amounted to strong serving, and powerful forehand and backhand driving from the baseline. He prided himself on his ability to play all-court tennis, but would never have dreamt of

---

*The description "arm in line with racket" means when seen from in front, and a full Eastern grip gives this result. However, Eastern grips place the palm and wrist behind the handle; viewed from above, arm and racket are less in the same plane than they are with an English Continental grip (see Appendix I).

playing the Big Game introduced some twenty years later by Jack Kramer and adopted by almost every leading player since. Serve-and-volley would have been too restrictive for Tilden, even allowing for the non-serving games. He was a virtuoso who liked to be free to use the whole keyboard.

Beautifully co-ordinated, Tilden made all his strokes smoothly, whether sweeping masterfully over a high ball or approaching a low one with lowered knees and seemingly uncoiling himself into full stretch. He had particularly swift and correct footwork and a fine freedom of action in his swing. His grip, whether original or modified, was conducive to a wide swing, and many photo-graphs of Tilden awaiting the ball also show his elbows characteristically lifted as though, when it came to making his shot, he could not bear having them anywhere near his ribs. Whether stationary or running, he swung his front foot across to the ball and placed it firmly on the ground before striking. Whenever possible he took the ball waist-high (where it could be driven hardest), just below the top of the bounce (where it was at its slowest point), and struck it from slightly outside and below; in his own words, for the forehand he hit the south-east corner of the ball, and for the backhand the south-west corner. He rolled his drives with long contact between ball and strings, and finished them with a full

Bill Tilden

follow-through. Of all later champions, probably the two most reminiscent of Tilden's tall figure and swinging Eastern stroke-play were Ellsworth Vines and Jack Kramer.

Tilden set new standards for orthodoxy in the Eastern style. The loop of his forehand was lower, and the backswing was no longer carried round behind the back. The wrist was used, but more as part of the arm, and less whipped; the knees were bent, and he preferred to move into the ball rather than hit from a fixed stance. Many present-day players regard the Eastern style as having stemmed from none other than Tilden; Rod Laver quotes his early coach and mentor, Charles Hollis, as saying: "Tilden was the father of the Eastern style, and in a sense we are all his disciples." Hollis, talking tennis rather than history to his group of youngsters, was quite correct.

It seems most appropriate that Tilden was orthodox—even if he had to modify the currently accepted orthodoxy that immediately preceded him. Of all his theories, probably his strongest belief was that orthodoxy was not restrictive—not only did it lead to soundness, it also provided the broadest base from which to develop any stroke or aspect of the game.

After 1925, with the young French stars overhauling him, Big Bill's efforts for American tennis were better appreciated, and despite further disputes with officialdom he became a more popular figure. One now becomes more aware of the human side of this formerly unbeatable tennis machine. Like Australia's Harry Hopman in later years, he had a great interest in the advancement of promising juniors, but he did not have Hopman's success, perhaps because he was too domineering. Crabby and wilful himself on the court, he admired the play and sportsmanship of his contemporary, Little Bill, and later of von Cramm. As a young man he heroworshipped Norman Brookes, and he has recorded his delight that after he met the great man this respect did not diminish. Taking a pride in his own game, he hated to lose and even when trailing in a practice set would stay on the court until he had won, no matter how long it took; yet he had to endure one of the game's most famous reversals. Returning to Wimbledon in 1927 after an absence of six years, he led Cochet in the semi-final by two sets to love, 5–1 and thirty-fifteen, and lost.

But Tilden always managed to come out on top in the end, and sure enough we find him finally reconquering Wimbledon, and Cochet as well. It was a long hard road, involving, in all, three more visits to Wimbledon and a professional tour several years later. First came failure. In the 1928 Wimbledon semi-final he led René Lacoste by two sets to one and 3–0, but eventually went down to Lacoste's wonderful steadiness. In the 1929 semi-final Cochet, hitting winner after winner from Tilden's fiercest services, defeated him in straight sets. In 1930 therefore, the thirty-seven-year-old Tilden was thought to have little chance of success in a field containing both Cochet, the holder, and Jean Borotra, the winner in 1924 and 1926. But in the quarter-finals Cochet was unexpectedly defeated by an unseeded player, Wilmer Allison, a young Texan. The nonchalant Cochet had become famous for the victories he had achieved after losing the first two sets, but the determined and hard-hitting Allison would not allow his name to be added to this list. Even though Allison defeated another good player in the semi-final (John Doeg, who was to become America's 1930 National champion and who is generally thought to have had the most powerful left-handed service the game has seen), Wimbledon had become so accustomed to its title being won by famous players that it was to the remaining semi-final that all eyes were turned. This was between Tilden and Borotra, and it was widely regarded as virtually the Wimbledon final. With Cochet out of the way, it was Tilden's great chance and, like the champion he still was, he was determined to hold it. In a dramatic match of fluctuating fortunes he won in five exhausting sets and then defeated Allison in a straight-sets final. Ten years to the day since he had been the first non-British player to win the Wimbledon crown he recaptured it.

It was the climax of Tilden's amateur career, and shortly afterwards he turned professional. He did not, of course, become an obscure professional; 15,000 people saw him play his first pro match under the blazing lights of New York's Madison Square Garden.

Cochet, who was ranked first in the world from 1928 to 1931, and was the only one of Tilden's amateur opponents to have beaten him more times than not, later joined Tilden's professional troupe, but did not play with the same interest and concentration as before. The implacable

Tilden certainly did, however. Defeating Cochet by a wide margin, he more than redressed the Frenchman's amateur-match balance against him.

It was said of Tilden that in his fifties he could still take on anyone in the world over three sets. It was also reported that at fifty-three, in 1946, he astonished Fred Perry—British triple Wimbledon winner in the mid-1930s and later a professional in America—by asking his advice on how he, Tilden, could adopt a Continental forehand grip to give him a more aggressive return of service. With no other experiments left to make, Tilden was perhaps thinking of leaving his beloved left court in doubles and of raking in a few wide serves on the other side with a brand-new forehand. Pages ago we mentioned his life-long desire to know everything there was to be known about the game of tennis. From Tilden's example, it is a pleasant thought that not only chess, but tennis too, can have limitless possibilities.

Tilden as veteran, 1944

9 | Honour of France

FRANCE, it seems, has always been a tennis nation. Lawn tennis stemmed from Tennis, and whatever Major Wingfield may have said about the game having been played in ancient Greece and by kings of England, France was the stronghold of Tennis from the Middle Ages onward, and from France came a number of terms connected with lawn tennis today. If not proven, it is highly probable that the word *tennis*, for example, comes from the French *Tenez!* (*Hold!* or *Play!*) and that *deuce* comes from *à deux* (at *two*, meaning that two consecutive points had to be won for the game). One is tempted to plunge further and say that *love* came from *l'oeuf* (*the egg*), but experts assure us it is more likely to have come from an English term for "nothing"— in the sense of "a labour of love", etc.

Service, oddly enough, did not come from the act of serving or delivering the ball, but from the ancient practice of having a servant deliver the first stroke. This was indeed service, though it's the sort of attention a modern champion would prefer to do without.

The method of scoring points by fifteens carries perhaps the most interesting explanation of all. In Tennis the points were originally called fifteen, thirty, and forty-five, the forty-five becoming shortened to forty. It seems that in the Middle Ages sixty was regarded as a whole or round number, in much the same way as a hundred is today; there was, for instance, the association, from the thirteenth century onwards, with the sixty minutes on a clock face. It took four points to win a game, so each was accorded a quarter of sixty, or fifteen. The six games for a set may well have come from six sixties being 360, the number of degrees in a complete circle; or, putting it the other way round, we can start with the circle of 360 degrees as the whole, divide it into six sixties (i.e., into six games) and divide each game, or sixty, into four points valued at fifteen each.

But back to lawn tennis. The French National championship was introduced in 1891, between the Renshaw and Doherty eras. Although the first champion had the unlikely name of Briggs, until 1925 the championship of France was the exclusive province of Frenchmen. This was mistaken patriotism, and almost certainly held back the French players' standard to some extent. France, however, lost little time in entering the Davis Cup competition. She was a challenger the first year the field was widened from its two original competing nations—1904, a year before the old name of Australasia (brought about by the presence of Brookes and Wilding in England) made its first appearance. She was also to the fore at Wimbledon earlier than any other non-British country, and the first non-British success was the men's doubles championship win in 1911 by Max Decugis and André Gobert. This was twenty years after the French championship had begun, but we should in fairness make allowance for the Doherty period of dominance from 1897 to 1906. Also, there was another famous British pair in action at this time—Smith and Riseley, who defeated the Doherty brothers in two Wimbledon doubles finals. With Brookes and Wilding coming next on the scene, the Frenchmen's win seemed to come about as soon as reasonably possible.

France's outstanding player of the pre-Great War days was Max Decugis, who won his country's singles championship eight times between 1903 to 1914, and with three different partners (Worth, Germot, and Dupont) won the doubles championship every year from 1902 to 1914 and in 1920 as well.

France's lawn tennis style descended like England's from Real Tennis. As for French standards of play, Decugis and Gobert won their 1911 title from the holders, Wilding and M. J. Ritchie, a pair good enough to have contested the doubles final four years in succession. By the early 1920s Tilden was describing the tall and powerful Gobert as a terrific hitter with flowing flat ground strokes, a brilliant overhead and volley, and one of the finest services he had ever seen. In the true conditions of indoor tennis on wood surfaces Gobert's play was of world standard. Outdoors, however, wind, sun, and the state of the court interfered with his fractional timing, his highly strung temperament, and eventually his whole game; his results were not what they might have been; certainly not enough to inspire France.

Perhaps W. H. Laurentz could have provided the inspiration. When only sixteen years of age he was good enough to defeat Anthony Wilding, then in the middle of his Wimbledon reign, but in the following year he suffered the cruel misfortune of losing an eye when a ball flew into it from the edge of his racket. He played in French

André Gobert and Max Decugis

Davis Cup teams until 1921, but not as a great star.

The honour of inspiring France, and indeed the world, fell upon the slender shoulders of a young girl, Suzanne Lenglen—the Incomparable Suzanne. She was twenty years old when she first appeared at Wimbledon in 1919, and the first impression she made there was one of shock— shock at the scantiness of her attire, which was as revolutionary then as the revealing styles introduced after World War II. But the sense of shock, even of outrage in some quarters, did not last long; by 1920 Suzanne was recognized as the leader of tennis fashion. The basis of her attire was a short-sleeved one-piece dress—later supplemented by the famous series of different-coloured bandeaux she wore wound round her hair, secured with a diamond pin—and her lipstick. But whatever she wore she was a player of wonderful artistry, and most experts agree that no woman player has yet been her equal.

Suzanne was rigorously trained by her father, Charles Lenglen, who had decided upon a tennis career for his daughter and was determined to make her a champion. Not even Tilden's relentless driving of himself equalled Lenglen senior's driving of young Suzanne; the Lenglens came to be regarded as the Svengali and Trilby of lawn tennis, the mastermind in the background controlling its subject's performances in public. Suzanne is supposed to have been schooled and drilled until she could land the ball on a pocket handkerchief placed on any part of the court, and it was her amazing accuracy, combined with her natural speed, co-ordination, and nervous energy, that mainly accounted for her phenomenal success.

She was only fifteen when in 1914 she won a French event called the Ladies' Hardcourt Championship of the World; in the same year, partnered by Max Decugis, she won the mixed doubles championship of France. At this point Monsieur Lenglen's dreams of fame and fortune were interrupted by the Great War. The French championships were not resumed until 1920, so that it was at Wimbledon in 1919 that Suzanne made her first real entry into world-class tennis.

Although she had never played on grass before and had not yet attained full strength and confidence, her performance was amazing. Her first match was in keeping with the subsequent commanding and unusual career of the Lenglens, *père et fille.* All eyes were on Suzanne; her opponent, who played with a borrowed racket, was completely outclassed, Suzanne conceded only one game, and M. Lenglen had to be restrained from trying to coach his daughter from inside the court.

Suzanne Lenglen, 1919

With only one hitch (the second set in one match went to advantage) she advanced to the challenge round. She had beaten first-class players by wide margins and Wimbledon's interest was thoroughly aroused; the title-holder was the redoubtable Mrs Lambert Chambers (née Douglass), seven times Wimbledon lady champion. The meeting between the amazing young French girl and the mature champion promised to be a thrilling match and proved to be an epic one.

Suzanne began in sparkling form to reach 5-3. Undismayed, Mrs Lambert Chambers pounded her deep drives across and drew to a lead of 6–5 and forty-fifteen. Suzanne countered, and eventually won a compelling first set, 10–8.

In the second set Mrs Lambert Chambers, wanting no more of this sort of nonsense, took a commanding lead of 4–1. Suzanne fought the score round to 4–all, but Mrs Lambert Chambers swept through the next two games for the set. She then sat down on one of the linesman's chairs with an air of "I'm ready whenever you are" while an almost exhausted Suzanne rested under the umpire's stand and ate lumps of sugar soaked in brandy sent down to her by her anxious father.

The third set began like the first. Suzanne's marvellous stroke-play brought her a 4–1 lead, then Mrs Lambert Chambers fought back strongly to 6–5 and forty-fifteen, with two match-points in hand.

At this stage one imagines an overwrought Suzanne's despairing glances towards her father at the side of the court, and Papa Lenglen's expression most emphatically forbidding defeat. Suzanne reached into the depths of her resources and attacked. She saved the first match point with a rather unkempt volley off the wood, and the second with a glorious backhand. From there onwards, Suzanne maintained her bare margin of stroke superiority and eventually closed the score at 9–7. For a brief moment the spectators seemed unable to believe that the sustained tension of the match was indeed over; then, in an explosion of applause, Suzanne's parents and Max Decugis were swamping her with ecstatic embraces, tears were flowing from Suzanne, there were more embraces, and yet more. The applause continued, for the British, whatever they may say, love an occasional show of Latin temperament.

The spotlight was on Suzanne and the Lenglen

Mrs Lambert Chambers, 1919

she was due to play, and turned professional later in the year.

In the early 1920s Suzanne was a greater attraction at Wimbledon than even Patterson and Tilden. All her matches had to be played on the centre court because no outside court had enough room for the throngs that attended her and on one occasion the hedges dividing the outside courts had been trampled down. Even the centre court's stands proved too small, and a long queue would often form. Such a queue became known as Wimbledon's Lenglen Trail A-winding.

The bigger the crowd, the more the Leading Lady enjoyed it, and she gave some memorable displays, not only of fetching leg but also of almost unbeatable tennis. Her 1923 Wimbledon crown involved her in six matches and twelve sets during which she lost only eleven games. In 1924 she won the first three rounds without losing a game and then amazed by losing the middle set of her match with Elizabeth Ryan. It was the first set she had lost at Wimbledon since 1919; a point gained against Suzanne was an achievement, a game an event, a set almost unbelievable. This was the tournament from which ill-health forced her to withdraw.

Returning in 1925, she won the title in five matches with the loss of only five games; included in this was a 6–0, 6–0 defeat of the holder—no doubt for daring to occupy one of Suzanne's thrones, even in her absence. In France in 1926 she topped her Wimbledon performance by winning the title in the same number of matches and losing only four games.

Never has one player, man or woman, achieved a dominance equal to Suzanne's. Never have matches been so one-sided and yet so well attended. It was all a matter of personality and play—for this was the Incomparable Suzanne.

Suzanne is one of the few women champions to have played in the English or Continental style. This style requires too much strength of wrist to be generally suitable for women players, the vast majority of whom are Easterners; even the Western style of using the same face of the racket for forehand and backhand is more popular and has remained in favour among the ladies far more than it has among men.

Whatever power Suzanne lost by not having her palm and wrist behind the racket handle was made up by her fine timing and weight control.

fortunes were assured, but what of Mrs Lambert Chambers and all that she represented? She declared that she had never played better in her life, and one likes to think that she was not too downcast by her defeat. She had had a long innings; she belonged to a generation which firmly believed that the game counted more than the result; and she had had a good game, the best of her life, in fact. In any case, her performance of seven ladies' singles wins at Wimbledon has been exceeded only once—by America's Helen Wills Moody.

Suzanne Lenglen, once safely through her trial by ordeal, emerged as the sophisticated and tempestuous Queen of the Courts. Dual monarch of England and France, she won the singles and doubles crowns in each of the two countries six times, the French triple crown (singles, doubles, and mixed) six times, and Wimbledon's triple crown three times. She probably would have bettered these figures if illness had not prevented her in 1924 from competing in the French championships or completing the Wimbledon tournament. Nor did she complete the 1926 Wimbledon; she withdrew after a dramatic misunderstanding with officials over the times when

A most graceful player, she was often referred to as the Pavlova of tennis. Powerful or not, she was a fast player and, particularly when at the net, attacked the ball with vigour. She hit her forehand harder than her backhand, but her backhand was if anything the more accurate stroke. She smashed and served accurately, often placing a controlled second service for an ace. Like Laurie Doherty, she was often restrained with the return of service, preferring to launch her attack later. Secure at all points in her own strokes, she concentrated on strategy. She had a game that was nearly perfect.

Suzanne Lenglen's influence on France's Four Musketeers is unquestionable; she was their "wonderful comrade and friend". Like Joan of Arc, she showed what France could do, and Frenchmen rose and became heroes. It was she who achieved the break-through without which the four young Frenchmen might have become good players but never world champions. Eleven years, from 1895 to 1905, separated their dates of birth, but all four arrived in France's Davis Cup team within a space of three years, from 1921 to 1923, and in the time of Suzanne.

Though their tournament successes were many, the Musketeers' greatest triumph was a collective one—as a world-dominating Davis Cup team. It was here that they won the hearts of their countrymen, were accorded their romantic name, and became the idols of Paris's Roland Garros stadium.

Jacques Brugnon, at the age of twenty-six in

The Incomparable Suzanne. (The thick racket handle—5¼ in was not unusual in the 1920s—makes the backhand grip look unusual.)

Toto Brugnon: Topspin drive with extreme Eastern grip

also successfully partnered Lacoste. He was the rock on which France's doubles success rested.

A doubles specialist, in championship company, is perhaps a little hard to understand today. With its Big Game of serve and volley, singles for the past twenty years has been played with doubles tactics, and the best pairs have consisted of men renowned for singles play. In earlier days, two singles players were less likely to form an outstanding doubles pair. We are inclined these days to view earlier doubles specialists with a certain suspicion and to wonder if they were not to some extent carried by the superior strokes of their "singles" partners. Toto Brugnon gave this kind of impression to many onlookers; as well as "bringing out the best in his partners" he was reported to have "subordinated himself to the brilliance and opportunism of his partner"; in other words, we hear more of his support than of his positive performance. Modestly, he used to say that he always played in the right court because his backhand was so awful. If he had known how many people would have believed him he might not have said it. He was in the right court for the good reason that a player of

A Brugnon high volley

1921, was the first of the four to carry France's colours. The following year saw the appearance of Jean Borotra and Henri Cochet, aged twenty-four and twenty-two respectively. In 1923 René Lacoste, aged eighteen, rose to complete the quartet.

United though they were as a team, France's Musketeers were four widely differing individuals and players. Volatile Borotra was a volleyer. Retiring Lacoste was a baseliner. Cochet played an all-court game of extreme nonchalance. The amiable Brugnon was a doubles specialist.

Jacques Brugnon was slender, of medium height, and wore a small dark moustache. He obligingly partnered any of the other three, and was more likely than anyone else to bring out the best in them; his partnerships with Borotra and Cochet became famous, and sometimes he his type would have been wasted in the left. What some onlookers may have seen as the unselfish Toto playing unobtrusively while his partner made killing volleys was not at all the Brugnon that a serving opponent saw. Of all the Musketeers, he had the most probing and dangerous return of service, a dipping topspin forehand that often dictated the form of the ensuing exchange.

This forehand was made with what we have chosen to call an extreme Eastern grip—that is, a grip well behind the racket, towards Western. It is an excellent grip for making topspin shots from balls that are short and high, such as services. With such a forehand grip, Brugnon, as would be expected, did have a certain amount of trouble with his backhand, but he was one of those quick-footed right-court specialists who can step round most services aimed at their backhand; and in these circumstances his return of service, either in dip or concealed direction, was often more difficult again to handle. If either of his opponents crowded the net closely to nullify his topspin drive he had his famous attacking topspin lob. In short, his doubles play constantly threatened his opponents with a broken service game, and as for holding his own side's service games, he had a reliable serve and overhead and was a gifted volleyer.

Although he had to compete for his position in Davis Cup teams against three of the world's leading singles players, Brugnon's record stretched from 1921 to 1934, and in only two of those years, 1928 and 1929, did he fail to play in a tie. He played the challenge round doubles match on six occasions and won the French doubles five times, twice with Borotra and three times with Cochet. He won the Wimbledon doubles four times, twice each with Borotra and Cochet, and between 1926 and 1934 he contested the final of this event seven times. He clearly qualified for the title of Musketeer—even if not in the leading role of D'Artagnan.

The D'Artagnan of the four was surely Jean Borotra, the Bounding Basque, the Frenchman who, in Anglo-Saxon eyes, personified his country. His play, personality, and expression were of quicksilver; he was witty and gay and completely charming. The darling of the Wimbledon crowd, he even anticipated their dearest wish and wore a beret in all his matches.

Borotra was above middle height, clear-skinned and somewhat sharp-featured. He lived a full life at great pace, and dashed everywhere—from a business conference to a taxi-cab, from train and taxi-cab on to the court and in to the net. He bounded for volleys, leapt for smashes, chased drives. Haring after a wide one at Sydney's White City in 1928 he nearly ran into a linesman, so leapt clean over his head, and then delightedly joined in the general laughter.

The one thing about Borotra that was not exactly elegant was his stroke-making, though even this, to the general onlooker, was concealed by his acrobatic fleetness and by his confidence and élan. His service action was somewhat jerky and his ground strokes, made with a short swing, were often cramped. An Eastern-grip player, he made a large change for the backhand, his wrist being right behind the handle for this stroke with the middle knuckles of all fingers pointing forward in the direction of the ball. Apart from the strength and safety of his smash (doubtless greatly aided by the height he could leap from the ground), his most effective stroke was a medium-to-high backhand volley. This stroke became known as the Borotra Prod. But let a ball reach Borotra higher than the net, and the Prod would despatch it in one stab.

Borotra's dashing methods forced him, in spite of his dynamic energy and superb physical fitness, to play in fits and starts. He had to make his run at the right time, and his standard pattern was to get a good start, pause, then come again like a high wind. This is easier said than done, but Borotra could pace himself and play these tactics to perfection.

You could reason that in, say, a five-set match in which he had won either the first two sets or the first and third and had let the other two go, Borotra would have been on the court as long as his opponent and so would be just as tired for the last set; also that if he had not exerted himself in the two sets he had let go, his opponent need not have done so either. But Borotra never let it work out that way; in a set he was prepared to lose he managed either to keep his opponent uncertain of his intention, or in a sudden change of front to leap to the attack and win the set and match if he got the chance. Furthermore, in sets he was letting go, he gave his opponent little or no opportunity to build up his confidence and no chance at all, if he could help it, either to practise a weak stroke or to guess what Borotra's final tactics might be. Typically, while taking the first two sets of one match from a not in-experienced Lacoste, he noticed a small characteristic in Lacoste's backhand—normally his stronger side—that might prove exploitable. He threw the next two sets in a way calculated to tire his adversary more than himself, playing to Lacoste's forehand but without any rallying. In the fifth set he routed Lacoste with a net attack directed mainly to his less penetrating forehand but cunningly mixed with sorties against his backhand in positions where it could be exploited by anticipating its direction. Working it all out later, the studious Lacoste confessed himself greatly impressed with Borotra's sagacity.

So well did Borotra exploit tactics like these that it became almost imperative for his opponents to prevent him from gaining a set lead; but because he always began his matches in top gear, only the very best could do this.

Borotra prods a backhand

There is, however, a clear line between tactics and what has since been called gamesmanship, and Borotra sometimes overstepped this mark, either intentionally or through heaven-sent opportunities that were more than his fun-loving nature could resist. When trailing on games, an embarrassed-looking Borotra would say to his opponent during a change-over, "You are playing beautifully—I confess it. But I? Nothing will go right. *Mon Dieu*, the people and the money they have paid to see such a poor match as this." Or words to that effect. The opponent would relax—and in an instant Borotra would be swarming all over him. After a lost fourth set—which he may have let go, while giving the appearance of being out on his feet—he would slump on his seat without looking up as though the only thing to be decided was whether he would forfeit or self-sacrificingly continue for form's sake. Then in the fifth set an unwary opponent would suddenly be met with a flood of tigerish Borotra volleys.

Though this type of play usually thrilled the crowds, it was not well received in one tournament, the 1926 Nationals in America, in which Borotra won a long five-set match against the popular Little Bill Johnston. The length of this match was due in no small measure to Borotra's continually playing for time to prevent Little Bill from getting in the groove with his devastating forehand, and he resorted to similar methods in defeating Richards in the next round, a semi-final. The American Press stated coldly that Borotra had "feigned fatigue". Tilden—who regarded Borotra as a tricky customer and who tended to become upset more over injustice to his friends than to himself—rose in wrath. He may have thought that young Vincent needed a shock to his confidence, but for anyone to take advantage of Little Bill's good nature was more than he could put up with. "Jean Borotra outstalled and out-smarted Billy Johnston," he stormed, his anger evidently getting the better of his choice of words. Perhaps Borotra thought that a little latitude should have been permitted to the underdog; and underdog he certainly was, for in the Davis Cup challenge round only a week or so earlier Johnston had overpowered him in straight sets. Perhaps he thought a little play-acting would do the all-conquering and serious Americans no harm.

Not that Frenchmen were exempt from his pranks, either. Brugnon was his faithful doubles partner, and against the gentle-natured Lacoste, with whom he sometimes walked off the court arm-in-arm, he may have confined his artfulness to tactics alone, but Henri Cochet was apparently fair game. In a tense situation in one Borotra–Cochet encounter, from somewhere in the stand a baby let out a cry just as Borotra threw up the ball to serve. Borotra caught the ball and, alive in a moment to the possibilities of the situation, prepared to serve again, in the patient manner of a resigned parent. The crowd began to titter a little. Up went the ball—and the infant obligingly howled again. Borotra walked over to the edge of the court and, to everyone's delight except Cochet's, solemnly wagged a reproving finger in the baby's direction. In his own good time he returned to serve to a Cochet whose composure and concentration were suitably disturbed.

On another occasion—in a semi-final of the 1929 French championship, with the score at 3–5 against him in the third set—Borotra slipped and went down on one knee. Deciding to make a good fall of it, he rolled to the court on his face. He got up, smiling and unhurt, and went back to serve. As he was about to throw up the ball, a surprised look crossed his face and he spat out a pebble. The crowd's involuntary shout of laughter coincided perfectly with Borotra's striking the ball, and the startled Cochet missed the return. Borotra repeated his act on the next serve and, with the dignity of the game exchanged for the pantomime of a circus ring, Cochet allowed himself to become annoyed and lost the set.

Borotra did these things, he enjoyed them, and crowds everywhere (except for that one occasion in America) loved them. It is likely that Borotra, so wrapped up in his performance, did not give his opponent a thought; any suggestion that it was a plot, deliberately contrived to put his opponent off, he would have laughed to scorn.

In this respect no one could control Borotra—not even Tilden, who, forewarned, was always on the lookout for the slightest suggestion that a disturbing incident was being intentionally developed. In the Wimbledon semi-final against Tilden in 1930, Borotra, in champagne form, led by two sets to one, then proceeded to take a rest in the fourth. He began to take longer and longer to towel himself between games with a great bath-towel at the umpire's chair. Tense,

Borotra as veteran

anxious to get on with the game, suspicious, and determined not to be fooled, Tilden sternly requested the umpire to keep play moving and strode out to his end of the court. Borotra hurried out, too—but as a picture of flustered repentance, mopping at his face with one end of the large towel the other end of which was held by a small ball-boy who looked for all the world like a page carrying a train at court. It was ludicrous and brought shouts of laughter. At every subsequent change-over Borotra played crowd-tickling variations on this theme, adroitly forcing Tilden into the role of the man who had caused it all. But Tilden kept his head and eventually took the match in the fifth set.

Showmanship aside, Borotra's record was more than enough to justify his entry to the hall of fame. Besides his Davis Cup performances and his 1924 and 1926 Wimbledon titles, he won the French singles twice, and also all three Australian titles in 1928. In the indoor championships that play so large a part in European tennis Borotra was at his best. The fast surfaces, giving a man on the baseline less time to make passing shots, suited the Basque's net attacks, and he won the French indoor championship twelve times and the British eleven.

Borotra was the real leader of the Four Musketeers, and kept them together. Unpredictable to the last, he did not quickly fade; he played more Davis Cup tennis than any of his compatriots, and his doubles appearances with Brugnon alone were said to have numbered more than a hundred. He has been rated by some as second only to Vincent Richards as a volleyer, but the two were of entirely different types.

René Lacoste, though shy in manner, exercised strong determination and self-discipline in his tennis. Of about medium height, sallow-complexioned and dark-haired, he did not enjoy good health, and though he was the youngest of the Musketeers—and the last, in 1923, to make his Davis Cup début—he was the first to leave the scene, all but retiring from competitive tennis after the French championships early in 1929 at the age of twenty-four. In that short period, husbanding his physical resources, practising diligently, planning his matches as though they were military campaigns and then playing them with great patience, he made tennis history.

From 1923 to 1928 he was never omitted from

Two angles on Lacoste's Continental backhand

a French Davis Cup team. He was runner up to Borotra in the French and Wimbledon championships in 1924, winner of both in 1925 and, though essentially a singles player, winner of both doubles titles as well. In 1926 he inflicted on Tilden his first Davis Cup defeat, won the U.S. National singles, and gained the world's top ranking at the age of twenty-two. In 1927 he regained the French title, played the major role in France's first Davis Cup win by defeating both Johnston and Tilden, and retained his U.S. National title. After regaining the Wimbledon title in 1928 by defeating Cochet, the holder, he began the 1929 season by winning the French singles for the third time. After that, he could go no further.*

Lacoste's tennis has often been described as rock-like. He was not a tennis "natural", and so it is not surprising that the game's most natural shot, the forehand, was not his strength. His forehand was never weak, but, being mounted on poor footwork and played from a wrist held a little too stiffly, it suffered by comparison with his backhand. This backhand, perfectly produced, was accounted the finest of all time. In later years it served as a standard of comparison for the famous backhand of Donald Budge—just as, later again, Budge's was the standard for young Ken Rosewall's.

Lacoste could, of course, serve, smash, and volley efficiently, but he founded his game on strong baseline defence. His backhand was significant in two ways. Firstly, although a back-

*To complete Lacoste's record accurately it must be stated that he reappeared in the French singles championship in 1932. Here he defeated the reigning 1931 Wimbledon champion (American Sidney Wood) by the revealing score of 6–1, 6–0, 3–6, 6–8, 7–5 (how the Roland Garros stadium must have rocked), but the effort finished his career. He lost in the next round and retired—finally, but still only twenty-seven.

hand may not be either as powerful or as flexible as a forehand, once mastered it becomes a more consistently grooved stroke and lends itself to greater steadiness. Secondly, most right-handed players find it easier to produce straight forehands and crosscourt backhands than the reverse. This applies both to swift net-approach shots and to deep drives in baseline rallies; thus, from both forehand and backhand and from net or baseline, the right-hander's natural target is his opponent's backhand—the solid Lacoste's most solid stroke.

Beneath his white-peaked cap, the serious-faced Lacoste enjoyed his tennis immensely. Nevertheless he was often described as playing like a well-oiled machine; as well as being amazingly consistent and accurate, his strokes were beautifully smooth. With his sweeping low-wristed shots all made with one grip, he was an English-style player. England's greatness had been so long in eclipse, however,* that by this time the name "English" was being overtaken by such terms as "Lacoste grip", "All-stroke grip", and eventually "Continental style".

Lacoste held the world top ranking for 1926 and 1927 and the United States singles championship for those years as well, but the Americans (and there were by this time a number of theorists about besides Tilden) did not go overboard about either Lacoste or his style. Lacoste might have been a marvellous young player, but he was a counter-puncher, and American critics tended to regard only a man who took the attack into his own hands as being a real champion. They granted that the Continental grip could give excellent balance between forehand and backhand, but argued that such balance was likely to go too far and result in a forehand below the standard an Eastern grip could produce. Lacoste's forehand wasn't as good as his backhand. What more was there to be said?

Lacoste, for his studious part, decided that more points were lost by error than were won by outright winners, and that the answer was to eliminate errors. Errors were least likely to be made from the baseline, so this became his operational area. One needed to be able to cover it, however, and the Continental grip provided

the greatest reach. Against a baseline opponent, deep driving from corner to corner in general provided the longest path, thus giving the ball its best chance of falling into court. Against a volleyer, down-the-line passing shots were the easiest to make and any chance to play them should always be taken, but one must also be able to roll the ball across a volleyer's body at angles more and more acute so that he would be drawn closer and closer to the net to protect these angles, until he came in just too far—and then one tossed firmly beyond his reach. It all took a great deal of practice. Well then, one practised a great deal. (Lacoste practised one stroke—a forehand passing shot—for two hours before his match with Cochet in the Wimbledon final of 1928.)

One's opponent? It was necessary to know his strength, his weaknesses, his whole game. And so the meticulous Lacoste kept a dossier on each, and we are told that he once refused an offer of a thousand dollars for his notebooks.

An intelligent man like Lacoste must have known far more about tennis and its tactics and subtleties than has been set down here; what has been given is only a general picture of Lacoste as seen by tennis followers of his day.

Though Lacoste's health forced him out of tennis at an early age, his stamina did not fail him during protracted matches. He was seldom out of form, and although his displays did not normally arouse the enthusiasm accorded at Roland Garros to Borotra or Cochet, Frenchmen had a comfortable feeling that Lacoste would never let France down. Because of his smooth stroke-play his long matches were never dull, and against anyone of lesser ability he appeared as much master of the court as did Borotra with his net assaults.

Henri Cochet, a small man of unworried mien and the last of the Musketeers to reach top form, became in the opinion of most critics the finest player of them all. He was a beautiful Continental stylist with a wrist as smooth as silk, and the forehand was his stronger side. He made his backhand with a small change of grip and with a little underspin, the disadvantage of which he largely offset by taking the ball early and by fine control of pace and angle. Because of his near-perfect timing he has been called the greatest rising-ball artist and the most effortless stroke-

*It may be recalled that Wimbledon's last English-style winner was Laurie Doherty in 1906 and that, irrespective of style, the last Englishman to win had been Arthur Gore in 1909.

maker the game has seen. Take a short back-swing, pick the ball up from an early bounce, send it with smooth follow-through skimming low over the net to the baseline, or short across the forecourt, giving the impression that the whole stroke was made with forefinger and thumb alone—that was Cochet, and no French-man with the slightest understanding of tennis quarrelled with the claim that no one, but no one, could low-volley and half-volley like France's own Henri.

As with many another champion of short stature, Cochet's service was lenient but his overhead deadly. He even had a winning back-hand smash—a stroke more often associated with players whose game is based on strong backhand stroking, usually including a powerful topspin drive. Cochet covered lobs as inclusively as most taller men could; low volleys and half-volleys presenting little difficulty to his Conti-nental type of play, he could afford to stand farther back from the net than other players and using a good leap, supply the necessary cover. He seemed to have no preference for any shot, nor for the direction in which he hit it. This, coupled with his early-ball play, made him a

Henri Cochet's Continental forehand: fingertips do not extend far up front surface of handle

most deceptive opponent. The better the opposition, the more he showed to advantage. To offer him a difficult ball seemed to be a mistake; more often than not, it only forced him into surpassing it. As this implies, he was a past-master at turning defence into attack. Probably no one has made the all-court game look so natural.

In the time of his greatness Cochet, though almost invariably the smaller man on the court, seemed to dominate his matches, whether winning or losing. "Cochet was hitting winners," they said, or "Cochet was making a lot of errors." No one ever seemed to consider his opponent's game. Thus we read accounts of Tilden in his later amateur years being unable to handle Cochet, "who seemed to be able to impose his will on Tilden". What was being imposed, of course, was Cochet's strokes.

In his earlier days Cochet's stroking passed almost unnoticed. The more laboured a man's style, the more obvious it is; if a man's strokes are awkwardly produced they attract greater attention. Cochet played with such ease that at first he was thought to have no style and very few strokes either. It could be seen that he had an incisive smash and volley, but his forehand drive was taken so early that it could scarcely be called a normal forehand at all; nor, for that matter, did he seem to have much of a backhand or service. By all previous understanding of the game he should have been on the defensive because so many half-volleys were inflicted on him—but, remarkably, he used them as part of his attack. Obviously he skimmed the ball over the net from anywhere to anywhere, but did he know exactly how he did it? He was once asked, the question being specifically about his service. "The service?" he replied. "Ah, yes. I throw the ball up—and then I hit it." And he would say no more, doubtless taking a straight-faced delight in leg-pulling. He wrote various articles on tennis, which show that although he was an advocate of naturalness, the mechanics of stroke-play were anything but foreign to him.

Although his low- and half-volleying could be compared to Vincent Richards's, Cochet's game as a whole was very much like that of the brilliant Dick Williams. Like the little girl with the little curl, he could be very, very good or he could be horrid; his form could vary not only from match to match but within one match. This prompted two theories. One was that beneath his calm exterior Cochet was really a temperamental man who swung between nervousness and extreme confidence. The nervous Cochet was sometimes tentative and mild and not very dangerous, at other times resigned to his fate and reckless. The confident Cochet was knife-bright and audacious, and nothing seemed beyond his powers. The other theory—more widely accepted—was that Cochet believed firmly in his ability and his star. Contemptuous of risks, he matched his ease of

A Cochet service

stroke with an off-hand manner. Most of his poor showings could be attributed to mere indifference and lack of training.

Cochet does seem to have been the most nonchalant champion ever to have graced the centre court of Wimbledon, whether in victory or defeat. Coming from behind, he would record a resounding, sometimes amazing, win and not turn a hair; beaten in the second round of the 1932 Wimbledon while holding the number-one world ranking and top seeding for the tournament, he turned up at the referee's office and calmly entered his name for the consolation singles event—and duly became the only Wimbledon champion ever to win it.

Whatever the truth of the theories about him, he was involved in so many full-length matches that he became known as "Five-set Cochet". Time and again he would lose the first two sets before the true Cochet began to emerge. Then he would return cannonball serves with the steadiness of Laurie Doherty, his mastery of angles and of half-court play would begin to exhaust his opponent, he would glide to the net (never did he rush it), and the final set usually saw him fit and fresh and playing at the top of his form. Small wonder, then, that he was described as a player who liked nothing better than to lose two sets with composure and then overwhelm his rival with a display of magic.

One can imagine the effects of this sort of victory on the crowds at Roland Garros, but it was at Wimbledon in 1927 that Cochet played his dangerous game to its very limits. His amazing sequence began against the stalwart Frank Hunter, when, down two sets to nil, he began that easy but paralysing glide to the net and settled the last three sets at 6–2, 6–2, 6–3. In the semi-final came his most famous five-set victory of all—over the mighty Tilden himself. Hitting like a cyclone, Tilden led two sets to love, 5–1, and thirty-fifteen. The bewildering Cochet then won seventeen successive points, six successive games for the set, and the next two sets as well. The final was to be against Jean Borotra, the holder, who was thought to have more chance of defeating Cochet than the ageing Tilden had had. Moreover, Borotra was a player who based his whole strategy on gaining an early lead and who was practically unbeatable if he could get both of the first two sets. A match between such a player and one who apparently liked losing the first two seemed a near approach to the old physics impossibility, with Borotra the irresistible force and Cochet the immovable object.

To everyone's delight, the opening sets, or at least their results, followed the expected path. Naturally enough, whatever people imagined, Cochet did not want Borotra to have his lead, but Borotra, refusing to be denied, took the first set at 6–4. Cochet could not contrive an answer to Borotra's volleying attack to his backhand, and the second set was also Borotra's at 6–4.

Borotra had spent a great deal of his stamina, and Cochet now produced some amazing backhand passing shots. The score reached the classical point of two sets all. In the final set Borotra would have to launch another onslaught, and Cochet would have to remain unruffled.

Each played his allotted part. Borotra, attacking, went to 5–2, and Cochet carried on. Borotra went to match point, and still Cochet carried on. This happened six times between 5–2 and 5–all. Wimbledon had seen nothing like it since William Renshaw saved six match points against Barlow some forty years earlier. Borotra's last match point was at 5–4, when he held the net

A Cochet low volley

position, only to see a down-the-line backhand skim past him and raise a puff of chalk. Cochet was the eventual winner at 7–5.

He had proved to be the immovable object. Or had he? One of the match points he saved was from a volley off the wood at the top of his racket. Many in the crowd thought it a double hit; Borotra thought so, too, and appealed to the umpire. The umpire gave the striker the benefit of the doubt—or did his human instincts cause him to give the verdict to the man who was one point down rather than end the match with a disputed decision? Possibly the former, but in deciding between forces and objects it is doubtful if scientists have ever struck a closer balance than Borotra and Cochet did on that memorable day.

During his great years, from 1928 to 1931, Cochet suffered some unexpected defeats, but if a man plays with fire he must sometimes burn his fingers. Whatever the theories about his temperament or his attitude, Cochet certainly had nerves of steel. Playing an earlier ball than anyone had done before, skimming the net, finding the lines with short crosscourt shots, picking up dangerous half-volleys, he played on the razor's edge. We have already seen Little Bill Johnston playing till he dropped and crashing his forehand drive across even when defeat stared him in the face, but courage in tennis, as in other things, comes in many forms.

If Lacoste had rocked the great Tilden on his throne, it was Cochet who effectively shook him off it. Cochet won the French singles five times, Wimbledon twice, the U.S. National once, and was undefeated in Davis Cup singles matches from 1928 to 1931. He partnered Brugnon in many an exacting doubles match, but liked to relax in mixed doubles; Wimbledon legend has it that he always entered with the prettiest girl in the tournament, and never got beyond the semifinals.

His style of play was considered the last word in modernity, and many began to wonder if its utter simplicity were not a better foundation than Tilden's wide range of more orthodox strokes. It was soon decided that it was not and that Cochet's success was founded on his personal gifts. His use of a Continental grip for maximum flexibility was also taken to be merely a part of the Cochet picture, and the Eastern remained as the standard grip in world opinion.

The all-court concept, however, had triumphed. The tennis world was convinced that in Vincent Richards and Jean Borotra it had seen the volleying game at its best. But Richards had been overcome by Tilden and Johnston, and Borotra by Lacoste and Cochet. Lacoste was a thoroughgoing baseliner, Tilden's game was all-stroke more than all-court, and both had shown that they had the beating of the volleyers. Then had come Cochet's truly all-court game, showing the volleyers to be brittle and at the same time always threatening to make the baseliners look like workhorses. Cochet's stroke-play might prove incapable of emulation, but his all-court tactics were certainly in the public domain. Tennis thinking had progressed one more notch. In summary, grant Tilden his range of strokes and Cochet his genius; the normal man should aspire to power of service and control of forehand and backhand driving like Tilden, and should come to the net like Cochet.

These, then, were France's Four Musketeers. They won Wimbledon six times—from 1924 to 1929—and five of the finals were all-French affairs; as for the Wimbledon's doubles finals, Brugnon was there seven times. They held the Davis Cup from 1927 to 1932. They went to America and won the National singles; Borotra and Brugnon ventured as far afield as Australia and between them carried off three national championships. And after France opened her championship in 1925 to the world's best, not one foreign name was allowed to desecrate the Gallic roll for a full eight years. It is sad to have to add that only three French names have honoured it since.

A NOTE ON "WORLD TITLES"

In 1913 the International Lawn Tennis Federation granted the title of World Grasscourt Championship to Wimbledon and that of World Hardcourt to Paris. At Wimbledon, this caused the introduction of two new events—mixed doubles and ladies doubles. In France, the singles titles remained reserved for French nationals only, the World's Men's and Ladies' Hardcourt Singles being added as extra events. Players who won both Grasscourt and Hardcourt World singles titles in the same year were Suzanne Lenglen, Tilden, and Johnston. World titles were abolished in 1923 (when the world's best tennis was being played in America), and in 1925 the French singles championships were opened to foreigners.

10 | Murder on the Centre Court

FOR Wimbledon, the year 1930 did not usher in a new decade so much as it signified the end of a twelve-year period in which the singles title had always been won by a famous player. From 1919 the list of champions had comprised Gerald Patterson, the two Bills, and one or other of the Musketeers; and if you ignored the break caused by the Great War, the list went back in similar fashion to Brookes and Wilding and other players of renown.

It was 1931 that brought a change to this comfortable state of affairs. That year the Wimbledon final was to be played by two Americans, Sidney Wood and Frank Shields, of whom only Shields had even been mentioned in the ranking lists of the previous year. Worse was to come, for Shields sprained his ankle in defeating Borotra in the semi-final and the final could not be played, so that the prized Wimbledon crown was won in negative fashion by default. Shields—tall, handsome, and popular, all in large measure—was deprived of his hard-earned chance at the title, and Wood, denied the opportunity of winning on the court, modestly chose to refer to himself as a half-champion.

Wood, even younger than William Renshaw had been in 1881, was only nineteen, the youngest player ever to have won the Wimbledon Championship. Four years earlier, at fifteen, he had been the youngest competitor to appear on the centre court. Clad in white knickerbockers and long socks (these were not the good old days of Horrie Rice but sophisticated 1927), he had walked onto the court with none other than the great René Lacoste. The schoolboy acquitted himself well, and the crowd gave the pair an ovation at the end of their match. They made a fine picture as they left the court, Wood embarrassed but inwardly pleased as punch, the generous Lacoste fairly beaming at having been matched with such a fine young player.

But youthful performances at Wimbledon were by no means the exclusive province of the males. In 1887 Miss Lottie Dod—a tall, strong girl in round bonnet, dress and smock, and black shoes and stockings—had won the ladies' singles championship at the age of fifteen. She must soon have decided that lawn tennis was only for the young, because after recording five Wimbledon wins she retired at twenty-one. Not to her needle and crochet-hook, however; soon she was lady golf champion of England, and eventually we find her listed as international hockey player, Olympic archer, and expert skater, horsewoman, sculler, and mountaineer.

The Sidney Wood of 1931 was sandy-haired and slender, and an attractive stroke-maker. He had a smooth cannonball service, a beautifully

Sidney Wood

69

produced backhand, and fine touch with his volleys. He was sometimes criticized for being too clever and for being beaten by more limited but straight-out play; but his stroke repertoire lacked an effective forehand drive, without which it is most difficult to play more "straight-out" tennis.

Today Wood would be called a Continental stylist, and to date he and Bobby Riggs (in 1939) have been America's only two Wimbledon winners in this style. But in the 1930s hardly anyone would have referred to Wood in such terms; he was an American, not a Continental, and he had the fast service that, Patterson notwithstanding, had come to be regarded as an American prerogative.

Though a player of world class, Wood did not win either a French or an American National title, or another Wimbledon. He was ranked in the world's first ten players from 1931 to 1935, and played Davis Cup over the same period. Like others before him and after, he had an unbeatable opponent in the form of ill-health, and by the mid-1930s his best tennis was behind him.

The 1931 Wimbledon ladies' singles title was won by Fräulein Cilly Aussem of Germany, a win enclosed in six of Helen Wills Moody's record eight Wimbledon victories. Fräulein Aussem was pretty and petite, and her trim appearance was matched by her neat stroke-making, with its preference for down-the-line shots from both forehand and backhand. But any woman who won at Wimbledon in those days only did so if Helen Wills had decided not to compete. Taking over from Suzanne Lenglen, this second Queen of the Courts began with four Wimbledon wins in succession from 1927 to 1930, won twice more in 1932 and 1933, equalled Mrs Lambert Chambers' seven wins by winning again in 1935, and capped her performance with an eighth win in 1938. She also won the American singles seven times and the French title four times.

If Suzanne had been a tempestuous queen, Helen Wills was a serene one. Never betraying her feelings on court she became known, as a young girl, as Little Miss Poker Face. Calm and good-looking, she was unusually objective in character. Always following whatever she considered the correct course of action, she remained undismayed if the result was not to her advantage and, if it was, completely unruffled by any criticism she may have aroused. Though her standards of play, appearance, and deportment were exceptionally high, her methods were readily accessible to all women players. She dressed neatly and in plain good taste, even giving a measure of style to an eyeshade—an unbecoming piece of equipment that women had long favoured but hesitated to wear until the practical and handsome Helen swept away their doubts.

Her play, though hard-hitting, was essentially feminine. There was no longer any need for women to look at Suzanne and sigh hopelessly; here was a new champion whose style remained within reach of the normal woman player. Learn to volley, ladies, so that you may hold your own in doubles, but in singles build your game on the baseline, which you can always cover. Take a

Helen Wills Moody

good Eastern grip of the racket and make a decent swing so that you can get rhythmic power without needing great strength in your wrist. For the same reason, make a substantial change for your backhand grip, and run your thumb up the back of the handle for support. Roll your strokes a little, for overall it is the least demanding method. Your speed of foot is limited, so develop your sense of anticipation as much as you can. For serving, leave the Continental grip, the wrist snap, and any attempt at making the ball kick, to the men, whom nature built to throw and serve differently from women; instead, throw the ball high enough to have ample time for a full and unhurried swing, and hit it from behind with plenty of weight and only enough sidespin to improve its chance of landing in court. This sidespin, for a lady, can be either from the slice side or it can be reverse spin. The sliced spin swerves the ball wider on the forehand side and in general lends itself to accurate placing but the reverse service is the least tiring of all to make and it finds an opponent's backhand with far less strain than any other.

Helen may not have proffered this advice in so many words, but her style eloquently conveyed it. In the context of top class women's tennis of the 1960s, it may make the great Helen Wills sound fearfully old-fashioned. One wonders. Later years provided women all-court champions and even those who were essentially volleyers, but all were duly surpassed by the amazing "Little Mo" Connolly, whose game was essentially similar to that of Helen Wills. The argument comes down to whether a woman can play better with women's methods or with men's. Male methods are undoubtedly more imaginative, but to date male execution has never been

Helen Wills Moody: A large change a grip for the backhand

completely achieved by women. Various women players who hit hard and attack from the net and perhaps even kick their services to some degree are often described as playing like men, but their differences from men in stroke-play and coverage of the net—wide, low, and overhead—are clear to any discerning eye. Time and further experiment may settle the argument. Meanwhile tennis history has shown the women's method to be vastly superior for the average woman player, and that world champions have drawn on both.

On which note we must take leave of the ladies. One of the most outstanding winners of the Wimbledon men's singles is waiting in the wings.

Ellsworth Vines—like many other American champions, a Californian—was tall, slender as a willow wand, and strong as whipcord. Relaxing

Ellsworth Vines

between games and even between points, he often presented a loose-limbed and gangling appearance, but his movements in play were swift and purposeful. Under a peaked white cap his lean and high-cheekboned face could look grim; but he had a ready smile, he was a courageous hitter and a first-class sportsman, and was widely popular.

Spearheaded by a tremendous service, his whole game was played at withering speed. Of more recent players, Pancho Gonzales would have ranked with Vines in build and service power; he would have exceeded Vines in agility at the net, though not in power; and would have fallen well short of him in speed of ground stroke. Vines could hit his forehand with pace and depth throughout a rally, drawing from Tilden the tribute that his forehand was the fastest he had ever encountered. Some British critics went so far as to describe Vines's tennis as violent.

Vines played in a long-armed and full Eastern style similar to Tilden's, but, not having to compensate for a maimed finger, his forehand grip was not quite so full (meaning arm-in-line-with-racket) as Tilden's, and he made less change of grip for his backhand. His great speed came from his height and strength, his long swing, and his excellent co-ordination and timing. The reason why his shots were faster again than Tilden's or Johnston's—or, for that matter, than any world champion's before or since—lay in the comparative flatness of his strokes.

He used a Continental grip for his service, holding the racket farther round towards a backhand grip than most other players—though not so far round as Roy Emerson of more recent times. Combined with a perfectly co-ordinated swing of large arc and great height, this grip allowed Vines a maximum wrist snap. He brought the head of the racket over the ball for control, and largely dispensed with sidespin and kick. In the terms of the day, Vines served bullets.

Similarly, his forehand and backhand were "flat". There is no such stroke as a perfectly flat drive; even if the ball is struck with the racket face square-on to the intended line of flight, the racket rises in its follow-through and thus some forward spin is always imparted to the ball. It is the minimum of spin, however, and so these shots are referred to as flat drives. They carry more speed and depth than slightly rolled drives,

and more again than topspin drives played with a little "up and over" in the swing. The penalty attached to driving flat is that it demands a small net clearance and is thus the least safe technique.

In basing his game on flat strokes Vines was not unsound. He had the height necessary to do so in both service and ground strokes. Flat drives are most comfortably made from about waist-high and they allow a reasonable margin of safety when taken above net height. A tall man is thus able to play more balls flat with safety than a shorter man, and although there may be only a few inches in it, this difference in waist height between tall and short men has a marked effect on the style of play available to them. While not as safe as rolled strokes, flat shots, if mastered, give not only greater speed but greater accuracy.

Vines was only nineteen when, in 1931, he swept the board in U.S. major tournaments to such effect that his American ranking rose from tenth to first and he became regarded as the logical successor to Tilden. The following year he descended on Wimbledon, laying the opposition waste with his "violent" game, smashing some lobs so hard that the ball bounced from mid-court into the royal box itself. In the quarter finals he was expected to be well tested by the powerful serving and all-round hard hitting of the Spanish player Enrique Maier. But a strong opponent only caused Vines to hit even harder. He won in quick time, 6–2, 6–3, 6–2, making the Spaniard's service appear almost innocuous compared with his own. Next he faced Crawford, victor over fourth-seeded Fred Perry, and hit him off the court in so devastating a display that Henri Cochet, watching from the stand, was heard to observe: "Pretty good. Wonderful. Never saw anything like it."

In the final, Vines was to oppose England's Bunny Austin, who had beaten Frank Shields of America and Jiroh Satoh of Japan. Austin was a smooth stroke-maker usually at his best against the hard-hitting American type of player, and he was given some chance of halting Vines's crushing run. He was also the first Englishman to reach the final for ten years.

Austin was allowed to show a little more of his art than Crawford had been, but only a little. Vines began uncertainly, and the score reached 4–all in the first set. Veteran onlookers described the match from then on as the greatest display of intense speed ever seen on a tennis court. Vines swept over Austin like a heavy surf gaining force with each wave. The score was 6–4, 6–2, 6–0. In his twelve service games Vines served thirty aces, the last one ending the match. The third set took only ten minutes. Some of Vines's drives beat Austin by half the width of the court.

Austin did not play badly; he seldom did. He simply could not get his racket effectively to the ball, and some of Vines's services he did not even see. One Davis Cup player described Vines's play as "terrifying". Evening newsboards in London bore the headlines MURDER ON THE CENTRE COURT. Power tennis has not been confined to the post-World War II era or to players in short trousers.

Vines's play in the 1932 Wimbledon final may have been terrifying, but his manner was restrained. Photographs of the finalists shaking hands at the net show Vines not in triumph but offering commiseration to the unfortunate Austin.

In his next important event, the Davis Cup challenge round against France, played about

The Vines service . . .

two weeks after Wimbledon, Vines met his first check and had to be content with only mixed success. Perhaps, though it means widening our lens, we should review this most interesting tie between the France of the ageing Musketeers and the resurgent young America typified by Vines.

Both Borotra and Cochet had met defeat early at Wimbledon—Cochet, it may be recalled, so early that he was able to win the Consolation Plate instead—but the Musketeers, united and playing for France at the Roland Garros stadium, were a different proposition. In the opening match a thirty-four-year-old Borotra amazed everyone by defeating Vines in yet another of his characteristic tactical victories. Managing, from a combination of his marvellous agility and the court's slow surface, to get Vines's service back into play better than others before him, Borotra found that the rest of Vines's game showed traces of inconsistency. Rather than rush the net in his usual fashion and risk forcing his opponent into playing well, he remained at the baseline more than usual and allowed Vines to make mistakes. These tactics paid, and Borotra was able to establish his normally unbeatable lead of two sets to nil. In the third set, we are told, Vines improved; but knowing the wily Borotra well enough by now, we would expect him to have rested in this set.

At 3-all in the fourth set, Borotra, feeling his stamina failing, decided that he would have to win quickly or not at all. He launched a comprehensive net attack, and the startled Vines found him covering everything from the widest of passing shots to the deepest of lobs—in short, providing a taste of the Bounding Basque at his inspired best. In near-delirium, the crowd cheered Borotra on to what was regarded as an almost miracle victory at 6–4, 6–2, 3–6, 6–4.

Now Cochet came in with Wilmer Allison of Texas. Cochet had failed at the last three Wimbledons, and it was Allison who had defeated him when he was strongly favoured for the 1930 title sensationally won by Tilden. This time Cochet made no mistake; he beat Allison in four sets, giving France a two-love lead.

On the second day the world's two outstanding doubles pairs, Allison and Van Ryn, and Cochet and Brugnon, fought a hectic five-set battle finally won by the Americans. This kept the tie very much alive, for a win by both Americans on the final day was certainly not beyond the bounds of possibility.

In the next match, his last Davis Cup singles, Borotra covered himself with glory. Coming back from the most un-Borotra-like position of two sets down, he won at 7–5 in the fifth and sealed France's win. Borotra's triumph was Allison's tragedy. Towards the end of the match all the breaks went against him. He reached match point (perhaps Davis Cup point to America) four times, only to be disappointed. And one of these points was possibly a Borotra double-fault. Allison made no complaint, but one feels for him nevertheless.

It was a pity that when Vines and Cochet walked out to play the final singles the tie was already decided, for if the scores had been two matches all, the Cup would have hung on the outcome of a combat between the world's two greatest singles players. Cochet was the current holder of the French singles and of the world's number-one ranking for the last four years, and he had not lost a Davis Cup singles since 1927. Vines was U.S. and Wimbledon champion, but had not opposed Cochet in either event. After Borotra's success against Vines, most observers expected a Cochet win.

This time Cochet did not dally in the early stages of the match; in a display of all his erstwhile wizardry he took the first two sets at 6–4, 6–0. Vines then hit out fearlessly. In the feast of tennis that followed, his deep driving denied Cochet the net and he took the next two sets at 7–5, 8–6. Once over the hurdle, the young American hit Cochet out of the match in the fifth set, to record a grand win that was head-lined in Press and newsreels as YOUNG AMERICAN BEATS FRENCH TENNIS MASTER.

Some critics held that if the tie had not already been decided Cochet would not have let his early lead go and would have won in either the third or the fourth set; others declared that Vines would have won anyway, so that the Cup had really hung on Allison's match points against Borotra, including the possible double-fault. Such things being incapable of proof, it can only be said that France won the 1932 Davis Cup by the barest of margins; and perhaps just as well, for she has not won it since.

Cochet followed Vines over to America a few months later in an attempt to deprive him of his National singles title. Both reached the final, and again Vines was the winner, this time in straight sets. Standing in close, Cochet reduced the angle available to Vines's service and had the satisfaction of limiting his aces to a mere half-dozen. But Vines had other weapons; time and again his big forehand drive or volley made clean winners and broke up Cochet's all-court mixture of attack and defence.

In two years, 1931 at home and 1932 against all comers, Vines, not yet twenty-one, cut a swathe never equalled in tennis. Then things began to crowd in on him. He married soon after his twenty-first birthday, and in 1932–3 visited Australia. The tour did him no good. Stale and over-tennised, he was badly in need of a rest. His concentration and play were below standard, and his mantle of invincibility was holed when he suffered defeats from Australia's champion Jack Crawford and from the sixteen-year-old boy wonder Vivian McGrath. On his return to America Vines was soon engaged in preparation for Wimbledon and the Davis Cup inter-zone

. . . *and backhand*

final. All America expected him to retain his Wimbledon title and to win not only the inter-zone final but the challenge round against France as well and thus bring the Davis Cup back to its homeland after its long absence. The season was meant to end with Vines winning the National singles title for the third time in succession. He would then have virtually no more amateur worlds to conquer, and before he sailed for Europe he received an offer from Tilden to join a professional troupe. The offer was large enough to interest Vines deeply; nothing was signed, but a verbal agreement was reached.

"See here," said Tilden. "If you win the lot the association will put great pressure on you to stay an amateur. Will you go through with our deal anyway?"

"I may lose them all," Vines replied. "Will you go through with it anyway?"

"Yes."

"So will I then."

The United States L.T.A., hearing of the professional approach to Vines and wanting to be sure that no American player was sailing under false amateur colours, has been reported (by Tilden) as having "pestered Vines almost daily all through his European trip to know if he had signed a contract, what he was going to do, etc." This was certainly unsettling for Vines, but as amateurism meant a great deal more at that time than it does now the L.T.A.'s attitude is understandable.

Enough has been said to indicate that Vines's preparation for his 1933 tour was far from ideal;

Vines as professional, 1939

between the 1932 and 1933 Wimbledons he had probably as much on his shoulders as a twenty-one-year-old could be expected to carry.

At first things went well enough. At Wimbledon Vines soon showed that if he was not as sharply accurate as he had been the year before his power was every bit as devastating, and he soon reached the semi-final. Here, for the third time, he disposed of Cochet. Again it was a whirlwind finish, with Cochet left standing as Vines swept through the fourth and last set at 6–1. In the final, however, he met an inspired Crawford and lost his title in a five-set match of which more will be heard in a later chapter; it was regarded as the greatest final in the fifty-seven years of Wimbledon's history, and many people felt content that Vines would beat Crawford another day.

Then came a period of misfortune and disaster. Later that month Great Britain defeated the U.S.A. in the Davis Cup inter-zone final in Paris by four matches to one, and Vines lost both his singles. In the opening singles he lost badly to Austin, 6–1, 6–1, 6–4. Trying to make amends against Perry on the last day, he led by two sets to one, sprained his ankle in the fourth set and, concealing the pain he was suffering, played on to the fifth before collapsing on the court. Back in America, a committee was formed to investigate his amateur status. It found in his favour, but all too late. In the third round of the National singles Vines, by now a shadow of his former self, was beaten by B. M. ("Bitsy") Grant, and the high hopes held for him a few short months before were in ruins. Grant was a player good enough to gain selection in later U.S. Cup teams, but as irony would have it, his game was based on steadiness to the point of retrieving, and as the smallest competitor in the event he barely reached Vines's shoulder.

What of Tilden's offer, made when Vines seemed certain to have been a great drawcard?

What was Vines worth now? Tilden stood by his terms without reducing them a dollar. As a player he knew that Vines would regain his marvellous form, but there is no doubt that as a financier he was being generous. Tennis champions are often men of considerable character, and Tilden was one such.

So was Vines. Though he must have longed to regain his amateur prestige, he confirmed his acceptance of the offer, determined that Tilden should not regret it. He recovered his form, drew record gates on his first tour, in which he defeated Tilden, again proved his mastery over Cochet when the Frenchman joined the troupe, and in a later series defeated Perry, three-time winner of both the Wimbledon and U.S. National singles. It is a great pity that he was lost to the world's amateur tournaments and to the Davis Cup competition after only two years of international play and at the early age of twenty-two. He was a great player, and any one of his most powerful strokes—his concussive service, forehand drive, and forehand volley—was a candidate for world all-time honours in its own section.

This has been a story of brilliance and mismanagement, but it has its connection with style. One reason advanced for Cochet's eventual overthrow of Tilden was that Tilden possibly had too many strokes to choose from and that this was perhaps to his disadvantage against Cochet's direct and early-ball type of game. Vines's fall in 1933 tends to show that he, by contrast, had too few strokes. Flat and fast, with the ball shaving the net and landing near the lines, they were all-or-nothing. More roll would almost certainly have seen Vines through against opponents not quite in his own class at a time when he was outwardly a world figure and inwardly a most worried young man.

The lesson of style here is surely that no matter how straight a champion's eye and how stout his bow, he needs a few reserve arrows in his quiver.

11 | The Great Jack Crawford

JACK CRAWFORD was one of the truly great figures of Australian tennis, and is generally regarded as the man who made the game a major sport in his country.

Born in 1908, he learned his early tennis in the small town of Urangeline in the Riverina district of New South Wales before making his home in Sydney at the age of about seventeen. A rangy six-footer when young, he had broadened to about thirteen stone or 180 pounds by the time he won the Wimbledon title in 1933 and was over fifteen stone, or 210 pounds, in his later competitive years. He was remarkably straight-backed and took small steps about the court for a man so tall. Mostly serious and courteous in manner, he also had the brand of dry humour common among the sportsmen of his day.

His personality was both impressive and likeable, but the inspiration he provided came mainly from his delightful stroke-play. In the 1930s his polished displays stimulated thousands of spectators and players, and no matter how greatly tactics may have changed in the meantime, Australian play to this day bears the stamp of his free and classic style.

Many Australians tend to date tennis from Jack Crawford's time. One still hears them comparing the modern serve-and-volley power game with "the game in Jack Crawford's day, when they wore long trousers, and even long sleeves, and used to play leisurely baseline rallies with flat-topped rackets". Although much of this is correct, it applied only to Crawford and those influenced by him, and not to either his predecessors or most of his contemporaries.

Except for the long trousers—which were worn by all Wimbledon winners before Jack Kramer in 1947—it was Crawford himself who set the clock back. His appearance at Wimbledon in long sleeves buttoned at the wrist aroused considerable comment and caused older spectators to recall the Dohertys. But Crawford chose to play in long sleeves simply because he felt

more comfortable starting a match that way. In heat of battle he rolled up the sleeve of his playing arm; he did not feel a need to roll up the other one, and he was a man who seldom did anything he didn't have to.

In like manner his sudden introduction of a flat-topped racket was received, in the 1930s, with near-incredulity. When it became obvious that he was serious about it, a theory developed that the flat head helped in playing awkward half-volleys near the feet. Soon what at first was seen merely as an ugly racket came to be regarded as an integral part of Crawford's game. In normal stroking the upward slope of the uppermost side frame accentuated the characteristic lowness of Crawford's wrist. He was a past-master at making

Crawford in the late 1920s: Low-wristed backhand volley

angled crosscourt shots from balls above net height (flat from the forehand, sliced from the backhand) and in these shots, at least the way Crawford played them, the broad flat-top seemed to provide extra snap in coming round and outside the ball. As we shall see in a moment, this may not have been as fanciful as it sounds.

The once despised flat-topped racket thus came to be seen as a graceful wand, and it was not long before sporting-goods manufacturers and sports stores throughout Australia plied a roaring trade in it. The racket trade gained, in fact, a dual benefit, for this old racket shape had never been previously subjected to the tight stringing used in the 1930s, and sometimes, after its guarantee period had safely expired, its top broke inwards under the strain, providing the dealer with yet another sale. Semi-flat-tops were then designed, to maintain both the Crawford picture and the manufacturer's good name, until with Crawford's eventual passing from the world stage the normal oval shape returned—to the relief of all concerned.

The hundreds of buyers of flat-tops soon learned that the new weapon did not improve their low- and half-volleying. These shots are mostly played with the racket at some angle to the perpendicular, and here the flat top of the frame hindered rather than helped: its corner struck the ground where an oval-framed racket would still have had clearance. But the great Crawford used flat-tops, so his devotees persisted in using them too.

Eventually the story behind Crawford and the flat-top came to light. Playing a social game at Sir Norman Brookes's home in Melbourne, Crawford was offered one of his host's old rackets. "They were well out of fashion when I used to use them," said Sir Norman. "See what you think."

Crawford was surprised to find that for wide balls just too far out of reach to be struck with the centre of the strings the flat shape gave more power, that it overcame, or at least reduced, the weak area normally existing between the centre of the strings and the top of the frame. He decided that, freakish or not, a flat-top was the racket for him; he had modern ones made, and a craze was born.

This was no fad of Crawford's. Apart from the possibility that it helped him to play his crosscourt shots better, the racket certainly fitted his game. Never has there been a champion so indolently content to reach for wide shots or high lobs, or one so loath to run or leap for them.

Crawford was a baseline player in singles, the whimsical reason advanced by many of his tolerant admirers being that it was too much to expect Jack to run all the way up to a distant net. (Once, however, he unconsciously jumped it—in his excitement at winning the Wimbledon title. "I didn't realize I could clear such a high barrier," he said later. "It was the first and only time in my life that I attempted such a feat.") But Crawford was not only secure in his baseline

A Crawford forehand

game (in his heyday his control of ground strokes was said to be unequalled); he could also use it strongly in attack. Against different types of players—those with cannonball services, those with weak ground strokes, those who crowded the net—he would stand in close and at times give the impression of commanding the net, almost in the manner of a volleyer.

In his period he was practically alone in playing from the baseline; almost everyone else was playing the all-court game. Crawford, with his particular brand of ground strokes, showed that he did not need to. It can't be helped if this destroys pleasant imaginings of an old-time Crawford running about well behind his baseline, playing long and elegant drives that would have been cut off in their prime by any of today's hundred leading players. A moment's thought shows that if he had played in this manner he could not possibly have beaten a player of Vines's all-round power in that historic Wimbledon final of 1933.

Time may have confused some aspects of Crawford's image, but opinion was divided over him in his playing days, too. He was an uncomplicated type of player, yet in his time he seems to have been all things to all men. Perhaps people came to see in him what they wanted to see, and obligingly he did not let them down.

He played all his strokes immaculately and with apparent ease, and any one of them could be taken to be his favourite shot. Some observers were convinced that his most telling stroke was a straight forehand penetrating his opponent's backhand; others that his best forehand was a deep crosscourt shot that landed in the last square foot of his opponent's forehand corner; others again that his strength lay in his amazing forehand variation of pace and angle. Some decided that his backhand was an even more beautifully produced stroke, while there were many who preferred watching him play doubles, because it was there that they saw more of his low-volleying artistry.

Nor could everyone agree on how he played his shots. Some said he had a long-swinging action, so easy that it looked almost careless; others that he had the crispest ground strokes they had ever seen. Sometimes he played his low volleys and half-volleys with a low wrist and well-bent knees, at others he seemed to flick them from where he stood. Even when he was on the receiving end of a smash directed at his shoelaces, it seemed to some of his admirers that it was he and not his opponent who looked to be in command of the situation. Onlookers thought he played with such ease that he avoided making the game too hard for himself or for his opponent. Many opponents, on the other hand, felt that he stood in so close as to be almost on top of them, and that the ball was always coming back before they had finished their own shots.

Crawford's footwork, for so large a man, was light. He played his forehand beautifully, either across his front leg or along it. To some his wrist was like velvet, to others it was like steel. He never looked fully extended, though in fact he concentrated so deeply in title matches that he never once heard a press camera click. His wristy play was considered too risky for anything less than his top form, and it was said that he lacked interest in tennis and probably would not last long. But his career turned out to be as long as it was distinguished; still using his wristy and rising-ball style of play, he competed in Senior* events until his late fifties. Those who once thought his game may have consisted of brilliant winners and careless mistakes later came to the view that his range of strokes and great flexibility served to make him supremely steady, for he seemed able to cope with almost any type of ball he received.

No occasion appeared too big for Crawford and none too small, but even his appearance was interpreted in different ways. Walking onto a centre court before a packed gallery, he could appear to some the picture of a composed and impressive world champion, and to others, at Wimbledon for instance, appealingly human; as one observer wrote: " . . . Jack Crawford, in buttoned shirtsleeves and with a curious flat-topped racket tucked under his arm, reminded one of a young man who had looked in for an afternoon's tennis at the Vicar's. No one wanted him to lose. . . ." The idol of thousands of young players, he was also the favourite of at least one elderly lady who possibly never played tennis in her life—the late Queen Mary.

---

*"Senior" is the more courteous, if sometimes confusing, term used at Sydney's White City for veterans' events. A nice touch is added in the case of the Senior Ladies' Doubles: it is open to ladies over thirty-eight.

There were, of course, many aspects of Crawford's play on which agreement did exist. His effortlessly flowing strokes gave him maximum pace for minimum effort, and he seemed to have the same action for attack as for defence. Free use of his strong wrist enabled him to disguise both the pace and angle of his shots until the last moment. His timing was remarkable. His weight, whatever it happened to be, always went into his shots, though never noticeably. His arm was attractively straight as his racket met the ball, and the racket, in his hands, looked like a toy. Nevertheless he was a player in whom people could evidently see almost anything they cared to look for—except pettiness or a kicking service.

Though Crawford's style must have resembled the graceful low-wristed English style of the

Crawford, with flat-top, English grip and extra weight all well in evidence

Doherty brothers, nothing like it had been seen in Australia, where it came to be regarded as the latest method of stroking. Other players who held their hands farther round behind the handle came to be considered more or less old-fashioned: they had to work hard to obtain pace, they were clumsy on low shots and vulnerable near their feet, and they ran right out of the court in recovering wide balls while all Crawford seemed to do was lean over and flick them in, round the corner.

If Brookes had been a master at tying his opponents up, Crawford was a master at stretching them out; like his own stroke-play the essence of his matches was freedom of action. He did not employ either the cannonball or the American Twist service. Putting the ball up fairly high in front of his right shoulder, he seemed to stretch his tall frame in a leisurely way before projecting a sliced or almost flat delivery designed to go away from his opponent and bounce as low as possible. In baseline play, too, he liked to run the ball away, after which he would often be in a position to step in and drive one of his many characteristic clean winners into an open court. He stranded volleyers with flat rising-ball drives either threaded down the line or flicked across court with a typical Crawford hook rather than with the more steadying use of topspin. Giving the impression of playing from inside the baseline unless he could be forced behind it, he scarcely needed the net position himself, except in doubles. Fencing with an adversary of equal calibre, he would use practically every square yard of his opponent's territory; he was a master of what was sometimes called chessboard tennis.

His effect on attendances became noticeable as he rose into the top rank, and the Australian Lawn Tennis Association wisely imported overseas stars to meet him. Successive French, English, Japanese, and American visits made headline news of the game, bringing substantial gate money to the leading Australian tennis centres and new players onto courts all over the country. Even greater was his effect on the Australian tennis style, though the fact that it has remained to the present time is largely unrealized. This effect is perhaps best considered in the short and long terms.

Almost overnight, it seemed, Crawford's style had copyists everywhere, particularly in Sydney's grasscourt tournaments. They walked after the ball instead of running for it, they attempted to take it much earlier than they could with consistency, they tried for crosscourt angles with a flat racket and missed the sidelines, they ignored the net when it was theirs for the taking, and they altered their grips as well.

Crawford's grip was what would now be called a free-wristed form of Continental, with a slight change for the backhand. As a young player Crawford stepped round a lot of backhands; later, by adopting a slice, he made his backhand solid against fast play and developed excellent touch with it. Further, being Crawford, he made it a long (longer than his forehand) flowing stroke of such grace that it became his most photographed shot. His admirers followed with grip, wristy forehand, and sliced backhand—and lost much of whatever power and effectiveness they had previously possessed. Finally they discovered a preference for playing doubles from the right-hand court—the one Crawford always took with Hopman, and later with Moon, McGrath, and Quist.

Crawford's wristy style proved too chancy for his early and impetuous imitators, as past players and critics had incorrectly predicted it would for Crawford himself. But no one seemed to mind in the least. They didn't win, but what odds? Hadn't they played a stroke-making game? That was the thing about Crawford's displays at the White City—the result of a match seemed to be of less concern to everyone than Crawford's tennis. Such, then, were the short-term effects.

The Crawford influence virtually obliterated the earlier Australian style of Patterson and Anderson from the grasscourts. It also invaded the hardcourts, where court preparation became more a matter of sufficient watering than of rolling to concrete hardness; both the chopping-and-cutting and the heavy-topspin styles disappeared, and Australian grass and hardcourt styles merged.

The idea that the Crawford style was the latest in modern play was strengthened in 1934 when Fred Perry became the next world champion and, visiting Australia, displayed an extreme "Full Continental" grip that needed no change at all for the backhand. Perry, too, had his copyists, but his grip was found too extreme for most players and the Crawford method thus came to be regarded as the sound modern grip. Long after Perry departed these shores, Crawford

was still playing and exerting his influence. It would scarcely be going too far to say that he exerted a spell.

Apart from the early rash copyists, a large crop of younger players developed in the Crawford style—though with more all-court play—and it would be untrue to say that the standard of Australian tennis as a whole did not improve. One of these younger players was Adrian Quist, whose style closely resembled Crawford's and who became one of Australia's greatest all-round players in singles and doubles.

Later—with the hard hitting of von Cramm, the "heavy ball" of Donald Budge, and the pressure of Jack Kramer—the Eastern American style again became acclaimed the world over. There can be no quarrel with this, since for most players the Eastern is both sound and natural and gives good results, and when it comes to world championship play there is nothing restrictive about it. Nor did Crawford dispute it; as obliging as ever, he agreed that if he had to learn tennis over again he would go along with the standard Eastern grips as providing the best basis for the game.

But the Crawford influence has clearly remained in Australia. The Eastern grip used by many Australians is not as far behind the handle as that used by the Americans, the wrist is often lower, and the general style of play is more flexible. Sedgman was an example of it. Hoad's forehand is Continental and his stroke-making most reminiscent of Crawford's. Despite the world-wide influence of Budge's rolled backhand, Rosewall's is sliced. In Rod Laver we even have a Continental-style left-hander. Emerson and Stolle, Australia's singles representatives in a Davis Cup challenge round as recently as 1966, are Continental-grip players.

This Crawford influence is not confined to top-class players. Any hundred Australian club players would probably compare more than favourably in style and freedom of stroke-making with a similar group of players from any other country. Australia in general has become a nation of stylists; a newspaper picture of some unknown schoolboy playing a low backhand volley is likely to show a stroke that before Crawford's day would have been considered most stylishly made.

The Dohertys being too far away for much more than fanciful comparison, it is interesting to compare Crawford's style with that of the

French master Henri Cochet.

Cochet used less backswing than Crawford on both service and backhand, and all told his strokes were plainer and made with less flourish. Nevertheless his strokes and Crawford's were strikingly similar. The service was not severe, but the return was pounced upon. The forehand was made with short backswing (Crawford's more rolling), the ball being taken early with a steel wrist in a velvet glove; languid, crisp, or at times even flicked, the forehand was the master stroke, carrying unexpected pace, change of pace, and control of both depth and angle. The backhand was sliced and, against a net attack, often played first slow and low across court to force an awkward half-volley, preparatory to a clean passing shot. Low and half-volleys were made with ease. Both men gave an impression that the display rather than the result was what mattered to them. Most unexpectedly, we find such a distinctive style in two men of entirely different build and from opposite sides of the world.

In his world-class days—from 1928 to 1939—Crawford was in nine of the ten Australian Davis Cup teams fielded, and so encountered overseas stars ranging in time from Tilden and the Musketeers to Donald Budge. He was ranked in the world's top ten players from 1932 to 1937, holding top place in 1933.

His career in Australian tennis was of course much longer. Beginning in 1925, when at the age of seventeen he won the under-twenty-one-years Australian junior championships (it was altered to under-nineteen in 1934), he was soon engaging the best senior players on equal terms and winning State titles. But he had to wait patiently for his first Australian singles championship; Jean Borotra of France and Dr J. C. Gregory of England took the 1928 and 1929 titles respectively, and in 1930 Crawford was unexpectedly beaten in the final by the greatest player Queensland had produced prior to Laver and Emerson. This was Gar Moon, tall and strong and tanned to the colour of mahogany, who played in the swinging lackadaisical manner often adopted by Crawford himself. After these early obstructions Crawford soon showed his authority, becoming the only man, other than Roy Emerson of later years, to win the Australian singles three years in succession. Fred Perry of England barred him from the title in 1934, but he returned the compliment by defeating Perry in the 1935 final for his fourth and last Australian singles championship.

Though gradually overhauled and passed, Crawford was the outstanding personality of Australian tennis until World War II and remained a drawcard until his last appearance in a championship event in about 1950. Even when his matches were relegated to outside courts he drew crowds, and always among them were loyal nostalgic supporters. Sometimes one of them could be heard asking a son or daughter to look at that and compare it with the hit-and-miss stuff you see nowadays.

Crawford's career was as full as it was long. Because he was renowned for a baseline game without powerful overhead strokes or severe high volleys, he might be thought to have been a singles player only. This was far from the truth. In partnership with Harry Hopman (the names of Crawford and Hopman were once as closely linked as those of Hoad and Rosewall were later) and then with Gar Moon and Vivian McGrath, he won the Australian doubles title four times; with Adrian Quist he won the French and Wimbledon doubles championships of 1935. His volleying was backed by surprisingly quick reflexes, and he was a low-volleying and half-volleying specialist; his rising-ball returns of service were so penetrating that he has been ranked with John Bromwich as one of the greatest right-court doubles players Australia has produced.

And if one felt that Crawford could never have been aggressive or sprightly enough to be a great mixed-doubles player, one would be wrong again. Besides a Wimbledon title with Miss Ryan, he won the Australian mixed doubles title three years in succession with his wife.

Crawford's calm manner did not fit him for being either magnificent in victory or gallant in defeat. Rather he was generous in the former circumstance and gracious in the latter, and because, in addition, he never spoke an ill word of anyone he became generally known as Gentleman Jack and was immensely popular.

As a good racing man he believed in luck, which he connected with most of his wins but never with his losses. Before his 1933 Wimbledon final with Ellsworth Vines a number of pointers gave him the feeling that it was to be his day. His favourite racket was just at the right played-in tension, and every string in it was sound (strings in those days were not as reliable as they became later). His favourite pair of trousers in which he had won his last twelve tournaments had been disturbingly overdue from the cleaners, but arrived at his hotel in the nick of time. On his way to the courts he chanced to look out of the rear window just as his car turned into Wimbledon, and there in the car behind him was Vines. His first thought was that it was a pity it wasn't a race day.

But whenever it was Crawford's turn to lose, Lady Luck, whether a participant or not, was never mentioned. In 1933 he beat Keith Gledhill of America for the Australian title, Cochet for the French, and Vines at Wimbledon; in the final of the U.S. National singles he led Fred Perry at the interval by two sets to one and was thus within one set—some have said within one string —of being the first man to win the Grand Slam. History records that Perry won the fourth and fifth sets and that, later, Donald Budge was the first Grand Slam winner.

What happened? Some said that Perry decided he had nothing to lose and, to use his own expression, "went mad"; others that Crawford unwisely waited through the interval in damp clothes while Perry took a refreshing shower;

Gar Moon

others again that Crawford had the ill luck of breaking a string in that favourite racket of his. Newspapers at the time used one or another of these theories or a mixture of all three, but although reporters were thirsting for copy direct from the players they could get no more help from Crawford than the opinion that Fred Perry had played very well indeed.

We come now to that ever-intriguing question of standard of play. Jack Crawford, the man from whom Australians so largely date tennis time, represents the standard of play by which they have most often sought to judge the moderns. Asked for his own opinion, Crawford has characteristically replied that he would have been very lucky to have troubled these fellows today, and this seems to have satisfied those who already hold such a view. But it loses rather than gains weight in coming from Crawford himself. One feels that if the questioner had referred to earlier days instead of later ones Crawford would have said that Cochet was past his prime when he beat him, or even that he would have needed luck to have beaten the Renshaw brothers. Until we come to consider the post-World War II champions we can only remind ourselves that Crawford proved himself capable of handling Vines's terrific service and volleying attack under the fast conditions of Wimbledon, and rest assured that if he were opposed by a modern serve-and-volley player we would almost certainly see our share of serve-and-passing-shots as well.

Crawford won eleven Australian titles and an almost countless number of State championships, and was in nine Davis Cup teams from the days of Gerald Patterson to those of John Bromwich. He won three Wimbledon and three French titles and, as we've seen, came within one set of gaining the first Grand Slam. Of all his successes, probably the best remembered is his defeat of Vines in Wimbledon's "greatest-ever" final—which, since it has been mentioned several times, calls for some description.

Crawford served first, as he did in all five sets. Games went to 4–all, with Vines attacking hard and Crawford managing to fend him off. Then Vines broke Crawford's serve in the ninth game and held his own for the set at 6–4. To the crowd it seemed that this could well be the pattern the match would follow—fine play, with Crawford sooner or later being forced to concede a service,

and Vines's thunderbolts then making the all-important difference.

Crawford, far from unbalanced by Vines's speed, settled down grimly to the task of winning the vital second set. He held his service lead for game after game, only to see Vines level the score with some of the thirteen blistering aces he was to serve during the match. In the twentieth game Crawford's poise and steadiness gained their reward and the set was his at 11–9. He gained an early break in the third set, which Vines then decided to let go at 6–2. Now it was anybody's match, and soon after the break Vines reasserted his claim to it. At 2–5 down, with Vines serving, Crawford decided to conserve his energy for the

Jiro Satoh

last set, in which, for the fifth time, he would have the opening service. After amost two hours' play the score stood at two sets all and twenty-three games each. Vines, having held his services by a wider margin than Crawford, had won considerably more points.

In the final set Vines attacked strenuously with his swinging strokes and Crawford parried deftly with his wrist. At 2–all Crawford was within a stroke of losing his service and facing almost certain defeat, but the score mounted with un-broken services until Crawford reached 5–4. Possibly deciding that this was his last chance,

Harry Hopman, Davis Cup player

Crawford lifted his play to its limits. Taking the final game to love for the Wimbledon title, he won all four points with shots that raised the chalk. His rising-ball groundstroke play had overcome one of the game's most powerful services, his accuracy having become narrowed to the very lines.

With Crawford, however, results can to some extent be placed on one side; there is little doubt that the classic displays of stroke-making he gave and the personality that gained him such respect and affection made an even greater and more lasting impact on the game of lawn tennis.

It is scarcely possible to discuss Crawford with-out mention of the remarkable Harry Hopman. Beginning his tennis at about the same time as Crawford, he was his close friend and doubles partner and also often his opponent in singles finals. He was chosen in five Davis Cup teams between 1928 and 1939; add his unique record of non-playing Davis Cup captaincies from 1950 to the present day, and it can truly be said of Harry Hopman that he has seen many champions come and go.

Slight, yellow-haired, and keen in manner, Hopman made a trim and nippy figure on the court. He had a snappy service, a severe smash, and was a grand volleyer, particularly on the forehand side, both in execution and in creating opportunities. His groundstroke game was de-signed mainly to gain him the net position, for which purpose he often employed a stroke that later became known as the net-advance chip shot.

His style of play can best be described as con-taining elements of both Eastern and English. He held his racket with an Eastern forehand grip in that the large knuckle of the index finger was behind the racket handle for force and power, but his wrist was decidedly more towards the top of the handle than that of either Tilden or Vines with their full Eastern grips or, for that matter, other Eastern players. Moreover, with their low-wristed forehand and backhand strokes and small change of grip from one to the other, Crawford and Hopman on first coming to prominence were often described as having their own style, in contrast with their predecessors; as Crawford's style was clearly English, there is some justification for saying that Hopman's strokes at least showed elements of this style.

Turning to the masters themselves, Hopman

supports the virtues of the Eastern style and no doubt regards his own game in that light, whereas Tilden regarded the essential difference between the American and English styles as being the lowness of the English wrist and would accordingly have classified Hopman as an English stylist. It is clear that Hopman, like so many Australians since his time, had a style that ought to be called by a name of its own—and what better than Australian?

Hopman's game was attractive. It did not have Crawford's grace or, on the forehand side, either

Harry Hopman, Davis Cup captain

his suppleness of wrist or perfect footwork, but it was brisk and second only in flexibility to Crawford's and possibly Gar Moon's. His matches were brisk and interesting, and at one time or another he could beat anyone in Australia except Crawford. A player's big guns meant little to him—weaknesses were what his sharp eye discerned in a moment, and his efficient game probed them throughout a match. In doubles he made full use of whatever happened to be his partner's strength to exploit his own volleying armory. Playing as a young man with the mighty Patterson, he was not in the least inhibited; the better Patterson served, the wider and more daring were the young Hopman's interceptions. Partnering Crawford, with his penetrating service return, Hopman would again blanket the net and often succeed in taking the volleying initiative away from the server. In mixed doubles—which he usually played with young Miss Hall, later Mrs Hopman—his partner had only to keep the rallies going for a reasonable time and Hopman would be certain to make more interceptions than his male opponent.

It was Hopman who introduced shorts to Australian championship tennis, though not with immediate success, the general opinion being that they would be better confined to the football field or to the beach. If long trousers look stuffy today, shorts at their first introduction looked jarringly discordant. Perhaps of more interest is the fact that Hopman did not noticeably improve his play when he changed to shorts; apparently earlier players were not, as is often supposed, hampered by wearing long trousers.

Since 1950, Hopman has been mainly identified with his success as a Davis Cup captain and administrator. But although his long experience in these fields must have added to his knowledge of tennis, he was a champion in his own right long before, and anyone who saw his intelligent play would have felt that there was very little Harry Hopman did not already know about the game.

12 | Two Hands Are Better than One

FRED PERRY, Wimbledon's next winner after Crawford, must wait for a moment, for at this point the game's most unusual style came into being. This was two-handed play, and because it came into championship tennis in the hands of a schoolboy its impact was all the greater.

It has long been accepted practice to wield bats, clubs, axes, and a variety of other implements with two hands, and for a time the tennis racket was threatened with a similar fate. Vivian McGrath, born in 1916, was the founder of the renowned line of double-handers that ran from the 1930s to the 1950s. As a small boy McGrath took his left-handed cricket or baseball-bat swing onto the court and hit tennis balls with it. Naturally a right-hander where one hand was called for, he learnt a normal service and forehand, but he always used two hands for strokes on the backhand side. Though it is hard to imagine anything more unorthodox than playing with two hands instead of one, so many variations of two-handed play came into being that McGrath could be referred to as the orthodox or at least the basic type of two-handed player. He developed a smooth, strong service, either sliced or kicked, a good volley and overhead, and a fair Eastern-type forehand, but his game was dominated by his remarkable two-hander. He could hit it flat down the line, fairly belt it down the middle, whip it sharply across court, and toss it unexpectedly with the same backswing he used for a drive. Most dramatic of all, perhaps, was his ending of rapid-fire volleying exchanges in doubles with two-handers of bullet-like speed.

McGrath was an unusually good player at thirteen, and by the time he was fifteen his name was well known throughout Australia. At sixteen he defeated Ellsworth Vines, holder of the Wimbledon and American crowns, in the quarter finals of the 1933 Australian championship, and in the same year he made the first of his five successive Davis Cup appearances.

His amazing success fired the imagination of other schoolboys, and the tennis boom inspired by Crawford spread rapidly to the younger ranks. Bunny Austin, the British Davis Cup star, may have been the man who officially introduced shorts to tennis, but quite independently all over Sydney an army of young would-be McGraths played in short white trousers and long school socks. Many of these young hopefuls also played with two hands, believing this to be the key to success, but it was not long before they ran into trouble; most of them being right-handed cricketers, their double-hander was a forehand and they soon found that their backhands provided insurmountable difficulties.

Dubbed the "Wonder Boy", McGrath played mostly with grown men, but as a schoolboy he

Vivian McGrath

88

had a selfless guide and mentor in Jim Willard, an Australian Davis Cup representative in 1930. His natural shyness soon gave way to an exceptionally calm exterior; it was said of him that a bomb could have exploded on the next court and he would not have noticed it. Olive-skinned with dark-brown curly hair, McGrath grew from a sturdy schoolboy to a slim and handsome 5 feet 10 inches. He became a great admirer of his Davis Cup team-mate and doubles partner Jack Crawford, and from his example smoothed his own stroke-making about as much as a two-handed player could. He was also influenced by Crawford's casual court manner, and probably became a little less purposeful than before.

McGrath was Australian champion in 1937, defeating, in a double-handers' final, an even younger player in seventeen-year-old John Bromwich. The score 6–3, 1–6, 6–0, 2–6, 6–1—was highly unusual for a match involving the dour Bromwich, indicating perhaps that McGrath's mixture of brilliance and casualness may have largely dictated the game. But although McGrath was Australian champion at the age of only twenty and already had several years of Davis Cup experience behind him, he was not destined to become one of the greatest players of tennis history or even of his own day.

Being the first of that string of outstanding youngsters we have since become accustomed to, McGrath was called upon to play far too much tennis and was burnt out before his time. At one period he seemed to be playing all the time, seven days a week; scarcely had he finished a week or fortnight of championships than he would be off on a mid-week exhibition tour of country towns; on Saturday he would turn out for his club, and on Sundays he would play with friends. Whatever the reasons for his early retirement, his stroke-play and his style undoubtedly handicapped him against players of world class. His forehand never developed to match the rest of his game, and his freak double-hander, once it lost its element of surprise, was found to be restrictive in reach.

McGrath was never seen overseas in the devastating form he could produce in Australia, and for this reason his two-handed style had far less influence abroad than it did at home.

Just as Perry's extreme Continental grip consolidated Crawford's English style in Australia, so did John Bromwich keep McGrath's two-handed play in the van. McGrath's success almost certainly encouraged Bromwich, but Bromwich had not copied McGrath's game in the first place. He began to play tennis before he ever saw his famous predecessor—before he ever saw anybody play, one is tempted to think. He had a left-handed forehand, a two-handed backhand on his right side, and as a small boy he served by throwing the ball up and hitting it with his two-handed backhand overhead. By the time he was old enough to serve with one hand he had already settled into this stance, and so he served with his right hand. This was a pity, if he was really left-handed, because his right-handed service and smash were awkwardly produced and never became strong; his sliced service, in fact, looked almost friendly—though it could swerve awkwardly enough and was often deeply placed.

Bromwich developed a game of great control. He was modest, sincere, and most determined by nature, and so was his tennis. His strokes lacked McGrath's freedom and, being made from a shorter backswing, their pace as well. His left-handed forehand was somewhat stiffly produced and mostly played from the wrong (left) foot but it was a far more reliable shot than McGrath's forehand and gave him a fair balance between forehand and backhand strengths. His two-hander did not match McGrath's for speed and topspin, and in moments of stress he sometimes sliced it a little, but it was his most reliable shot in a game thoroughly reliable all round.

Fair head down, long jaw set determinedly, Bromwich hunched his shoulders over his two-hander and so literally got down to his work that after a match his right knee always showed green smudges from the turf. He never minded how long a rally lasted; his determination seemed to increase with the number of strokes. The keynotes of his game were conviction and consistency edged with astonishing accuracy.

Given the steadiness of his game and character, you might expect his court demeanour to have been phlegmatic, but this did not follow. A true sportsman, he never blamed anything or anyone but himself for his mistakes and defeats—but how he blamed himself! Whereas McGrath was calm — almost bland — Bromwich could bring forth every known facial expression of horror and self-disgust at his errors. Someone watching him during a close and exciting match once asked whether Bromwich was playing tennis or Hamlet—and for some time afterwards he was known as the great tragedian. Surprisingly, too, for such a workman among stroke-makers, he had fads about his racket. The manufacturers had to reduce his racket handles to little more than the diameter of a golf club. More surprisingly still for a man who swung his racket with both hands, he was fussy about its balance; there is a story that when the manufacturers once wanted to clean up one of his grimy-looking rackets because it was hardly a good advertisement for them, Bromwich refused to let them, fearing that its balance might be fractionally altered. He also liked his racket loosely strung. As a specialist in control, he used exceptionally long contact between strings and ball, and the looser stringing increased this. A

A young Bromwich gets down to his work

well-remembered image of Bromwich's double-hander includes his low approaching run, his almost hypnotic attention to the ball, so that he almost seemed to be drawing it to his racket, his left leg placed well across and his right knee brushing the grass, and finally his loose-stringed racket sweeping the ball away with such long contact that it looked as though he were using a lacrosse bat.

From 1937 to 1950 Bromwich played in seven Davis Cup teams, starting as a lad of eighteen and finishing as a tried campaigner of over thirty. He won the Australian singles in 1939 and 1946, both he and Adrian Quist winning this event on either side of World War II. The war penalized Bromwich badly, occupying the years of his playing life from twenty-one to twenty-six and largely accounting for his absence from the lists of French, Wimbledon, and American singles

winners. But the lost war years were probably not solely responsible for this: once again, style demands to be considered as a factor. Though a superb player and a great advertisement for the two-handed game, Bromwich suffered like McGrath from the limitations of reach that his game inevitably imposed on him. For shots wide of his two-hander he used one hand (a left-handed backhand, never a right-handed forehand), but this was mostly a retrieved shot only; he could not cover the court as extensively as a single-handed player.

Bromwich was a marvellous doubles player. In partnership with Quist he won the Australian doubles three years in succession before the war and five years in succession after it, and also the Wimbledon and American doubles. Partnered by Sedgman, he had a second success in each of these events, and yet a third, in America, with

An older Bromwich gets down to his work

O. W. Sidwell. Some critics have rated him the master doubles player of all time, others the greatest right-court exponent, and the more conservative have called his double-hander one of the game's finest returns of service. Whichever opinion you accept, it justifies the two-hander as an individual stroke, for the recognized stock-in-trade of doubles is powerful serving, smashing and volleying, and John Bromwich was outstanding in none of these.

Discussion of Bromwich leads us straight to Adrian Quist, his singles rival, team-mate, and doubles partner. Quist was born in Adelaide in 1913 and came on the tennis scene at the same time as McGrath, the two playing their first Davis Cup series in 1933 in company with Crawford and another South Australian, Don Turnbull. (South Australia produced yet a third Davis Cup player in the 1930s, a brilliant volleyer named Len Schwartz.) Quist played in more Cup teams than either of the two-handers—nine in all, from 1933 to 1948. Apart from these matches and his record doubles successes with Bromwich, he was Australian singles champion in 1936 and 1940 and again as late as 1948 when he was thirty-five years old. Before teaming with Bromwich to win the Australian doubles title eight times he had won it with Don Turnbull in 1936 and 1937—thus finally holding it ten times—and before that he had won the French and the Wimbledon doubles with Crawford in 1935. After wondering for a moment or two whether Quist may have been an even better doubles player than Bromwich, we can agree without misgiving that this pair was one of the best of all time.

Though short in stature, Quist was beautifully built for sport: strong, springy, and finely co-ordinated. Despite his Nordic name, he was dark-eyed and olive-skinned. He put a lot of thought into his tennis, concentrated hard, and played purposefully. As a stylist he was clearly from the Crawford mould, with the slight difference that he made no change of grip at all between forehand and backhand. After trying out all grips he concluded that the hammer grip, the popular name at the time for English or Continental, was the best for him. He liked to play the ball early and he was not tall; the hammer grip was suitable on both counts since it entailed no change between forehand and backhand and

gave maximum reach. In Crawford, Quist had a model for his strokes, and with plenty of solid practice he took full advantage of it. He was too intelligent to ape Crawford. For a time he used a flat-topped racket (along with hundreds of others) and he based his ground strokes on

Bill Sidwell

Crawford's, but he remained his own man. In fact, when he came to the top he provided a better model for young players than Crawford did; the classic style was there, but supported by more apparent purpose. Crawford's fluidity was delightful to watch, but his almost contemptuous slapping at rising balls with a loose wrist and a flat racket-face invited disaster when practised by lesser men. Quist, like Crawford, sliced his backhand, but as a shorter man he rolled his forehand more; his service was stronger than Crawford's and carried plenty of kick; his volleying was more powerful; and all-court play in singles and interception in doubles formed a much greater part of his game than it did of Crawford's. His overhead was one of the most solid of his day.

Combining to a large extent Crawford's strokes and Hopman's tactics and agility, Quist was a formidable opponent for anyone. He passed Hopman, shared early honours with McGrath, gradually took over from Crawford, and later matched Bromwich. His left-court doubles play was strong and reliable, his usual

Adrian Quist

method of service return being to stand well towards the sidelines and attack strongly with his forehand; if the server reached his backhand Quist's slice could then be played at an acute angle. This doubles forehand was discernible to some extent in Quist's singles play, his forehand down the line being hit noticeably harder than his crosscourt.

Quist and Bromwich, indissolubly linked by their many successes as a two-man team, have a secure place in tennis history. In 1939, when Bromwich was only twenty, they gained Australia's first Davis Cup success.* The 1939 match, played against the Americans at Philadelphia, remains the only Davis Cup challenge round that has been won from a position of two matches down. It took place amid the strange atmosphere of Australia's entry into World War II. The following account of it comes in essence from Adrian Quist.

The Philadelphians were sympathetic towards the Australian team. Hopman and Quist had been photographed staring down at the newsboards announcing their country's declaration of war in support of Great Britain, and when the tie was played that afternoon the Australians were given a reception fit for heroes about to exchange racket for rifle. But however well-disposed the crowd may have been, Australia was down two-nil at the end of the first day's play, Bobby Riggs having defeated Bromwich in straight sets and Frank Parker, a backhand-strength player of unsettling steadiness, having downed Quist in five.

Without detracting from the Americans' play, it has to be noted that the Australians felt tense, far from home, and that they should probably not be playing tennis at a time like this. (Twenty-five years later a young American, Dennis Ralston, was called upon to appear in the finals of a State championship in faraway Australia immediately after hearing the news of his President's assassination. Better than anyone, Quist and Bromwich knew how he felt.) Nevertheless, Quist's match with Parker had been a close one

and he felt himself and Australia to be most unlucky when the last set went against him at 7–5 and faced Australia with almost certain defeat.

The Americans had not announced their doubles pair, having previously been in some trepidation over this match. Riggs and Elwood Cooke, who had won the Wimbledon doubles title only a few months earlier, were expected to be the choice. But Quist and Bromwich had not competed at Wimbledon, and in the U.S. National championships immediately preceding the challenge round they had soundly defeated Riggs

Adrian Quist

*Crawford and Hopman were also members of this team, but the two younger members, Quist and Bromwich, won the challenge round. It may also be recalled that in 1919—when the United States generously stood aside immediately following the first World War—the winning Australian team was still officially Australasia, even though it contained Australian players only.

and Cooke in a semi-final. Casting about for someone to upset the steady Australians, the U.S. selectors lit upon two young men who were probably the hardest hitters in America—Jack Kramer, then aged eighteen, and Joe Hunt.*

This pair duly took the court against Quist and Bromwich, and with powerful serving, youthful enthusiasm, and the all-round confidence engendered by their team's leading position, proceeded with the American onslaught. The first set was theirs, and though the Australians managed to level in the second the young Americans were in no mood to be denied. Gaining an early service break in the third set, they went to a 3–1 lead—and by that time the applause for the Australians, trailing from the outset of the tie, was indeed sympathetic.

The turning point came at 3–2 with Hunt serving at thirty-fifteen. In the previous rally Hunt had broken a string. Changing rackets, he decided to feel the new one out a little and for the first time that day sent down a three-quarter-paced serve, which Quist was able to get into play with certainty. Hunt volleyed, Bromwich

*Hunt later won the 1943 U.S. National championship before being tragically killed in a Navy air crash.

lobbed, Hunt missed the smash, and eventually lost the game. From that point on the Australians took charge, winning the set and the next as well to take the match and keep the tie alive.

"Look here," Bromwich said to Quist. "This isn't over yet. If you beat Riggs, I reckon I can win the last one."

On the final day Quist went to two sets to love over Wimbledon champion Riggs in a good match of all-court tennis. Australia had now won the last five sets played. Riggs gradually overhauled Quist to square the match at two sets all. Confident that Bromwich would be as good as his word in the last match, Quist felt the weight of the world on his shoulders. In the final set he advanced to 4–2, then captured Riggs's next service for an all-but-one lead of 5–2. At match point he managed to get the ball over Rigg's head with an unretrievable lob—which was out by a whisker. Riggs took the game and held his service in the next. It was 5–4 as Quist went out from the umpire's chair to serve. There was no thought of applause; tension had taken its place. Quist served out the game.

All sympathy now goes to Frank Parker. After the first day he had not expected to play again, believing that a substitute would be given

The 1939 Davis Cup challenge round: Riggs (foreground) v. Quist

the honour of playing the last singles. Now the whole tie suddenly rested on his performance. Bromwich, coming from behind, was almost straining to get on the court; Parker went on in do-or-die duty.

From different motives, each chose the same type of game. Bromwich, determined to win, was not going to miss a ball; Parker, determined not to lose, was not going to miss one either.

The rally for the first point consisted of some twenty to thirty strokes. It was eventually won by Bromwich—and after that there seemed no way for Parker to win. Long rallying continued, and one exchange was exaggeratedly reported to have lasted the better part of a hundred shots. But most of the points, however long, went to Bromwich. The match, which was Bromwich's at 6–0, 6–3, 6–1, must have been the longest of only twenty-four games ever played.

The Davis Cup was won for the first time by Australia, and it had been won as never before or since. But in spite of the tensions and the drama it produced, it was Australia's most quickly forgotten victory—forgotten as war closed in.

Quist and Bromwich were to have another famous overseas victory, but this time more in the nature of a sentimental triumph. Visiting England eleven years later in 1950, the Old Firm of thirty-seven-year-old Quist and thirty-one-year-old Bromwich took the Wimbledon doubles title as a fitting climax to their long and world-famed partnership.

Returning to our discussion of two-handed play, it could be said that except for those seeking the sensation of a truly whacking double-hander, Quist's play was more impressive than that of

The 1939 Davis Cup challenge round: Kramer-Hunt (foreground) v. Quist-Bromwich

his early contemporary, Vivian McGrath. It therefore seems that the two-handed style might have ended with its original exponent had it not been for John Bromwich.

For better or worse, however, two-handers attract great attention, and more than one overseas article praised Jack Crawford for "playing so elegantly in a land of freak and ugly styles". An Australian's first impulse is to resent this remark, but it is thought-provoking. Australia had produced two left-handers, Brookes and Hawkes, who played in a manner all their own, two lopsidedly forehand players in Patterson and Anderson, two patterns of orthodoxy in Wilding and O'Hara Wood, an attractive tactician and flexible stroke-player in Hopman, two classical stroke-players in Crawford and Quist (and on occasions two classical sleep-walkers, one is inclined to add, in Crawford and Moon), and the two double-handers on opposite sides, McGrath and Bromwich. Even if two-handed shots are fairly claimed to be natural rather than freakish, it was an unusually mixed bag to have offered the world.

And there was more to come. Close on Bromwich's heels appeared another Australian double-hander in the person of hard-hitting Geoff Brown. Different again from either of the other two, Brown was a right-hander who played a hurricane two-handed forehand on his right side and, having thus placed all his eggs in this one basket, was forced either to use a backhand with his right hand stranded halfway up the handle or to make a forehand from his formerly untrained left hand. After much experimenting he chose the second course, and made a far better job of it than could reasonably have been expected.

Brown was a devastating player. Sometimes he leapt off the ground in delivering his crashing

Frank Parker: Bunched fingers, but the low racket head with closed face makes this stroke more Eastern than Continental

double-hander, and although only lightly built he had a cannonball first service which, after a rapid backswing, he seemed to hit while the ball was still on its way upwards. In his first Wimbledon attempt in 1946, made when he was twenty-two, he reached all three finals without losing a set; he then suffered the misfortune of losing all three, but in his courageous five-set singles final against Yvon Petra he won many friends. He gained Davis Cup selection in 1947 and 1948.

After Brown it seemed that two-handers were dying out, and then Pancho Segura, only moderately successful as an amateur, rose to the heights as a member of Jack Kramer's professional troupe in the 1940s and 1950s and displayed what some critics described as the greatest individual stroke seen up to that time. This was a right-handed two-handed forehand whose direction, pace and intention (whether the shot would be drive, drop-shot or lob) were all concealed until the last possible moment. Both solid and brilliant, it was a match-winner.

On his left side Segura had a strong orthodox right-handed backhand. One may wonder how this could possibly have been, since Segura's right hand had perforce to be halfway up the racket handle to play his two-handed forehand. What he did, almost in the manner of a juggler, was to change the position of his hands between strokes, bringing the right hand to the butt of the handle for the backhand, and for the two-handed forehand throwing this hand to the top of the racket grip and placing the left one at the butt. Where there's a will there's a way, and if there is to be a way we can rely on the champions to find it. *Partially find it* would be more correct, for there was no way in the world for Segura to reach as wide on his two-handed forehand side as a single-handed player could.

It is now time to offer some conclusions about the dramatic departure the double-handers brought about. Are two hands better than one? In the cases of McGrath, Bromwich, Brown, and Segura, yes, for each at his peak had probably the finest single shot of his day, and without his two-hander none of them would in all probability have become a champion. So yes for one stroke alone, and yes also, it could be argued, for doubles. For balance between forehand and backhand, no; two of the four players (McGrath and to a lesser extent, Brown) suffered for lack of it. In the matter of reach, no, for here all four

players were at a disadvantage; so no for singles, the basis of championship tennis. And no, finally, from the aesthetic point of view. Do what he may with his other strokes, while playing his double-hander a two-handed player loses the graceful and balanced appearance that his non-playing arm should provide, and even though he may feel natural he looks ungainly. Viv McGrath hit his two-hander standing up straight and tall, but even so . . . .

The two-handed style burst upon us in the early 1930s in the hands of an exceptional youngster, was given a trial of over twenty years, and has been little seen since. Nevertheless it left its mark on the orthodox single-handed style, particularly in Australia, where the two-handers had most influence. With the added support of the extra hand, all the two-handers of top class were able to play firm rising-ball shots from a short backswing. Single-handed players adopted this shorter backswing for their backhand strokes, the backhand grip itself providing sufficient purchase or leverage. But this grip had to be adequate, and so, to avoid a large change from the forehand, Australian players have since tended to place their forehand grip less behind the handle than Americans.

This Australian adaptation of the Eastern

Geoff Brown

American grip, virtually making it more a form of English or Continental grip, has already been attributed to the influence of Jack Crawford. But it was undoubtedly the two-handers who introduced the shorter backswing, and this probably had something to do with the adoption of the Australian grip, because when it comes to styles of play it's amazing how one thing can lead to another.

Pancho Segura: This stroke will be played with one hand; his double-hander was on the forehand side

13 | Black, White, and Red

HAVING sacrificed some chronology to the two-handers, let's turn now to one of the halcyon periods of tennis—from 1934 to the outbreak of the World War II, when the dominating figures were Fred Perry, Gottfried von Cramm, and Donald Budge. Perry and von Cramm were born in 1909, Budge in 1916. Black, white, and red were eventually to become enemy colours; meanwhile they applied well enough to the British, German, and American champions. Perry was once aptly named the Black Panther, von Cramm was an immaculate sportsman, and Budge a flaming redhead.

Tall, with sleek black hair and keen eyes that flashed from a bronzed face, Perry was fleet-footed at the baseline and catlike at the net. Something of a fashion-plate, he wore creams that were long and wide at the cuffs in the very latest style, and always razor-creased; shorts, no matter how well cut, he could not abide.

His game is generally accepted as stemming directly from table-tennis, which he played in world-class company before applying himself seriously to lawn tennis. He favoured an extreme Continental grip, which he used unchanged for all strokes, advancing both the forefinger and thumb as far as possible along either side of the racket handle in much the same way as they are normally advanced along the sides of a table-tennis bat. He was probably the only champion ever to await service holding his racket in one hand. Again as in table-tennis, he took a very early ball and played wide forehands from an extended right leg.

He was a most confident player—perhaps because of the ball control that table-tennis allows in large measure, perhaps because he escaped the torments of ever being a promising junior, or perhaps, after all, because confidence was in his nature. Once, just before taking the court, he remarked to a group of officials that he expected to beat his man 6–2, 6–3, 6–4—a nice, convenient score, didn't they agree?—and

bettered his prediction by one game.

Perry did not have a big American or Australian service, either cannonball or kicking. He served an orthodox slice of low bound, concentrating on getting a large proportion of first balls into play and on making the second ball as similar as possible to the first. His backhand was also basically a sliced stroke, though he developed a fair amount of pace with it.

On his forehand side he invariably drove. With his extreme Continental grip he had no need to slice under a low ball and, with the reach that this grip afforded, plus his speed of foot and his strong wrist, he rarely had to cut round a wide one, and his early-ball technique avoided high bounces. Even his forehand volley was played in the manner of a very short forehand. It was thus said of him that he used few strokes but that those he did use he played well. He had, however, one outstanding shot: his running forehand drive—a stroke used against wide balls by another dashing player, J. C. Parke, about a quarter of a century earlier. When playing this shot well, Perry was a picture of exuberance.

But his favourite method of play was to gather in a rising-ball forehand en route to the net and arrive there a split second after his own shot had crossed it. When this shot was working well it gave him greater pleasure than any other. On an off-day it produced a crop of errors, but Perry always preferred playing like a millionaire to playing like a miser. Attack was his nature, but he could also play grand defensive tennis when the situation demanded it.

Reminiscing years later, Jack Crawford said that of all his tennis he enjoyed his battles with Fred Perry most, that Perry was hard to beat anywhere and almost impossible to beat at Wimbledon, and that Perry's was the most effective forehand he had encountered. This is praise indeed from a forehand master like Crawford. If Perry received a ball on the forehand side that was at all short he could almost always gain ascendancy in the ensuing exchange and win the point. This made his forehand side, except for shots of excellent length, a danger area for his opponent, and he used to provoke shots into it by positioning himself towards the backhand side of his own court.

Though his strokes lacked the elegance of Crawford's or von Cramm's, Perry's play was highly attractive, particularly to those who like the crisp Continental style. Backing his strokes with speed of foot, all-court versatility, and an outright zest for match play, he achieved great success. He won Wimbledon from 1934 to 1936, defeating Crawford once and von Cramm twice —his 1934 victory making him the first Englishman to win the title since A. W. Gore in 1909. He was, as we already know, United States champion in 1933, and he repeated this success in 1934 and 1936 by defeating Allison and Budge respectively. The Australian championship was

Fred Perry: Table-tennis or extreme Continental grip (this forehand drive will be made without slice)

his in 1934 and the French in 1935. Most heartening of all for tennis in the British Isles, Great Britain won the Davis Cup, after a lapse of twenty-five years, from 1933 to 1936, with Perry the outstanding performer.

Perry's name is so often mentioned in connection with the Continental grip that anyone would be likely to believe him to have been practically its only user. This impression probably stems from the extremeness of his grip which, in Australia at least, was known simply as the Perry grip.

Each generation tends to regard its world champion as the greatest of all time, and Australian tennis followers of the mid-1930s were no exception. To them Perry was the top, the zenith. Anyone of earlier vintage who mentioned Brookes was listened to politely but unbelievingly. Brookes was a serious-faced old man with a tweed cap, tight trousers, and a slack racket; the handsome and vibrant Perry was as modern as tomorrow. No comparison could be imagined. Today, however, Perry's wide and immaculate trousers bear more relation to Brookes's narrow ones than they do to Rod Laver's shorts—and even sleek hair is no longer modern. All champions are superseded in their turn, but all past champions, with the possible exception of the old-fashioned Crawford, were modern in their day; they were young and strong, and most of them inflicted a few salutary defeats on the very players who were later to supersede them either by superior merit or only by advantage of age.

It is impossible to discuss Perry without reference to his Davis Cup team-mate Bunny Austin. Austin did not win any of the world's four major championships (though he was runner-up twice at Wimbledon—to Vines in 1932 and to Budge in 1938), but he had an excellent Davis Cup record. In Britain's four challenge-round wins from 1933 to 1936 he won six of his eight singles matches, losing to Cochet and Quist, but defeating Wood and Shields (the 1931 Wimbledon finalists), Crawford (the 1933 Wimbledon winner), and Allison and Budge (the 1935 and 1937 winners of the American National championship). His failure in championship tournaments was put down to lack of stamina. He could play a five-set Davis Cup match as well as almost anyone, but he could not stand up to the long series of matches encountered in tournament play. He campaigned for some time to have championship matches up to the semi-finals reduced from the best of five sets to the best of three, claiming that the existing system was boring to the spectators and so tiring to the players that the semi-final and final matches suffered as a result. His campaigning came to nothing in his time, but in the 1960s the early rounds in Australian State championships were shortened as he suggested.

Austin was truly a pioneer. He was an early lone wearer of shorts, and he played with a racket of novel design for which a lighter and more rigid frame was claimed because two supporting strips of wood ran from the top of the grip to the shoulders of the racket hand. The result looked like a snowshoe, but in Austin's hands any racket looked beautiful, and it was not his fault that the new design was a commercial failure. With his slight build and fair curly hair, he made a somewhat boyish figure on the court, and his flowing forehand and backhand drives and graceful volleys were produced in the exquisite manner of the Dohertys.

A third Englishman to merit special mention in connection with Great Britain's return to world supremacy in the mid-1930s was G. P.

A Perry backhand—made this time with an inadequate grip

Hughes, her leading doubles exponent. Partnered in turn by H. G. Lee and C. R. Tuckey, Hughes played in all of Britain's four winning Davis Cup teams. With Perry he won both the French and Australian doubles titles, and with Tuckey the 1936 Wimbledon—mostly playing right court.

Tall, with flat black hair, Pat Hughes was one of tennis's leaders. He captained Britain's Cup teams, controlled his partnerships with Lee and Tuckey, and stood no nonsense from the sometimes fractious Perry. His championship days behind him, Hughes became a power in international tennis, both in England and on the Continent.

The German championships were first held in 1893; Germany entered the Davis Cup competition in 1913; and we have already paid homage in some degree to Otto Froitzheim, Germany's grand old man of tennis. Froitzheim played in Davis Cup teams in 1913 and 1914 and again, on Germany's long-delayed readmittance to the competition, in 1927 and 1928; and he won the German singles championship as early as 1907 and as late as 1925. He was a master conserver of energy. He had a deep and bounding service, he loped smoothly to the ball, and he drove with such quiet ease that his opponents did not realize they were being forced out of position. His lazy-looking volleys seemed to go just, but only just, out of reach.

In the 1930s, however, few spectators recalled Froitzheim as they sat in packed stands applauding the world's latest tennis idol, Baron Gottfried von Cramm. Rather did the title of Baron, the "von", and the air of glamour that came to surround von Cramm and all his achievements invoke fanciful comparisons with the famous air ace of World War I, Baron Manfred von Richthofen.

Tall and handsome, fair-haired and blue-eyed, von Cramm became the Adonis of lawn tennis—a role that had been Tony Wilding's some twenty years earlier. But if the crowd in its admiration tended to neglect the Baron's opponents, von Cramm himself did not; his courtesy never faltered.

Von Cramm was a stylist of the front rank. Straight-backed, he bent his knees in perfect timing on both forehand and backhand as he swept into rising-ball drives made with an Eastern grip, long backswing, and firm wrist.

The follow-through was also full, often ending with a characteristic lifting of the racket head in the direction of the ball's line of flight rather than continuing farther round towards his shoulder.

Like most rising-ball experts, he seldom looked hurried, and like most players who use a long swing, he had a lot of power. His volleying, too, was severe and graceful, and he had a menacing service that combined cannonball and slice for the first delivery, and swerve and kick in the second. Tilden was prepared to grant him the strongest and most attractively moulded strokes in the world.

Among the champions we have met so far, rising-ball play has been connected with short backswing; the longer-swinging and more powerful hitters have normally played the ball at the top of its bound or a fraction later. Von Cramm combined a long swing with a rising ball, and for success with such daring stroke-play he needed iron nerve and intense concentration, to say nothing of a good court surface and true bounce. His style produced tennis that at times could sweep aside any player in the world. He never used defence—probably because he had none and possibly because it was against his instincts—and

Bunny Austin

G. P. Hughes

was accordingly unable to maintain his continuous attack without conceding many errors. If he could be contained his errors would cost him the match, but it took a giant to hold him. Though Borotra's net play may have appeared more daring, von Cramm was probably tennis's most adventurous champion.

Von Cramm played his matches with the deep concentration his style demanded, and in tournament play many of his early-round matches against lesser players were terribly one-sided. But no one was ever disgruntled, for even when he was being annihilated an opponent was given the feeling that the Baron was pleased and honoured to be on the court. Small wonder that no player was better liked by his competitors. The notion of taking advantage of anything not directly vetoed by the rules of the game never entered von Cramm's head, and the following incident was typical of his outlook. In the 1935 Davis Cup interzone final between Germany and America, with the score at one singles each, the doubles between von Cramm–Lund and Allison–

Van Ryn was expected (correctly) to be the deciding match. It was fought to five sets, the last three of which went to advantage, and was won by Allison and Van Ryn after von Cramm had seven times carried his side to match point. In the midst of the struggle Van Ryn hit a ball out. Game to Germany was called, and accepted by umpire, linesmen, the crowd, Lund, Allison, and Van Ryn. But von Cramm calmly informed the umpire that the ball had touched him and that the point was America's. At the time this was regarded as an outstanding gesture of sportmanship, but as von Cramm's career progressed, most people agreed that it would never have occurred to him to do anything else.

Among von Cramm's many enthralling matches were his French championship wins in 1934 and 1936, over Crawford and Perry respectively, and his battle with his close friend, Donald Budge, in the 1937 Davis Cup inter-zone final—sometimes regarded as the greatest Cup match of all time. The winner of the inter-zone final between the powerful American and German teams was regarded as virtually certain to take the Davis Cup from a British team weakened by the loss of Fred Perry. The score stood at two matches

Close-up of a von Cramm forehand

all when von Cramm and Budge took the court for the "Davis Cup decider". Attacking fiercely, von Cramm won two closely contested sets at 8–6, 7–5. Budge stood firm and took the next two at 6–4, 6–2. Von Cramm opened the decisive set with service and, attacking on practically every point, swept to a 4–1 lead. Changing ends either to hold service or be irretrievably down, the twenty-one-year-old Budge calmly told his captain: "Don't worry. I won't let you down."

Nor did he. While Tilden in the stand was being torn between patriotism and his admiration for von Cramm's stroke-making, Budge raised his game to its highest pitch and, on occasions taking desperate chances, eventually won at 8–6. Seven days later America defeated Great Britain in the challenge round by the handsome margin of four matches to one and regained the Davis Cup for the first time since the Four Musketeers had defeated Tilden, Johnson, and Hunter in 1927.

The match against von Cramm had been Budge's greatest match to date. It was also possibly von Cramm's most disastrous. Had he won it, he would no doubt have led Germany to her first Davis Cup success; he might then have become so popular at home that the Nazis could not have taken their subsequent course of action against him.

Von Cramm has often been described as the champion who was magnificent but unlucky. He was magnificent in that, despite his adventurous play, it was in important matches that he rose to his greatest heights; yet it was in the most important tennis—the Davis Cup competition and the Wimbledon championships—that he must be accounted most unlucky.

In the 1935 Wimbledon he came through to the final round with wins over McGrath and Budge, neither of whom could withstand his powerful forehand crosscourt driving; he then found the agile Perry too good for him all round. In 1936 he defeated Crawford and Austin, and again opposed Perry in the final. As von Cramm had recently defeated Perry for the 1936 French championship, a "battle of the century" was expected.

Only one game, involving ten deuces, was played before von Cramm tore a ligament in his leg and was barely able to walk. To stay on the court meant not only accepting unseemly defeat but aggravating the leg injury and reducing his

country's chances of success in the Davis Cup inter-zone final to be played against Australia a few days later. Von Cramm did not hesitate. He would not force on Perry the mortification of winning his third Wimbledon title in succession by an unsatisfactory forfeit, nor would he deprive the British crowd of triumph in their champion's performance. Perry, for his part, offered no embarrassing sympathy to von Cramm; he played as though his opponent were fully fit. The score, 6–1, 6–1, 6–0, was mercifully short.

In 1937 Perry, with a wonderful list of performances behind him, with von Cramm and Budge hard on his heels, and with a fortune awaiting him in Tilden's professional troupe, left the amateur ranks. Was the 1937 Wimbledon to be von Cramm's? Budge was given the first seeding, but there was little between the two.

Von Cramm again defeated Crawford and

The von Cramm service

Austin on his way to the final, but Budge justified his seeding and von Cramm was defeated once more. Perry and Budge had proved themselves capable of withstanding von Cramm's attack, and he found himself Wimbledon runner-up for three years in a row. A few days later he made his gallant but unsuccessful attempt to upset Budge, now acknowledged as the world's leading player, and to win the Davis Cup for Germany. But if he was unlucky on the tennis court, he was to be even unluckier off it.

As a Prussian baron, von Cramm was not exactly Nazi material, and never at any stage did he pretend to sympathize with the party. In 1938 he was arrested on a dubious charge of perversion and imprisoned for twelve months. Released in 1939, he entered the annual London championships held at Queen's Club and, encouraged by his success there, entered for Wimbledon. Budge had by now become a professional, making von Cramm the likely winner, but his entry was refused and the title was won by Robert Riggs of America, whom von Cramm had defeated, 6–0, 6–1, at Queen's Club only a fortnight earlier.

During the war years he survived three further Nazi interrogations. In 1951, thirteen years after his previous Wimbledon appearance, a forty-two-year-old von Cramm entered the famous tournament for the last time so that goodwill could be expressed on both sides. Though defeated by Czechoslovakian Jaroslav Drobny, 9–7, 6–4, 6–4, he played in his former brilliant fashion and left the court to ringing applause.

Von Cramm continued to play Davis Cup tennis until 1953. He became, in fact, the competition's senior member, playing, in all, thirty-seven ties and over a hundred matches. For comparison, Crawford and Quist each played between fifty and sixty matches, and Perry and Budge about fifty and thirty respectively.

Descriptions of von Cramm's unique career, his personality and his misfortunes, have carried us away from our theme. Von Cramm was a beautiful if perhaps overadventurous Eastern stylist. With a strong nerve and the clear conscience that is one of the rewards of unfailing sportsmanship, he was an ideal vehicle to carry the long-swinging/rising-ball style of play to world honours. This he did—as testified by his six world rankings backed by two French and six German singles championships—but his copyists have been few. Nor has this style of play ever won Wimbledon, and it is a nice question whether it had its greatest opportunity to do so in von Cramm's magnificent hands or whether it had no chance at all in his unlucky ones.

J. Donald Budge, the red man of this chapter, has already been introduced in some degree. It remains to present him in his own right.

His record speaks for itself. In 1937 and 1938 he won two Wimbledons, two American Nationals, and was a member of two winning Davis Cup teams; in 1938 he became the first player in

A von Cramm backhand

Donald Budge

best be described as having played with an extreme Eastern grip. This grip was not naturally suited to handling balls deep and wide to his forehand corner, but Budge, long-legged and fast on his feet, was able to cover such shots more than satisfactorily.

He hit his forehand hard and with a controlling measure of topspin, but the stroke never became as natural or as well produced as his backhand. It was an orthodox shot, going by the mechanics of "racket back, left foot forward or across, and then swing forward—up and through the ball, for rolled speed". In this there is nothing to criticize except perhaps some loss of the instinctiveness one comes to expect in a great champion's stroke-making. But Budge's forehand, though somewhat lacking in flexibility, was never a weakness and no opponent was able to break it up.

His ground strokes called for a wider change of grip from forehand to backhand than would have been acceptable to an early-ball player like Cochet. Budge made this change, however, concentrating on power from each wing, and opponents soon found that, particularly from his backhand, he hit a very heavy ball. This term

Budge volleys

history to win the Grand Slam, and the only one until Rod Laver in 1962.

Budge's great interest as a youth in California was baseball, and it was from this sport, in which he was a left-handed batter, that his world-famous backhand evolved—though, unlike Vivian McGrath, he made this stroke with one hand. Making a straight backswing in line with the ball, he hit either a flat or a rolled Eastern backhand with the straightest of arms and with great power and accuracy. It was his finest shot, and most critics have rated it even greater than René Lacoste's.

On the forehand side Budge began his tennis with a Western grip, but as the calibre of his opponents increased he decided, in 1935, at the age of nineteen, to become an Eastern player. The change he made was not large, and he can means that, from a combination of smoothness, timing, and weight co-ordination, the ball is found to be travelling a lot faster than a receiver would expect. It could be called hidden power.

It should not be imagined, though, that Budge's game was in any way ponderous. Vines had been the hero of his youth, and for a time he copied the great man's leisurely movements. "Then I saw Perry bounding about and I saw him take the ball on the rise," says Budge, "and immediately I began to walk faster."

In keeping with his extreme Eastern forehand grip, which placed his hand well behind the racket handle, Budge's service grip, although

Budge: Extreme Eastern forehand grip

Continental, was nearer to the Eastern position than the Continental grip used for service by most other champions. It produced a smooth and powerful service with less wrist snap than Vines's; with Budge's weight well behind it, it was fast and, once again, distinctly heavy.

Budge played an all-court game of sustained power, volleying and smashing severely. His temperament was reliable under pressure and all told he was an aggressive and determined player. He first came to fame in 1934, when at the age of eighteen he reached the final of the Pacific Coast championship and forced world champion Fred Perry to five-sets. By 1935 he was being called "another Vines", as Vines, only three years earlier, had been labelled "another Tilden". In 1936 he won an epic Davis Cup match over Crawford at 11–9 in the fifth set. In 1937 he equalled a record held only by Laurie Doherty, Tilden, Vines, and Perry by winning both the Wimbledon and U.S. singles in the one year. Duplicating this feat in 1938, he set a new record with his Grand Slam.

It is hardly surprising that, like other great champions at the height of their fame, Budge was hailed as the greatest player of all time. His studied rather than natural forehand may cast doubt on so high an assessment, but it has the

Budge serving to Jack Kramer in a Royal Command match for King Gustav of Sweden

support of expert opinion. Jack Crawford used to say that Budge was the best player he had met although Fred Perry was the hardest to beat at Wimbledon; Budge was also the choice of Adrian Quist, a man with Davis Cup experience from 1933 to 1948; and, as late as 1968, so shrewd a judge as Jack Kramer put Budge, Vines, and Tilden in a class above all others, implying, perhaps, that the red-headed Budge was his selection as the world's greatest player. True, Budge reigned when Kramer was at his most impressionable age, but most people would be prepared to accept Kramer's judgment to the extent that if Budge was not the world's greatest he was mighty close to it.

This raises the old question whether a player's strength is better placed in his forehand or in his backhand. No matter how small the difference between the two sides may be, every player has some degree of preference for one over the other. Supporters of the backhand say, firstly, that a poor forehand can never in itself be as weak as a poor backhand, and, secondly, that a player's

Bobby Riggs

backhand side (presuming right-handedness) is the natural direction in which practically all his opponents prefer to hit their shots—forehand or backhand, right-handed or left-handed—and that therefore a player is better equipped if his strength and preference are in his backhand. The first of these arguments is clearly not applicable to world champions. Nor can the second apply to the greatest of the great, since surely the true champion must dominate and not be dictated to. The forehand can be brought into play more often than the backhand, it is capable of more power than the strongest backhand, and it is decidedly a more flexible shot; more can be accomplished with a wonderful forehand than with an equivalent backhand.

Hence, in theory, it is impossible that Budge, a backhand-preference player, was the world's greatest. Perhaps he was one of those practical exceptions that have upset so many good theories: Crawford, Quist, and Kramer, all forehand players themselves, were well aware of the theory, but have still chosen Budge.

In a time of great tennis personalities Budge more than held his own. He was popular with spectators, competitors, officials, team-mates. The influence of his style, however, was not allowed full rein. Though many players modelled their backhand stroke production on his, none but arrant copyists adopted his forehand. More importantly, World War II called a halt to championship tennis, and when at last it resumed Jack Kramer introduced a different concept of singles play in which, mistakenly, ground strokes largely went unnoticed.

Such were the three great overseas figures who supplanted Jack Crawford as the world's leading player in the middle and late 1930s. There was yet one Wimbledon to be played, that of 1939, before the curtain of war descended in September of the same year.

In the absence of Perry, von Cramm, and Budge, the win of twenty-one-year-old Robert L. Riggs, of America, over his fellow-countryman Edwin T. Cooke generated no great enthusiasm as a Wimbledon final. But Bobby Riggs was not one to remain unnoticed for long. He followed his singles win with the capture of the men's and mixed doubles, and Wimbledon suddenly found that it had a new record-holder who had won the triple crown at his first appearance and had not surrendered a set in any of the final matches.

Riggs's earlier loss to von Cramm at Queen's Club had not shown his true form, and he did not win the 1939 Wimbledon as a rank outsider. He was seeded second to Austin and so was one of the favourites for the title, although in a field of lower quality than those of preceding years.

Riggs also won the 1939 and 1941 U.S. National titles, but it was in professional tennis that he really made his name. Although opposed by two all-time greats in Budge and Jack Kramer, against whom one would expect him to have had little chance, Riggs at one time and another had the beating of them both.

He turned professional late in 1941 and was beaten in a series of matches by Budge, who also won the 1942 professional final. In the 1946 final, after war service by both players, Riggs defeated Budge in less than an hour. True, Budge was out of condition, but not everyone can boast of a win over such a player, at his peak or not.

In 1947 Jack Kramer bestrode the amateur world and, when he turned professional, anyone could have been excused for dreaming of a series of matches between him and Budge—two lanky and colourful power players, the pre-war and the post-war champions, each of whom had already been acclaimed as the greatest player of all time. But Riggs had other ideas. He was determined that he would be the man to cut up the financial cake with Kramer, and after defeating Budge in a stern five-set encounter in the U.S. professional final of 1947 he emerged as the leading professional. He then further confounded the critics by defeating Kramer in straight sets in their first professional encounter and by winning most of their early matches. Kramer, however, settled down to the new conditions, won the series comfortably, and went on to become professional champion in 1948 and 1949.

Although Riggs may not have defeated Budge or Kramer at their top, it cannot be denied that he gave two of the game's greatest exponents a thorough shaking. Kramer never lost his respect for Riggs's tennis. "When that little guy has the bug to play, watch out," he once said.

Riggs was a great match-player for a big occasion, particularly if he felt he had been underrated, and at such times he often backed himself with hard cash. The sense of injury he sometimes suffered was not altogether unfounded, and it went back a long way. Californian tennis authorities had come to think that champions should be tall and hard-hitting like Vines and Budge, and they tended to ignore young Bobby Riggs as being too small. They sponsored others for experience in the Eastern grasscourt tournaments, but not Riggs. By 1936, when Riggs was eighteen, he was ranked number four in America, but in 1937 he was omitted from America's four-man Davis Cup team. His successes in America that year did not cool his resentment: he was gunning for some of those team members when they returned.

Even without the spur of injustice, Riggs never lacked self-confidence. But because he was of small stature and prone to wise-cracking, his brand of confidence was described as cockiness. He loved to let his opponent dictate the tactics— to play the match just as it suited him best—and then to beat him at it. His wonderfully controlled game, in a time of big hitting, certainly gave him grounds for confidence. He played in a Continental rather than an Eastern style, gripping the racket handle with fingers well spread for solidity and control; his service (sliced or kicked), his volleying, and his overhead were all sound, and he was a good quick-footed court-coverer. He knew the game thoroughly and could always make the most of his stroke equipment, of an opponent's weaknesses, or of any opportunity that presented itself. Next to the two-handers, he could probably conceal better than anyone else the difference between his preparation for drive or toss. He developed an attacking rolled lob—and once this shot, with its going-away bounce, was over an opponent's head there was little point in his chasing it.

Riggs made his own contribution to tennis, though probably the game could not hold too many like him at any one time. But even as one says this, one can imagine the pert young Riggs of twenty-five years ago cracking back with something like: "I set my own standards; and there's no second prize for anyone else."

14 | Interlude

IF we were to pass from the Wimbledon of 1939 straight to that of 1946 all sense of time and proportion would be lost. Though the National championship was continued in America and the French championship resumed in occupied France, tennis in this period lost its place on the world's stage. The untimely interruption of Budge's style, the tribulations of von Cramm, the return of the Davis Cup to Australia after two decades of endeavour, the loss of Bromwich's best playing years—all were trifles compared with the war and its issues.

But the interlude does provide us here with space for a brief discussion of professional tennis of the times, into which we have already recorded the disappearance of Suzanne Lenglen, Vincent Richards, Tilden, Cochet, Vines, Perry, Budge, and Riggs. When Suzanne and Richards, backed by three lesser-known players, performed in a number of exhibition matches in 1926, they became the first "touring professionals" in a domain hitherto consisting of coaches, teachers, practise players, and club groundsmen. Suzanne retired not long afterwards, and a United States Professional Tennis Association, which Richards had helped to form, soon passed from the tourists' hands to the coaches'. By 1930 the professional playing side had expired.

Tilden was the first of a new group of playing professionals, and it may be wondered who, besides Vincent Richards, would have been available to oppose him; a series between these two would have been regarded as merely re-forming their Davis Cup association.

How many people today have heard of Karel Kozeluh or, for that matter, of Hans Nusslein? Each was a world champion—professional world champion.

Among the teaching professionals of the world various tournaments had from time to time been held. Of these, the only one to become important was a tournament staged annually on the French Riviera, and any player who won it with any consistency came to be regarded as the world professional champion. At odd times a professional would claim that he could defeat any amateur in the world, but no such claim was ever put to the test.

Into this nebulous picture strode the remarkable figure of Karel Kozeluh of Czechoslovakia. Stern and tall, with a craggy face set off by abundant tufts of tawny-coloured hair and bushy eyebrows, he became the clear-cut holder of the title of world professional champion from 1925 to 1930. Having also visited the United States and beaten Vincent Richards several years before Tilden turned professional, he was Tilden's natural opponent. And so began the first of those renowned series of matches in which the world's leading amateur, after accepting a lucrative

Karel Kozeluh

contract, challenges the world's leading professional.

Kozeluh was a member of a well-known Czech tennis family of whose six sons only one, Jan, was an amateur (he represented his country in Davis Cup matches from 1924 to 1930). Karel, who took a pride in being a professional in his art, commanded every stroke in the game, but his service was severe rather than devastating, and he had no great flair for net play. He was a baseline master and could hit the ball from any part of his court to any part of his opponent's, with no preference as to the direction of his shot, the height at which he hit the ball, or whether he took it on the rise or on the drop. When rising-ball play became popular he showed his independence of thought by letting the ball drop noticeably lower than his opponents did. When asked why he preferred a falling-ball to a rising-ball game, he replied that he played whatever was better at the time—that he was not bound by hard and fast rules but met the circumstances with whatever they called for. Others might choose one of the two games, but for him—both. He went on to say that he often purposely let the ball drop "to draw my opponent to the net, since I have unbounded confidence in my passing shots". As for the rising-ball and beyond, he asked: "Can I not half-volley with the best?" Clearly he was a man who did not lack faith in himself.

Kozeluh said that unless forced by a volleyer to use topspin (and he regarded volleyers as pests), he always stroked the ball flat. Though he acknowledged the value of topspin and underspin for variety in the games of others, he added that he himself used spin on service alone and for the rest relied solely on pace. By this he meant change of pace, at which he was adept, and this, combined with the different heights at which he took the ball and his wonderful tactical use of the lob, gave his game plenty of variety. Tilden—possibly in the first flush of enthusiasm for the professional game—credited him with being steadier even than Lacoste and with having an even greater backhand.

A Continental stylist who used no change of grip for any stroke, Kozeluh had one most unusual characteristic. He made practically no use of his left arm, leaving it hanging by his side as he made his strokes; in lifting the racket for his backswing he used only his playing arm.

When the Tilden/Kozeluh series began in 1931 it soon became evident that Tilden was too good for his rival. After he had won the opening match and several thereafter the promoter, becoming perturbed, called to see him. Tilden, in usual fashion, beat him to the draw.

"If you're going to say what I think you're going to say," he announced, "the answer's no."

Waving aside the accepted principle of promotion, that the margin between two competitors must never be allowed to grow too wide, Tilden declared that he would beat Kozeluh every time he could. The discussion ended with agreement on only one point: that Tilden was probably a darned fool.

Tilden had held that honesty of purpose would prevail, and he was proved right. The tour attracted good crowds and was a financial success. Perhaps Tilden's long-established pride of performance and hatred of losing any match he could win allowed him no other course. He defeated Kozeluh by the large margin of twenty-seven matches to six. Later, in a short tour with Richards, he won all ten matches played.

But Tilden's large winning margin should be set aside. The amazing thing about this first professional series was that Kozeluh was able to win six matches. Neither he nor the German professional Hans Nusslein, who came on the scene a little later, could have had the match practice of the ex-amateur champions they opposed. For them there were no large tournaments like Wimbledon. That they could rise to the heights they achieved is amazing.

Hans Nusslein won the world professional championship in 1935. He played in the company of both Vines and Perry in the second half of the 1930s, and Tilden placed him a shade above both of them over 365 days a year, though each was capable of higher peaks than he. Tilden also placed these three a little above von Cramm and Budge, the leading amateurs at the time; but when comparisons between the professional and amateur games are made by an interested party we are entitled to have reservations about them.

Nusslein's game was based on accuracy and simplicity. He did not possess a crushing service or smash, but hit flat, beautifully made ground strokes from either wing. These were of such consistency that he seemed capable of keeping the ball going indefinitely without error, and of such accuracy that it was fatal for an opponent to undertake any but the best-prepared net attack against him. Our picture shows him covering a wide ball—from the right leg, but well balanced and in control. He volleyed well, mixed drop-shots into his game, and half-volleyed superbly from any part of the court.

Tilden has said that the three finest exponents of the backhand drive in the thirty-odd years he played, allowing that he had not played against Budge, were Nusslein, Kozeluh, and Lacoste. These three were also his nominations for "finest baseliner", and Nusslein gained two further top positions under "accuracy" and "average standard over a year". (Tilden's forehand-drive ratings are also interesting. They were Vines, Johnston, and Hunter, none of whom, we note, was an English or Continental stylist.)

Nusslein played what is still regarded as the typical European game: he was a Continental stylist, he was not powerful overhead, and he based his game on accuracy and consistency rather than on power. In the 1930s era of Eastern-grip dominance, blazing speed, and all-court versatility his game was almost as outmoded as it would be today; yet in the hands of this rising-ball master it held its own among the world's best, even on the fast surfaces of indoor courts.

The man responsible for this was a pleasant fellow, sturdily built, fair-haired, and deeply sun-tanned. Though well known in America, he never gained the top position of opposing the latest amateur champion to turn professional. Perhaps he typifies an element lacking in professional tennis despite its high technical skill. Matches between professionals—even those who have been famous amateurs—have never been accounted equal in importance to Davis Cup ties or the big national tournaments. Somehow they have lacked the necessary dramatic point and context.

Hans Nusslein

114

We have seen that tennis up to World War II, besides its baseline and all-court players, had already included volleyers and big-servers and also serve-and-volley players. Though unmentioned so far, the term "Power Game" had once been applied to Red McLoughlin, the Californian Comet, and "Big Game" to both the all-embracing game of Big Bill Tilden and the crashing forehand driving and volleying of Little Bill Johnston. By the time Wimbledon reopened its gates in 1946 these were long-forgotten terms, and now one heard them used on all sides as something brand new. In the years that followed, older players and observers tried to explain that they were not new, and eventually, perhaps, went too far by declaring with exasperation that the modern Big Game itself contained nothing new to tennis. Post-war audiences of varying ages have by and large remained unconvinced of this view. May the Big Game discussion contained in the following chapter bring some semblance of reconciliation between the two generations and their opposing viewpoints.

15 | The Big Game

FITTINGLY, the post-war Big Game was introduced by Big Jake Kramer, who emerged as the big name when world tennis recommenced in 1946. It would have been equally fitting if he had also won that year's Wimbledon, but, seeded second and soon regarded as favourite, he suffered a badly blistered hand and was defeated before the quarter-finals in a stern tussle with Jaroslav Drobny of Czechoslovakia. He served effective notice, however, that the title was not likely to elude him the following year; nor did it, and he soon became the most famous player of his time.

But if the 1946 final was not won by the technical Big Game, it provided plenty of hard hitting. The finalists were Geoff Brown of Australia, with his cyclonic two-handed forehand and cannonball service, and the six-foot-five Frenchman Yvon Petra, winner of the last three French wartime titles. Petra's game hinged on impulse rather than soundness, and he too possessed a service of considerable muzzle velocity. The story has been circulated that in the slugfest that developed between these two, one of them served four clean aces in a row, only to see (or not to see) the other return the compliment in the very next game. Whether strictly accurate or not, the story at least indicates the mood and tempo of the match.

Petra was a far from typically European player. He had learnt his tennis in French Indo-China, where he was born in 1916. On the court he resembled Ellsworth Vines, being long and lanky and affecting the white peaked cap of his former idol; similarly, his game was based on a blistering service struck from a great height and backed by a powerful forehand drive and a strong net attack. His forehand, however, was Continental rather than Eastern like Vines's, his backhand was vulnerable and his nature highly excitable.

His 1946 Wimbledon progress included defeats of Australia's two hopes, Dinny Pails and Geoff Brown. Jaroslav Drobny had exhausted himself in overcoming Kramer, and when he was defeated by Brown, Pails, the first seed, was a clear favourite for the title. But on his way to the courts to meet Petra in a quarter-final he became badly confused in London's labyrinth of underground railways and eventually arrived an hour late and much shaken. A walk-over had by then been awarded to Petra, but he sportingly refused to accept it and the match was rescheduled for the same afternoon. Perhaps both players should have been able to approach it calmly—Petra from the sustenance of a sporting action, Pails because he was now in the happy position of having nothing to lose—but such attitudes are easier to suggest than to achieve, and both men were badly unsettled when the match began.

Yvon Petra

116

Pails remained unsettled, and Petra won at 7–5, 7–5, 6–8, 6–4. It was hard luck for the popular Dinny, but he could have no complaint against a man who had given him a second chance and then beaten him. A fluent Eastern stylist, Pails won the Australian title the following year and also reached the Wimbledon semi-final, where he encountered an invincible Kramer.

Petra survived another unusual match in his semi-final against Tom Brown—America's last survivor and the subsequent winner of the doubles with Kramer and the mixed doubles with Louise Brough. In an uneven display, Brown won the first two sets and Petra the next two. Serving at 5–4 in the final set, Petra's excitable nerves gave way; after losing the game he proceeded to protest against decisions given by umpire and linesmen. The score of 5-all stood, but Brown, unnerved by the incident, lost his next service. Staking all on service and volley, Petra managed to hold on and win.

Meanwhile Geoff Brown, having defeated Sweden's Lennart Bergelin in the quarter-final and Drobny in the semi-final, had, despite his sometimes neck-or-nothing hitting, come through the other half of the draw without conceding a set.

Petra being clearly an erratic player, Brown was advised to moderate his hitting and keep the ball in play. These tactics reacted against his game, and he lost the first two sets. With defeat at his elbow, he opened out and took the third set with cracking aces and double-handers. In the fourth set Petra, not to be outdone in big hitting or effectiveness, went to a lead of 5–4 and forty-fifteen on his service. Brown's reply was to hit two outright winners from Petra's two next services, even the game score, lead 6–5, and then break Petra's service to love to square the match at two sets all.

Petra appeared to have lost his chance, but then an overexcited Brown lost his service in the opening game of the fifth set. Petra, holding his own services, again reached 5–4 with his service to follow. A breathless crowd waited to see what Brown, the most gallant little hitter since Bill Johnston, would produce.

He was given no chance to produce anything. Reaching into the sky, Petra fired down four aces to end the match in the most decisive fashion in Wimbledon's history and to become France's first winner since Henri Cochet in 1929.

Dinny Pails

117

Petra's triumph was soon followed by disaster. He was unsuccessful in the French championship (which in 1946 was held after Wimbledon) and the U.S. National; in 1947 he underwent a foot operation and was never the same player again. By 1948 big tennis was behind him and he was a coach.

Geoff Brown had need to call on his reserves of philosophy; this was the Wimbledon in which he reached all the finals without losing a set and did not succeed in winning one title.

Jack Kramer, yet another "Tilden" and the third from California, now took over the scene, drastically changing the course of championship tennis from that day to this. Based on serve-and-volley tactics, his methods completely upset the balance between net and baseline play that had existed since the height of the net at centre and posts was fixed in 1882.

Born in 1921, Kramer became U.S. boy champion in 1936 and interscholastic champion in 1938. A year later he was handed over to Ellsworth Vines for coaching, and from Vines he learnt the cannonball service and controlled speed that, together with the Eastern grip, had formed the basis of the "Tilden game". He won Davis Cup honours early, representing the United States, as we have seen, when he was barely eighteen. Then came a series of set-backs. Favourite for the 1942 National title, he developed appendicitis and could not play; a finalist in 1943, he suffered a severe attack of food poisoning shortly before the match; in 1944–5 he served with the U.S. Marines and played no tennis; in 1946, as we know, he lost at Wimbledon through a badly blistered hand and the tenacity of Jaroslav Drobny.

The Wimbledon set-back was to be his last. In the U.S. Nationals the following September he swept through all opposition with the loss of only one set, and with the assistance of Ted Schroeder recaptured the Davis Cup from Australia in a challenge round in which he won all his matches in straight sets. In 1947 he completed a triple Wimbledon, National, and Davis Cup success. At Wimbledon he was overwhelming, defeating Geoff Brown, 6–0, 6–1, 6–3, Pails, 6–1, 3–6, 6–1, 6–0, and, in the final, Tom Brown, 6–1, 6–3, 6–2. Frank Parker held him off temporarily in the National final, but the last three sets were Kramer's at 6–1, 6–0, 6–3. In the Davis Cup challenge round, all Pails and Bromwich could

manage against him were five and seven games respectively. He had never been other than direct about his intention of turning professional when a suitable offer was made, and he did so in November 1947. For a record fee of $70,000 he left an amateur tennis world largely in agreement that King Kramer and his Big Game had provided the greatest tennis in the history of the game.

Kramer resembled Tilden in his tall and lean appearance, his strict observance of training, his superb physical fitness, his strong will to win, his stroke production and controlled speed, and the close and objective study he made of the game. The main difference between them was that

Jack Kramer

118

Tilden's game was all-stroke and all-court with a preference for the baseline whereas Kramer's was based on consistently attacking from the net. People who had seen Tilden on the court were struck by a second difference: Tilden acted as though it were good of him to appear before the crowd, while the decks-cleared and straight-shooting Kramer played as though it were good of the crowd to have come to see him, and gave them the best value he could.

Before discussing Kramer's Big Game tactics, let's first examine his strokes—the equipment used to implement these tactics.

Playing powerfully in an orthodox Eastern style, Kramer used a full Eastern grip for his forehand, with arm and racket much in line in the manner of Tilden and Vines. From a shorter backswing than Tilden's he used more roll than Vines and, particularly for his crosscourt forehand—a shot that at first did not come naturally to him—he employed a long follow-through for control. On all types of stroke he was clearly stronger on the forehand side, and a close observer might have noticed that his backhand grip was, if anything, only just adequate.

He had an excellent service with plenty of pace and full mastery of flat, sliced, or kick variations. It is detracting little to say that his service was not as fast as the cannonballs of Patterson, Vines, or Gonzales; it was at least comparable to Tilden's and thus could be classed as a big service. Cochet, Crawford, and Perry would perhaps have been pleased to have Kramer's second delivery as their first; with either his first or his second ball he could put pressure on the receiver. His rhythmic action appeared so controlled that no matter how fast the ball flew he never seemed to be exerting his last ounce of energy. He

A Kramer low volley

practised his service diligently, and many people saw exhibition films of him serving at speed and knocking over a ball box placed almost anywhere in either of the service courts, or sending ball after ball through a set of small hoops fixed at different points above the net. These demonstrations of accuracy were all performed with his sliced service, but with considerable pace.

Kramer was a severe and accurate volleyer. He had both power and touch, and his reach and agility allowed him more than ample net coverage. He was a fine all-round player in strokes, physique, and temperament, and most critics agree that without using his Big Game tactics he would still have been the world champion of his day.

If Australians have dated tennis from Jack Crawford, they have also dated it from Jack Kramer, regarding the one (however incorrectly) as personifying peaceful baseline days, and the other the beginning of the modern game. Many present-day Australians—and perhaps others as well—credit Kramer with having established the volley in singles play. This is completely wrong, but such is his fame in this connection that there are even some—non-tennis playing, of course—who imagine he invented the stroke.

In what way, then, did Kramer differ from his volleying predecessors? Let's recall a few of these, and their methods. Spencer Gore won the first Wimbledon from the net, but as the net posts at the time were about five feet high his performance can scarcely be taken into account. Brookes combined twisty left-handedness and uncanny anticipation with a penetrating exploitation of his opponents' weaknesses, and so reduced the effectiveness of the would-be passing shots he had to meet. Part of the tactics behind McLoughlin's net game was the covering of his backhand ground stroke. Similarly, Borotra was without doubt a talented volleyer, but his ground strokes were not equal to those of his world-class opponents; for him it was a case of net or nothing.

Kramer's net game was not built on conditions such as the height of the net, nor on subtlety, nor yet on necessity: it was founded on sheer pressure. He followed all his serves, whether first or second, to the net. His serve being powerful, he was thus always advancing behind a difficult ball rather than merely a short one. His service returns, or the first suitable ground stroke there-after, were likewise shaped to be followed in; and like his service they were strong. Once at the net, he preferred severity, aiming to win with his first volley if possible; he calculated that the longer he was at the net in any single rally the more chance he had of being passed. "I win fast, or I lose fast," he said, and it was not often that he lost.

Kramer's strokes and methods combined to make his play justifiably known as the Big Game. About this and its other name, the Power Game, Kramer, as an astute man with his eye on a professional career, said nothing to hinder their growing use. However, as Vines and others had been harder hitters than Kramer, neither title was perhaps as accurate as the less exciting term "Pressure Game" would have been. The most obvious components of Kramer's game were a fast first service and a single winning volley, but the term "serve and volley game" tells only half the story. Kramer's strong accompanying ground strokes should not be overlooked.

They were badly overlooked by many who tried to follow his methods. An unsound idea developed—and spread amazingly—that ground strokes were no longer needed, that a player with a powerful serve and volley could hold all his service games and then only needed to break one of his opponent's services for the set. Sometimes this happened, and at least one Wimbledon—Robert Falkenburg's in 1948—was won in very much this way. But time was to show that more often the theory worked in reverse—that the player without ground strokes never broke one of his opponent's services and that when he had the misfortune to lose one of his own it was his opponent instead who won the set on a service break. Such players often followed the unlucky part of Kramer's pronouncement and lost fast. Still, even a serve-and-volley-only player came to be termed a Big Game player.

It may be wondered why such lightning net players as Cochet and Perry are not described as Big Game players. Again it was because their methods were not Kramer's. They did not follow every serve to the net, not even every first service. More often their means of advance was to pounce on the service return, whip it deep to the baseline, and play their winning volley from the comparatively long drive they had forced on their opponent. Kramer, on the other hand, played many of his volleys against the fast service returns of opponents standing well inside the baseline. There was more smash-and-grab and Big Game atmosphere in this, particularly when the exchange began with a towering service.

But even though Cochet and Perry were not big servers, one may still wonder why it was left to Kramer to found a lasting Big Game as late as 1946—seventy years after the first Wimbledon and nearly fifty years after the Doherty era. Plenty of men in the meantime had had big serves—Tilden, who had also studied tactics from every angle; Vines, who had also followed his cannonballs to the net; and power players like von Cramm and Budge. Why did none of these develop the Big Game?

Tilden went to the net to finish off a rally, and would have thought himself as lacking in judgment as a junior if he had gone up only to be passed. He believed ground strokes to be the unshakeable foundation of a winning game. Unless the net was obviously his for the taking he stayed back, secure in possessing a greater range of ground strokes than any of his opponents. Vines, von Cramm, and Budge went to the net far more often than Tilden did, but their attack was governed by what they considered the

Jack Kramer

121

odds for success on each individual sortie to the net. Kramer allowed that this reasoning was correct for individual net sorties, but held that it neglected the overall odds on a complete match. He argued that even if he were passed sometimes, his persistent presence at the net exerted such pressure on his opponents that the overall odds for success would eventually pass to him. This was part of what the businesslike Kramer called "percentage tennis"; its other tenet was that you should play only those strokes that paid more often than not.

To keep an opponent under pressure to produce passing shots demanded the powerful strokes Kramer so assiduously developed, for no one overawes a good baseliner simply by rushing up to the net behind any and every shot. Kramer boldly put his theories to the test and proved them correct. Since his day the Big Game has been universally adopted in championship and professional tennis played on fast court surfaces such as grass or wood.

It should be noted, though, that it has no great significance in everyday tennis or in championship hardcourt tennis. Even a power player like Lew Hoad could not sustain these tactics on the slow Roland Garros courts, and he won his only French championship, in 1956, from the baseline. Nor is Rod Laver's Roland Garros record impressive. Nevertheless, although the Big Game applies in only a small proportion of the world's tennis, it encompasses the most important spectator events; besides the Australian, Wimbledon, and U.S. championships, the Davis Cup challenge round, since 1934, has been played almost entirely on grass. Similarly, professional matches have mainly been played on fast surfaces.

As a professional Kramer became undisputed champion of the world by asserting his superiority first over Riggs and later over Gonzales and Sedgman. He took over the promotion of the troupe and saw to it that professional tennis did not fall from pure tennis into exhibitionism. His organization being thoroughly reputable, young Australian stars were able to move from amateur fame and Harry Hopman's dependable guidance to professional fortune and the solid protection of Jack Kramer's integrity.

Kramer was at pains to explain his financial affairs openly, from the contract amount offered to an amateur to the division of gate money among the players. On the matter of contracts, the following conversation between Kramer and Pancho Segura was once retailed:

"Jake," said Segura, "I want a signed contract with you this year."

"Sure, Pancho. Why?"

"I've been playing for you for ten years on a handshake, and now the word's going round I can't write."

Since Kramer made a great contribution to tennis, it seems churlish to qualify this. Nevertheless—and paradoxically, because he stood to gain heavily from the popularity of the game— his influence set the game back in two distinct ways.

His Big Game was exciting at first, and its efficiency in the hands of a player good enough to exploit it on fast surfaces has been unquestionable. But what was formerly exciting has since come to be regarded as a monotonous succession of short points, often consisting only of a service, a return, and a winning volley, and sometimes of only a service and an overambitious attempt at a return. There is speed and there is agility (sometimes almost acrobatics), but many critics have said that there is no real racket-work any more. There was, after a while, a decline in the popularity of championship men's singles, and later of tennis as a whole.

Secondly, and ironically, the very excellence of Kramer's professional organization drained from the great amateur tournaments too many of the top players, most of them at an early age and before they were seen at their best. Tennislovers greatly regretted this, and spectators *en masse* chose to stay away from an amateur game they no longer regarded as first class.

Kramer did his best to rectify both of these unfortunate results. In an attempt to reintroduce rallying into the game, his professionals played to various modifications of the established rules, and he campaigned vigorously for open tennis so that the top players could be seen in the top tournaments at the best grounds. He failed to achieve either of these objectives.

Meanwhile the Big Game was by no means dull, and in the hands of Bob Falkenburg, Ted Schroeder, Budge Patty, and Dick Savitt—each of the last three in less exaggerated fashion than his immediate predecessor—it won for America the next four Wimbledons, from 1948 to 1951.

Robert Falkenburg is remembered largely in

Bob Falkenburg

connection with the stalling and time-wasting tactics he used, particularly against John Bromwich in the 1948 Wimbledon final. Falkenburg for his part found the Wimbledon crowd biased and unsporting.

Very tall—records give his height as somewhere between 6 feet 2 inches and 6 feet 4 inches —Falkenburg had a flat cannonball service of terrific pace, but he lacked the stamina necessary to sustain his big-serving and net-rushing game. To pace himself in close matches, like Borotra before him, he often threw a set; but he had none of Borotra's charm, and his court manner aroused antagonism. He practically ensured the crowd's opposition to him in his Wimbledon final against Bromwich by his performance in the semi-final against his fellow-American Gardnar Mulloy. Since his game involved many a desperate lunge for the ball, he fell over a great deal, and against Mulloy he took a long time in rising, sometimes dragging himself to his feet. It was no way to win friends, either in the stands or on the court, and both Mulloy and the crowd were clearly fed up with it.

The Wimbledon crowd has long cherished several aspects of its own behaviour. It is quiet during rallies, it supports the underdog, it does not applaud mistakes, and it always applauds good shots, no matter which player makes them. That is as far as it can go, for polite or sporting applause can never equal the enthusiasm of applause that's spontaneous. Wimbledon hopes that it is as generous as any other crowd in the world, but it never claims impartiality. It normally favours the older player, believing the younger will have another chance later. Also, Wimbledonians will confess to an Australian that when the last representative of Great Britain is out of the tournament (it is sad that except for the Doherty and Perry eras it has always been "when" rather than "if"), they always support the Australians as next-of-kin.

In 1948 John Bromwich was the crowd's favourite. He had been a grand young player before the war, had served his country for four wartime years, and now, approaching the end of his championship career, was playing perhaps his last Wimbledon; he was almost thirty, Falkenburg only twenty-two. Although Falkenburg had not created this situation and could scarcely have altered it in his favour, his semi-final display had assuredly weighted the crowd's

natural support of Bromwich.

The final (like practically every match in which the unorthodox Bromwich was involved) provided a complete contrast in styles and tactics. Bromwich's service could be broken, but having one of the most accurate returns in the world he was a difficult player to hold service against. Falkenburg relied on holding his service in any set he wanted to win. Bromwich played a baseline game consisting of patience and steadiness and accurate passing shots; Falkenburg played the Big Game.

Falkenburg won a tense first set at 7–5 and threw the next 0–6. He won the third, and took little interest in the fourth. The applause was heavily in favour of Bromwich; the crowd did not like Falkenburg's delays, but Bromwich showed no sign of irritation. The standard of play was poor, the match anything but exciting.

Bromwich was winding up the match in the fifth set. Serving at 5–3, he went to forty-fifteen, steadily, almost by routine. The next rally developed favourably for him; he played the ball deep to Falkenburg's backhand and took the net. Back came the return, higher than the net as it reached Bromwich and very close to the sideline. Bromwich, his foot over the line, was in two minds whether to hit the shot or not; he hit it— and dragged a double-handed volley low into the net. Forty-thirty. Bromwich hit a short ball from Falkenburg right into the backhand corner, almost a winner. Falkenburg sprinted wildly for it as Bromwich covered the net. Falkenburg got his racket to it in another attempt at a down-the-line passing shot. It crossed the net outside the sideline but within reach. Bromwich let it go. Slanting inwards the farther it travelled, it went deep enough to land in the corner.

A rejuvenated Falkenburg won the game. An overcautious Bromwich began slicing his double-hander instead of rolling it, and a stunned crowd watched Falkenburg become Wimbledon champion at 7–5 in the fifth set. Lifting his game marvellously, he had come from 3–5 and fifteen-forty down to win the last four games running against the world's steadiest player. The crowd applauded the new champion, although at the presentation ceremony it was the award of the runner-up medal that aroused most enthusiasm.

There was much criticism of Falkenburg. His appearance of being almost out on his feet before whipping over a mighty cannonball savoured strongly of foxing. There was sympathy for Bromwich, but he brushed it aside and took all the blame for his loss. A player who does not take his chances, he said, does not deserve to win. Feeling that he had let himself down, he was determined to betray no one else, and he grimly won the men's doubles with young Frank Sedgman and the mixed with Louise Brough.

Falkenburg, incensed by the criticism he received, replied with a strong blast against Wimbledon's officials and spectators, whom he described as the most prejudiced he had ever encountered. Nevertheless both he and Bromwich competed in the 1949 Wimbledon championship, and met in the quarter-finals. A grudge match was widely talked about, and the centre court was packed. This time the tennis was excellent. Falkenburg won the first two sets, the second at 11–9. The day was hot, and the crowd had to wait while Falkenburg threw not only the third set but the fourth as well, though his behaviour this time gave no cause for complaint. The fifth set was played amid great excitement, and at last a great shout announced that Bromwich had been "avenged". There were no accompanying expressions of triumph or surliness from the players. Seated on the court after the last shot—he was down again—Falkenburg waved a salute, and moments later both players, smiling broadly and following the custom of Borotra and Lacoste, left the court arm-in-arm.

"If you can meet with triumph and disaster ..." is the well-known motto on the Wimbledon gate. Australians have a similar if less dignified saying: "After the Lord Mayor's carriage comes the rubbish cart." This applies to all players, high or low, and John Bromwich helped to illustrate it in the next round—his semi-final against Jaroslav Drobny—by being soundly defeated while displaying possibly his worst form in a championship match.

The 1949 winner was F. R. Schroeder, yet another Californian. Frederick Rudolf was too heavy a name for this likeable character who was universally known under the more friendly name of Ted. At one time he was also known as Lucky Schroeder because he won a large number of five-set matches and gained selection in American Davis Cup teams without playing in as many preliminary tournaments as his harder-working (on the court) rivals.

No champion decries luck, but with champions there is always more to it than that. In Davis Cup matches Schroeder fulfilled the selectors' confidence, and his five-set wins resulted from determination and nerve. In the first round of the 1949 Wimbledon championship he encountered such stern opposition from Gardnar Mulloy that in the fifth set he was beset by severe cramps. Often having to force his fingers apart with his left hand to be able to grip the racket, he won one of his "lucky" matches. Lucky or not, he was better off than the second-seeded Gonzales, who was summarily knocked out in the fourth round by giant-killer Geoff Brown.

At match-point down in his quarter-final against Frank Sedgman, Schroeder hit one of his hardest services and, knowing that it would be right, followed in whole-heartedly. "Footfault" was called. He returned to the baseline, banged down a hard second serve, advanced, and killed

Ted Schroeder

the return. After defeating Sedgman in five sets, he won a semi-final against Eric Sturgess of South Africa and the final against Drobny, both also in five sets. For a man who played less tennis than any other champion, the lion-hearted

Budge Patty

Schroeder certainly made a meal of it while he was at it.

He was of sturdy appearance, bronzed, and with crew-cut hair. In his T-shirt and very short shorts, and particularly when he was wearing spikes, he looked more like a track athlete than a tennis player. He had a beautifully made backhand and a sound forehand played with an Eastern grip rather more towards Western than normal. He served with an Eastern grip, bending his knees well for power or kick. As with most Big Game players, his ground strokes were little noticed in comparison with his dynamic net attack.

Schroeder was U.S. junior champion in 1939 at the age of eighteen. He partnered his young friend Jack Kramer—there was only twelve days' difference in age between them—to win the National doubles in 1940 and 1941, and in the following year he was National singles champion. After this, apart from winning the doubles for a third time with Kramer in 1947 and losing the singles final to Gonzales in five sets in 1949, he did not visit Forest Hills again. He played in no French or Australian championships, and it took some persuasion to get him to Wimbledon, where, after winning the title and being asked if he would return to defend it, he replied that he might come back, in about twenty years' time, as an umpire perhaps.

It was thought at one time that Schroeder might join Kramer's professional troupe, but he did not. His main interest seems to have been in the Davis Cup. He played in winning teams from 1946 to 1949 without losing a singles match and in two losing ones in 1950 and 1951. He has since remained well known in Australia as a visiting Davis Cup commentator with a rolling voice, a rolling gait, and a well-stoked pipe that he seldom lights.

Budge Patty, who at twenty-six succeeded Schroeder as Wimbledon winner in 1950, had earlier followed him as U.S. junior champion in 1941 and 1942. After his younger days in California he chose to live in France, and it is in the honour rolls of France and England that we find his name rather than in those of his native country, whether in championships or in Davis Cup teams.

Patty was tall, handsome, elegant in bearing, dress, and stroke-making. Although an Eastern stylist, he played his forehand with a lower wrist than other American champions. He also used less backswing in his strokes. This was most noticeable in his service: he took the racket straight up from knee to shoulder, more in the manner of a smash than a normal service action, in which the racket is looped behind the back. In other days his early-ball ground-stroking backed by superb volleying, particularly on the forehand, would have made him a suave all-court player of the Cochet type, but the Big Game had proved that no one could afford to stay back, and at Wimbledon Patty came to the net after every service and at every opportunity, in the fashion more or less dictated to every champion since Jack Kramer.

Even if only in the manner of a Prodigal Son, Patty showed how valuable training can be. As party-goer and playboy he lost many a match through lack of stamina, and after weakening against Drobny in the third round of the 1949 Wimbledon he seemed to have reached the end of his tennis road. From then on, however, he trained rigorously. Not only did he become the next Wimbledon champion but he and Drobny hold the record for the longest uninterrupted battle staged in Wimbledon's history—a four-hour marathon in the third round of the 1953 meeting that we shall come to in due course.

If Budge Patty was a natural all-court player, Dick Savitt, the 1951 Wimbledon champion was a baseliner coerced into the Big Game. Tall, heavy, swarthy, he took his time with his service, turned well sideways in preparation for his somewhat laboured Eastern forehand, and

Dick Savitt

changed grip thoroughly for his backhand. He hit all these strokes powerfully from a fairly long backswing and held them with ample follow-through. But, as grasscourt championship singles since 1947 could no more be won from the baselines than could any form of championship doubles since the days of the Dohertys, Savitt, though initially an improbable volleyer, took the net, covered it adequately, and volleyed strongly.

Savitt was well known in Australia, not only for winning the national championship a few months before his Wimbledon success, but for his unwitting connection with a battle of tactics between the rival selectors on the eve of the 1951 Australia/U.S. Davis Cup challenge round.

An interesting and somewhat complicated situation had arisen. Of the contenders for the Australian team, Sedgman was a certainty while Ken McGregor of South Australia was on the whole more entitled to the second place than Mervyn Rose of Victoria, although it was Rose rather than McGregor who had shown that he was more likely to beat Savitt. Savitt was a more probable choice for the U.S. team than either the fading Schroeder or the rising Seixas, but if Australia chose Rose to beat Savitt, would the Americans foresee this choice and omit Savitt? Deciding that the Americans would never have the nerve to discard Savitt, the Australian selectors, though by no means unanimously, chose Rose to counter him.

They had, however, met their match in the gentle art of ploy and counter-ploy. The Americans' reckoning was that the Australians would work things out exactly as they did. They therefore omitted Savitt. They chose Schroeder and Vic Seixas for the singles to defeat Rose, and Schroeder and Tony Trabert for the doubles.

When the teams were announced, Savitt held his fire for a time, leaving the field to an Australian tennis public highly incensed over the omission of McGregor. In the challenge round an upset Mervyn Rose played badly and was beaten by both Schroeder and Seixas, justifying the American selectors. Rose directed all his annoyance at himself—to his left-hander's backhand, to be precise, which he declared he would in future always hit hard even if he sent the ball into the back fence for the rest of his life.

Winning his two singles and the doubles with McGregor, Sedgman became Australia's hero of the hour, distracting public attention from the Australian selectors. The selectors were delighted, happily contemplating another profitable Davis Cup promotion in Australia. The Americans were disappointed, but, having won the battle of tactics and almost the match as well, they were not entirely dissatisfied.

But Savitt, by the time the Cup was finally lost, was ready to burst. Angry over his omission from the team, furious at having been treated as a pawn in the affair, he exploded; the range of his criticism spread, and eventually he left Australia an embittered man.

Australians felt that it would only be a temporary bitterness, for sport usually manages to wash away such feelings. Savitt was given a good welcome when he returned in 1952, but he did not retain his Australian championship title. It was won by the other man who had been tactically omitted from the 1951 Cup, Ken McGregor.

Mervyn Rose

128

No account of the great American players of this period would be complete without reference to that outstanding doubles pair, Talbert and Mulloy. Bill Talbert, a doctor, was a skilful enough singles player to reach the finals in both the 1944 and 1945 U.S. National championships; Gardnar Mulloy, a lawyer, gained five world singles rankings and at one time had the reputation of being the hardest man to beat in any tournament.

Doubles, however, was their forte. Together— Talbert in the right court, Mulloy in the left—

they won the U.S. National doubles four times between 1942 and 1948 and were selected in U.S. Davis Cup teams from 1946 to 1953. Talbert, an attractive Eastern stylist and an aggressive player without weakness, alternated in partnering Margaret Osborne and Louise Brough to win the U.S. mixed title four times in succession from 1943 to 1946, and, partnered by his young protégé, Tony Trabert, also captured the 1950 French doubles championship.

His playing days behind him, Talbert captained the winning U.S. Davis Cup team of 1954,

Bill Talbert

129

and to the present day he continues to exert a strong influence on American tennis. Mulloy, with his powerful overhead and lean hard physique, was a champion who stayed in the top flight for a long time. Born in 1914, and four years older than Talbert, he appeared in Davis Cup teams until 1957, earlier in which year he shared a grand comeback success with Budge Patty when they won the Wimbledon doubles as an unseeded pair.

Both were popular—sturdy Bill Talbert always, as a model sportsman for youthful Americans. Popularity came to the self-willed and domineering Mulloy later in life when, asking no quarter, he would take on players who had not been born when he made his first trip to Wimbledon and when, as an irascible veteran, he once removed his glasses and wordlessly offered them to an erring linesman.

Gardnar Mulloy as veteran

16 | Eastern Octopus

THE post-Kramer years saw almost every champion and would-be champion attempting to play the Big Game and continually seeking the net. Those backed by strong services and ground strokes succeeded; those without adequate ground strokes played no more than a serve-and-volley game. There were many matches in which the service returns of both players were adventurously wild rather than sound, so that for a short period the Big Game degenerated and in some quarters was scornfully called the serve-and-miss game.

At the same time it cannot be denied that during this period the general standard of serving and volleying improved greatly. Kramer's play had also firmly implanted in all players a desire for speed (how controlled depended on the individual) and his style of stroke-making was analysed and emulated. Analysis leads to fundamentals—and in tennis the fundamental is the grip, mainly the forehand grip. Since Kramer used an Eastern American grip, many players thought it essential to Power Tennis and the only one worth using.*

It was at about this time in Australia (the immediate post-war years) that grips came to be classified under recognized names and to be generally spoken about. Previously they had been given any convenient name that came to hand—the Crawford, the Perry, the Budge, the hammer, and so on. Now there were three names on the tip of almost every player's tongue—the Western, the Eastern, and the Continental—though many who rattled off these names had no idea that the first two were abbreviations of Western and Eastern American, and few indeed knew that the Continental had once been known as the English.

The Western was summarily dismissed as cumbersome and outmoded, and was mentioned merely by way of introduction. The Continental received almost similar treatment, players probably confusing it with Continental nationality—and anyone who was at all up to date knew that European tennis could not compare with the game played by the reigning group of American power players. By a process of rapid elimination the Eastern was left as the only possible grip for the forehand drive. As further support (if any was needed) it was pointed out that the master player, Tilden, had founded it, that the last great players before the war, von Cramm and Budge, had used it, and that now, with Kramer and Schroeder and company, its superiority was fixed. It thus seemed a criticism of a champion, almost a rudeness, not to call him an Eastern player, and forehand grips as far behind the racket handle as those used by Gardnar Mulloy and later by Vic Seixas were included in the Eastern family. A little later these grips—which, if not quite Western, were at any rate extreme Eastern—became called "modified Eastern" to distinguish them from the more usual Eastern. This was reasonable enough, because the wrist and palm were in essence behind the racket handle—the basic characteristic of the Eastern grip. But if a grip can be moved a little farther behind the handle—that is, to the right—and be called a "modified Eastern", it is likely to receive the same name when it is moved somewhat to the left—particularly if the name is a popular one. Sure enough, as the years went by that was what happened. What once had been a form of Continental (or English) grip, became called a modified Eastern. Confusion, all unrecognized, had set in.

With the name Eastern encroaching on Continental territory in one direction and on Western in the other, a cynic might have wondered if these three grips should not have been called Centre Eastern, Left Eastern, and Right Eastern

*History was repeating itself. British tennis writers of the early 1920s had ascribed American players' superiority over British players mainly to the fact that Tilden and Johnston gripped the racket with their wrists well behind the handle.

to allow almost everyone the satisfaction of having a fashionable grip.

It will be seen that the "Left Eastern" grip, bringing the hand towards the top surface of the handle, tends to introduce play that is more flexible but somewhat less powerful than the play resulting from a genuine Eastern grip. As these are Continental-grip characteristics, a more accurate name than "modified Eastern" would have been "modified Continental".

To have branded an innocent grip with the name Continental was bad enough in the first place. To put a three-syllabled adjective in front of it would be the last straw. No average player describing his own humble grip would presume to use so pompous a term as "modified Continental"—let alone a busy coach trying to explain the various grips to a group of pupils.

A large number of Australians use this "modified Continental", "modified Eastern" or "Left Eastern" forehand grip, and from now on, to distinguish it from either the Eastern or the Continental, we will refer to it as the Australian grip.

Some of the confusion about grips has undoubtedly been due to a rough-and-ready definition that calls a grip Eastern if the thumb-and-forefinger "V" lies anywhere on the top surface of the handle, Western if the "V" is on the right bevel, and Continental if it is on the left bevel. This is confusing because it neglects the more important factor of the palm's position in relation to the handle. Many a player holds his racket with the "V" on the right bevel and, playing an orthodox backhand with the opposite face of his racket, is an Eastern, or extreme Eastern, player; no one would think of describing his style as Western.

Some players are uncertain whether a "shake-hands" grip gives an Eastern grip or perhaps, after all, some form of Continental. The answer is that it gives an Eastern grip. When two people extend their arms and shake hands their palms meet fully in the equivalent of an Eastern grip; if for some strange reason both decided to shake hands with a Continental grip, only the upper portions of their palms would touch; if with a Western grip, only the lower portions.

Again, if a player has the "V" of his thumb and forefinger in the centre of the top of the racket handle (the standard position for the Eastern) but bunches his fingers so much that

his wrist is above the handle and no longer behind it, his grip is much more akin to a hammer grip (one of the Continental family) than it is to the Eastern (which, it will be remembered, is founded on the wrist as well as the palm being behind the handle).

In terms of measurement, the differences between the "V" positions in Western, Eastern and Continental grips are small, and when any one of these grips is modified the difference between it and the next standard one is, of course, even smaller. This makes the whole matter seem of little consequence. But once you see the differences in terms of palm position their importance becomes apparent. No one would beat a carpet hanging from a clothesline with a Continental grip; nor would anyone hammer a nail with a Western. Just as different grips have their uses in backyard and workshop, so do they induce different characteristics when used on a tennis racket.

The strengths of any grip and style stand out in the game of a champion, and this is the main reason why each new champion attracts a host of lesser players to his style. With lesser players, it is a style's weaknesses that come to notice. An Eastern champion, for example, portrays power and reliability on both wings; the lesser Eastern player is either handicapped to some degree by the comparatively large change of grip between forehand and backhand that the Eastern style involves or, if he does not change grip sufficiently for the backhand, by a definite lop-sidedness in strength. A Continental champion's flexibility and dexterity appear marvellous; the lesser Continental player often shows a weakness on the forehand, particularly on high balls.*

Grips, styles, and characteristics usually go together, but tennis players being human, there are exceptions. Some Continental stylists are power players, and some Eastern players have weak forehands. A few players using some form of Continental forehand grip make a substantial change for the backhand and may drive from both sides with a higher wrist and lower racket head than is normal for the Continental style.

*Continental-style champions avoid high balls by rising-ball play, thus making advantage out of adversity. This has given rise to the misconception that the Continental grip is especially suited to rising-ball play. It is— between rapid-fire forehand and backhand—but not necessarily in itself.

A few Eastern-grip players will be found hitting forehand and backhand with short crisp strokes and a low wrist. Nevertheless, the vast majority of tennis players match the photographs and notes provided in Appendix I; and it is also sincerely hoped that these make all of the foregoing discussion clear.

In present-day championship tennis the three fundamental forehand grips are no longer the Western, Eastern, and Continental; they have long been Eastern, "modified Continental", and Continental. Leaving the Western to rest in peace, how much better it would be to rename them, respectively, American, Australian, and English, hoping that in the interests of simplicity other nations would not protest.

This chapter has set out to show that the term "Eastern" has become too widely used, not to discount the genuine Eastern grip or style of play. It has also tried to clear confusion, but its very detail may instead have caused impatience, and there may be some who would prefer to go back to where they started, referring to the Continental as only the extreme grip used by Fred Perry and calling almost every other grip Eastern. This would not be good enough, for it would imply that everyone between Perry and an outright Westerner like Little Bill Johnston played almost the same game. Allowing the addition of the term "modified Eastern" would not be enough either—for then such players as Sedgman and Gonzales (left of Eastern), and Budge, Mulloy, and Seixas (right of Eastern) would be classified under one heading. Which, as Euclid so often put it, is absurd.

17 | Southern Sunshine

AUSTRALIA has always been a land of sunshine, but by 1946 precious little of its light had been reflected from the gleaming surface of the Davis Cup—not so much as a ray since the 1919 "Patterson and Anderson" victory at Double Bay. So when the 1946 challenge round began at Melbourne's Kooyong courts Australian hopes were high. Australia had won the Cup in the years immediately before and after World War I; she had won it again in 1939, but it had gone straight into storage; now, in the year after World War II, she hoped to complete the pattern and thus provide her tennis public with a chance of seeing Davis Cup tennis again the following year.

The Australian team was a good one. Neither of its singles players, Bromwich and Pails, was expected to hold Jack Kramer, but it was thought that both could beat whoever was chosen as America's second singles player, and that the old firm of Quist and Bromwich might be a better-balanced combination than Kramer and whoever was chosen to partner him.

"Lucky" Schroeder was fortunate to be chosen over Frank Parker and Gardnar Mulloy, who had better tournament performances—and then proceeded to make hay of Australian calculations. In an excellent opening match he defeated Bromwich, and on the second day he partnered Kramer to beat Quist and Bromwich. Kramer defeated first Pails and then Bromwich setless, and Mulloy, substituting for either a generous or a lazy Schroeder, completed the rout by beating Pails in the last match. Bromwich and Pails being essentially baseliners rather than the more usual all-court type of Australian player, the Big Game tactics of Kramer and Schroeder stood out sharply and made Australians realize that their tennis was out of date. America having won 5-0, the Cup went into the northern hemisphere once more and was not seen by another Australian crowd until 1951.

In this period Australia was not the only loser so far as the game itself was concerned, for in many other parts of the world, too, it became apparent that the sporting spirit normally associated with first-class tennis had declined. There were a few jovial characters about, such as Victorian Colin Long, who played Davis Cup tennis from 1946 to 1948—but all too few. It was evident that the "killer instinct" had been born, and players were described as fighting to win instead of playing to win; the winner "whipped" the loser, no matter how close the score; some players saw nothing wrong in querying linesmen's decisions, and crowds were inclined to follow suit; there were a few sit-down strikes on the court; here and there team jealousies were reported, and some players saw nothing wrong with needling an opponent simply because there was nothing against it in the rules. The newspapers played up many minor incidents, it is true, but it would be unfair to lay the blame on them. Whether it was the players' fault or merely a sign of the times, the type of unfailing courtesy that Budge and von Cramm had shown towards each other and their opponents was now missing from the scene.

Given time, these clouds would have dispersed of their own accord, but there is no doubt that a young Australian named Frank Sedgman hastened their disappearance. Blessed with a most attractive court personality which the rigours of fierce competition could not disturb, he was also a fine player and was mainly responsible for starting Australia's remarkable run of Davis Cup successes from 1950 onwards.

Sedgman had a full range of sound strokes backed by great physical fitness and endurance, and by a determined and unruffled temperament. His service was his main weapon; the rest of his strong and energetic game depended on it to such an extent that his top rivals used to say that Sedgman was as good as his serve. Parting his arms to put the ball up and take his racket back, he would throw high and then pause, often being photographed in this characteristic position with arms outstretched and poised to strike. His service was a mixture of slice and kick; it was fast and well controlled, concentrated on achieving depth before angle and on landing a good number of first balls into play.

Sedgman's hard training in the gymnasium and on the road enabled him to sustain an almost tireless serve-and-volley attack. He had solid ground strokes too, and his backhand was among the best of his time. His forehand was not as outstanding comparatively, but it was yet a stronger shot and carried more rolled pace than his backhand. It was never a target for an opponent's service; Sedgman, a left-court doubles player, stood well to the sideline and played as many service returns as possible with his forehand.

Sedgman was called an Eastern player, but we have already seen that this term was somewhat loosely interpreted. His low wrist and straight arm allied with his small change of grip between forehand and backhand made him more Continental than American. His forehand bore no resemblance to either Schroeder's or Seixas's, nor his backhand to Tony Trabert's. He played in the Australian style.

He regarded himself as an Eastern player, but he probably began with a grip that was clearly Continental. In an article written about his career he said that often when he was playing badly he found he was slipping back to the Continental. It is a matter of interpretation whether the unnoticed Continental grip was making him play badly or whether he was instinctively returning to his more natural grip in time of need. One also wonders if the reason why Sedgman did not achieve quite the same mastery over his forehand as he did over his other strokes was this slight lack of naturalness in his grip. On the other hand, he might never have reached the top with his original forehand.

Anyway, reach the top he most certainly did, after setting his foot on what was probably the first rung of the ladder in 1939, when, at the age of twelve, he attended an after-school coaching class run by Harry Hopman at Kooyong. There was not much of note about little Sedg at the time, apart from his wide smile and willingness to work, but when Hopman reopened his class at the end of the war a seventeen-year-old Sedgman and a thirty-nine-year-old Hopman began laying the foundations of an interesting period of tennis history.

More than any of his playing contemporaries, Harry Hopman had always believed in physical fitness, and in young Sedgman he found a gifted junior who thrived on the hard training standard he set. When the severest Hopman workout was over, Sedgman was likely to say that he might drop in to the gym that evening for an hour or two. By the time he was eighteen he had greatly improved his physique and had increased his weight by more than a stone. Before he was nineteen he had won, with John Bromwich, the Wimbledon doubles. Hopman's unique record as a Davis Cup captain has been closely associated with his success in handling young players, and there can be little doubt that he was greatly encouraged by his early training of Frank Sedgman.

In 1949 Sedgman became Australian champion, downing a veteran John Bromwich to the tune of 6–3, 6–3, 6–2. At Wimbledon he held two match points against the eventual winner,

Frank Sedgman

Ted Schroeder, and at Forest Hills again ran Schroeder to five close sets.

Nineteen-fifty was the year in which Hopman began his amazing run of success as Australia's non-playing Davis Cup captain and coach. In that year's challenge round Sedgman defeated Schroeder and Tom Brown, and partnered Bromwich in a doubles victory over Schroeder and Mulloy.

In 1951 Sedgman and Ken McGregor, his new doubles partner, won the doubles titles of Australia, France, and Wimbledon. And then began an even greater period for Sedgman. At Forest Hills he gave an almost faultless display of power tennis in defeating Art Larsen, the holder, in the semi-final and then Vic Seixas in the final,

winning each match in about forty-five minutes and becoming, in devasting style, the first Australian to hold the U.S. National singles title in the seventy years of its history. He also won the doubles with McGregor, giving the pair a Grand Slam in doubles, and became a triple U.S. winner by taking the mixed doubles with Doris Hart.

Back in Australia, he took the lion's share of victory in the 1951 Davis Cup challenge round. In 1952 this Golden Boy of Tennis, as he was then known, became triple Wimbledon champion, U.S. champion, successful defender of the Davis Cup, and professional for a record fee. Aided by organized Australian tennis and guided by Harry Hopman, he became the first Australian player to follow the smooth highway from

Frank Sedgman

136

promising junior to reputable professional, and was shortly followed by his team-mate McGregor.

The loss of this handsome and impressive pair created a void in Australian tennis, but the southern sun continued to shine. The mantle of Sedgman and McGregor now fell on the shoulders of two phenomenal youngsters, Lew Hoad and Ken Rosewall, who had come to be regarded almost as the two elder stars' young brothers and who were affectionately dubbed the Tennis Twins. Both were born in November 1934, Rosewall on the 2nd, Hoad on the 21st.

The Twins first met when they were only ten years old as champions of their districts in a curtain-raiser to an exhibition match at Sydney's White City. Hoad has amusingly described the occasion. He had cleaned his sandshoes, his mother had specially pressed his shorts, his father had polished up his old racket. Even so, Rose-wall won 6–0, 6–0. Not long afterwards they met again, still ten years old, in the final of the under-thirteen schoolboys' championship of New South Wales, and the result was the same. Hoad's story is that he could not win a game from Rosewall until he had played him three times and that not everyone can claim to have even as good a record as that against the Little Master.

The Twins became world tennis news in the 1952 Wimbledon doubles championship when, at the age of seventeen, they opposed two strong, no-nonsense players in Dick Savitt, holder of the Wimbledon singles, and Gardnar Mulloy. To everyone's surprise, the lads won the first two sets. Then, as if this had been no more than encouragement to youth, the men powered their way through the next two sets at 6–1, 6–3. But in the final set Hoad's easily made but powerful service and forehand, Rosewall's accurate backhand return of service, and the volleying and

Ken McGregor

137

Lew Hoad as Twin

winners, generously sprinkled in his younger days with errors. Below this surface, he worked much harder at his game and concentrated in match play more deeply than spectators may have imagined. His free and wristy style gave him a flexibility second to none, and no shot was beyond him. Sir Norman Brookes was of the opinion that his range of strokes was second only to Tilden's. To anyone who cared to look beyond his big serving, net attack, and all-round power, Hoad's stroke production was highly reminiscent of Jack Crawford's—particularly on his forehand and backhand (until he later added a backhand topspin drive), and in his low- and half-volleying on either side.

positional play of both boys won them the match at 7–5.

A year later the Twins almost emulated the Sedgman/McGregor feat of winning the Grand Slam in doubles, only the last title, the U.S. National doubles, eluding them. Next came the 1953 Davis Cup challenge round, played at Kooyong in Melbourne, when Hoad and Rosewall were nineteen and one month. From two matches-to-one down, Hoad achieved Davis Cup immortality with a remarkable five-set win on a rain-soaked court over Tony Trabert, and Rosewall won a tense deciding match against Vic Seixas. Australia had lost world champions Sedgman and McGregor and had retained the Cup with two nineteen-year-olds. From 1953 onward no references were made to them as twins or lads; they had established themselves as men and were known as Hoad and Rosewall.

Lewis Hoad, "colourful blond", "built like a truck driver" (literal meaning unknown, but implication clear), was so much a power player that the words "Hoad" and "power" became synonymous. He had a free style and an apparently unconcerned manner, and he hit a crop of

Rosewall as Twin

138

Ken Rosewall, as a stripling, received the ironical nickname of "Muscles", but hard training and playing soon developed him into a strongly built young man who never lacked stamina. His game was founded on a beautiful backhand, which he played with a slight slice. This slice should have been a weakness against the overwhelming preference for net play brought about by the Big Game, but Rosewall had such control of touch and change of pace with his backhand that he was able to achieve the same angles and passing shots as other world-class players with rolled backhands. He became known as the Little Master, and as we have already

A Hoad forehand volley

139

noted, his backhand effectiveness was compared to Budge's and Lacoste's.

Being a player who never liked to give anything away, Rosewall practised hard to improve his forehand and his service. He succeeded so well with the forehand that he became a successful first-court doubles player, changing sides with Hoad late in their partnership* and eventually partnering dyed-in-the-wool second-court players; but he was never able to develop a powerful service, either in speed or twist. His lack of height aside, this was not surprising. He was naturally left-handed—and a service action is essentially similar to that of a throw, the basic test of left- or right-handedness in games. Rosewall developed an accurate sliced service, well-placed for angle and depth, but it never became powerful.

Because, in an era of Big Game tennis, young Rosewall was a baseliner who hit many beautiful passing shots, he was likened by some observers to Crawford. There was some degree of similarity in the backhand, though Rosewall's was neither so long in swing nor so sliced as Crawford's, but, as already mentioned, it was Hoad's strokes that really held the Crawford likeness. This view later gained backing from Hoad himself when in a book on his tennis career he said that as a boy he had copied a Sydney player whose strokes were said to be an exact replica of Crawford's. Thus does the stroke-play of great stylists descend to others, even though it may be partially cloaked by differences in tactics between baseline and Big Game.

Hoad's power and Rosewall's accuracy upset another precept of basic style. Hoad was a Continental player (perhaps by now we should say English), using one grip for all shots, and yet was a power player; Rosewall was an Eastern-style (American) player, but his main attribute was accuracy. The normal roles were reversed, but there were perfectly simple explanations. Hoad was a strong man with an exceptionally powerful wrist, and Rosewall, being naturally left-handed, was not even playing with his stronger arm.

In the top game of singles Hoad and Rosewall

*This unexpected change was not connected with return of service; it was intended to give Hoad's overhead more scope. It was not a successful move, and led to Hoad's later preference for Rex Hartwig as a right-court partner.

made greater names for themselves than either their youth or their doubles combination could have brought them. In 1952 at Wimbledon, Hoad fully extended the great Drobny in a power-laden match; soon after, at Forest Hills, he defeated Art Larsen, the 1950 National champion, and Rosewall defeated Vic Seixas. In 1953 Rosewall was Australian and French champion, an enthusiastic France claiming him as their own since it was plain that he had the volley and half-volley of Henri Cochet, and the backhand and lob of René Lacoste. At Wimbledon, however,

The Hoad forehand

140

The Hoad backhand

Rosewall lapsed and it was Hoad who did better, taking the ultimate winner, Seixas, to 7–9 in the fifth set.

By 1954 it appeared that Hoad and Rosewall —particularly Hoad, who by then had emerged as the stronger player—would have the tennis world at their feet. But they were not to win any of the four major championships, and in the Davis Cup challenge round at the year's end they were outplayed by Seixas and Trabert. In the 1955 championships their only success was Rosewall's Australian title, but aided by Rex Hartwig, who partnered Hoad in the doubles, they returned a slashing 5–0 Davis Cup win over their old rivals Seixas and Trabert, and Hamilton Richardson.

In 1956 Hoad, now regarded as the amateur world's most outstanding player, set out to win

Rex Hartwig

the Grand Slam. Using all other tournaments for match practice only, he concentrated on being in peak form for the major ones. In relentless procession he became Australian and French champion, defeated Rosewall in a glorious Wimbledon final, and advanced to the U.S. final, where again he found himself facing Rosewall. Hoad won the first set, then Rosewall came into his own with the almost flawless tennis he was sometimes capable of, and Hoad's Grand Slam was lost. For three or four days Hoad felt that the world had fallen around him, then, characteristically, he forgot all about it.

After another 5–0 Davis Cup win over the U.S. came a temporary parting of the ways, Rosewall alone accepting the large offer made to both men by Jack Kramer to join his professional troupe. In 1957 Hoad retained his Wimbledon title with a high-octane display in which he blasted his compatriot Ashley Cooper off the court in less than fifty minutes at 6–2, 6–1, 6–2. Cooper was a fine player, and being two years younger than Hoad and having everything to gain and little to

Rosewall: American forehand

lose, did not give up easily. He was the current Australian title-holder, and next year, in 1958, he became Australian, Wimbledon, and U.S. champion. Cooper and Malcolm Anderson—who made history by winning the 1957 U.S. title as an unseeded player—became Australia's new Davis Cup mainstays and soon were also sought by the Kramer troupe.

Hoad's hurricane winning of the 1957 Wimbledon made him indispensable to the touring professionals, and immediately after Wimbledon he accepted an even larger offer than those made earlier to Sedgman and Rosewall.

The departure of Hoad and Rosewall from the amateur ranks in their early twenties created a depression in Australian tennis. True, there were other fine young players who provided an almost uninterrupted Davis Cup success, but no one could now be persuaded that the professionals were past their best, nor that the amateurs were providing more than second-best play. The game seemed to go stale, the once exciting Big Game to degenerate and become stereotyped. There were no more breathtaking Hoad/Rosewall battles in which the burly blond, a fuzz of fair hair glistening in the sun against his bronzed legs and forearms, tried to crush a black-haired Rosewall, calm and sturdy and always capable of

Rosewall: Backhand master

producing finely threaded passing shots. Against the best of the Big Game players, Rosewall had been forced to take his share of the net to prevent his opponents from having it almost at will, and he was a first-class volleyer, too; but because he was a passing-shot master his games with Hoad were always poised on the brink. Would Rosewall hold and capitalize on inevitable errors, or would Hoad storm his way to victory? One could never be sure.

It has often been debated which of the two was the better. Hoad rose to greater heights, but he was never certain of victory over Rosewall. Rosewall was the better as a youngster, Hoad overtook him and surpassed him at the peaks of their amateur careers. Rosewall did not win Wimbledon, but Hoad's only success in America was a doubles win with Rosewall, the singles winner. Hoad had the wider range of strokes, more power, one of the great serves of tennis, and a beautifully easy style. Rosewall, too, was a stylist, crisp and decisive. His backhand was second to none, and his opponents had to work as hard against him as against anyone else to gain a service break. His forehand was weak only in his earlier years. Later, with a straighter arm and more use of wrist than of elbow, it became a solid stroke, its crosscourt version far better made than before. As to its effectiveness, one can only quote his compatriot Fred Stolle's remark that although Rosewall's forehand was supposed to be a weakness he would exchange any of his own strokes for it.

Rosewall was more successful as a professional than Hoad, and if professionals are right when they say they have improved greatly since their amateur days, it could be thought that Rosewall was finally the better player. But the comparison is not valid in this case, for late in his amateur career Hoad suffered a severe injury to his back that later hampered his mobility, if not noticeably his power. As passing time gives better perspective, Hoad, the more dynamic player, will probably be placed above Rosewall. The matches won by Hoad possibly provided the greatest tennis of these two players' meetings.

One thing alone seems certain: that had it not been for the existence of the other, either Twin would have been acclaimed as the marvel of all time. Most of their defeats were inflicted by one of them upon the other. Of their contemporaries, who but Rosewall could withstand Hoad's powerful range of strokes and eventually surpass him? Who but Hoad could dent Rosewall's apparently unbreakable steadiness? Each destroyed what might otherwise have been the other's near invincibility. Their continued goodwill towards each other was no less admirable than their tennis.

Mal Anderson

18 | American Reprise

In the immediate post-war years American women players were not long in showing the world that Jack Kramer's Big Game tactics could be applied to their tennis as well as to the men's. Between wars there had been only one famous serve-and-volley lady player—the tall, blonde and shapely Californian, Alice Marble, who won Wimbledon in 1939 and her own country's championship four times. Then the graceful Pauline Betz, of Ohio, took over world leadership in her domain, and the baseline game, backed by deft volleying as the occasion arose, reigned supreme once more. It was no use arguing any further, the critics decided: the net game was no good for the girls. They couldn't cover the net, and they couldn't be expected to. They couldn't reach as far as men could to cover passing shots, couldn't leap as high to cover lobs, and if they stood a little farther from the net, their wrists were not strong enough for successful low-volleying.

Just as critics and coaches had the situation agreeably weighed up, the girls decided that what was sauce for Jack Kramer was going to be sauce for them too. Louise Brough, of Oklahoma, and Margaret Osborne du Pont, of Oregon, swept in, serving, smashing, and volleying severely, and using their ground strokes mainly to pave the way for net advances. From 1948 to 1950, Louise Brough, with her sometimes anxious court manner and sunny smile, was Wimbledon champion while Margaret du Pont, attractive and serene, was American champion. The two were close friends and they formed an almost unbeatable partnership, creating the most outstanding championship performance ever recorded by winning the U.S. ladies' doubles championship nine times in succession, from 1942 to 1950, and a further three times in succession from 1955 to 1957. The Wimbledon doubles fell to them five times, but by comparison this hardly seems worth mentioning.

Equal in skill to these two players and claiming the Australian championship (1949), the French (1950), and Wimbledon (1951) was Doris Hart, a world favourite who, in her climb to the top, had gallantly overcome the effects of infantile paralysis suffered during her youth. A classical stylist with sweeping and beautifully produced forehand and backhand drives, she made up in grace and power what she lacked in mobility from her childhood illness. An all-court player rather than a serve-and-volley specialist, she had a fast swinging service, strong volleys, and, for a woman, a severe overhead.

The former critics of women's attempts at net play were silenced, and like their male counterparts the modern girls were accounted the greatest of all time. Their modern game proved it. Suzanne Lenglen could never have stood up to such power and Helen Wills Moody's baseline game would have had no chance. Future champions would have to be bigger and better editions of the modern net game, said the latest critics.

Men really ought to give up making predictions about women. Into the scene, walking swiftly and nodding her head, stepped the clearly feminine figure of sixteen-year-old Maureen Connolly; she played a feminine game—and drove everyone else off the court.

Holding her racket just a little short of full length, she played an orthodox American forehand, dutifully changing grip for the backhand and running her thumb along the back of the handle for support. She hit forehand and backhand with sustained power, either flat or slightly rolled for control, and a steady stream of these drives was the basis of her game. Not for her the Continental grip for service that gave Doris Hart her swingers and Louise Brough her kickers; she retained her forehand grip and sent down a plain service with a slight slice for control (and if she had played in the 1920s she probably would have used slight reverse spin).

There was no mistake about it, though: Maureen Connolly hit the ball hard. The world's most heavily armed battleship of the days was the U.S.S. *Missouri*, colloquially known as "Big Mo"; sturdy little Maureen won herself the nickname of "Little Mo", and made it the better known of the two.

She slammed her forehand drive again and yet again. But were we imagining things, or did her backhand have even more power? Didn't she move even better when her right side was forward, and didn't she show a backhand preference when the ball was straight in front of her? Wasn't there the same telltale break in her service action that there was in the actions of Bromwich and Rosewall? Yes, when "Little Mo" became famous enough to have her life story written she revealed that she was naturally left-handed. A professional coach named Wilbur Folsom discovered her as a small ten-year-old hitting balls about with rare abandon and with her left hand. It was Folsom who laid the foundations of her game and arranged for her to be coached by Eleanor Tennant, known as "Teach" Tennant, former coach of Alice Marble. It is not clear which coach changed Maureen into a right-hander, but if it was Folsom he certainly had "Teach" Tennant's support. As far as Miss Tennant could see, left-handers did not become champions; they were mostly all forehand, occasionally they were all backhand, and they never seemed to get the balanced strength on both sides that was essential for a singles champion. A man might now and again be able to cover this weakness by his net game, but a left-handed lady champion? Never.

Left-handers would be justified in pointing out that their group has little chance to prove its worth if its most promising members are stolen from it. We shall, alas, never know if Maureen Connolly would have been Wimbledon's first left-handed lady champion.

But what a champion she was. Beginning with the 1951 U.S. championship, for which she

Louise Brough

146

Maureen Connolly

defeated Doris Hart, the Wimbledon holder, in 1952 she won both the Wimbledon and the U.S. titles and in 1953 a Grand Slam of the Australian, French, Wimbledon, and American championships. In 1954 she did not defend her Australian title, but retained her French and Wimbledon crowns. Then came tragedy. She injured a leg badly in a horse-riding accident and, barely out of her teens, could play no more. American tennis had lost its brightest star.

If Suzanne Lenglen, the all-court player of the 1920s was not the greatest woman player of all time, then "Little Mo", the battering-ram baseline player of the 1950s, would gain the vote of most critics.

Althea Gibson

With Maureen's accident, two of the tennis world's favourites (Maureen had been too young to supplant them) returned to the winning list. Though neither was happy over the enforced absence of Little Mo, gallant Doris Hart crowned her achievements by winning her country's national championship in 1954 and 1955, and Louise Brough set the seal on her career with another Wimbledon win in 1955.

Serve-and-volley tactics reigned supreme in 1957 and 1958. Althea Gibson saw to that, by winning both the Wimbledon and U.S. singles in each year.

The ladies' scene had been dominated by America. Their menfolk's run of Wimbledon successes had been checked by Frank Sedgman in 1952, and when young Ken Rosewall opened the 1953 season by carrying off the Australian and French singles championships, two of them, Vic Seixas and Tony Trabert, decided it was time Americans did something about it. Accordingly, Seixas won the 1953 Wimbledon singles and Trabert the U.S. National; the following year, Trabert won the French singles and Seixas the American and together they relieved Australia of the Davis Cup; in 1955 Trabert proved himself the player of the year by winning the French, Wimbledon, and American titles.

Vic Seixas, dark-haired and handsome, was born in Philadelphia in 1923 and made his first Wimbledon attempt in 1950 at the age of twenty-seven. At times during his career his keenness caused him to express a certain amount of displeasure on the court, inviting more than one Wimbledonian to refer to him as Vexatious. His rise to the top was due mainly to his fighting spirit and brilliant volleying, but once there he encountered great difficulty in beating two players—first Sedgman and later Rosewall. Sedgman, who, as we know, was at his best in 1951 and 1952, was too strong for Seixas in all of their three major clashes, defeating him in straight sets in the final of the American championship and in the two Davis Cup challenge rounds of 1951 and 1952.

Just as Dick Savitt's path had been obstructed by Mervyn Rose, so Seixas often found himself thwarted by the young Ken Rosewall. Rose had been able to anticipate better than anyone else the direction of Savitt's ground strokes; Rosewall, opposed by one of the best net players in the world, skimmed shot after immaculate shot past him. Receiving congratulations after at last defeating Rosewall—in the 1954 Davis Cup challenge round in Sydney—Seixas cheerfully remarked that he knew he could do so, for he really didn't expect to be beaten by the same man nine times running. It was a most sporting compliment from a married man of thirty-one to a youngster no more than a few weeks out of his teens.

Seixas was above middle height and slender in build, but his game gave an impression of compactness. He held his racket a little short on all strokes, playing them close to his body, though not in cramped fashion, and delivering his service swiftly, without much preparation or stretching. This service—made, like his volleys, with a Continental or English grip—while not powerful was well produced. The first ball carried plenty of snap and the second seemed almost incapable of landing anywhere but in court. It was an American Twist or Kick service, but unlike many others of its family it was completely unlaboured. He cracked the first ball hard; for the second he whipped on more twist, sending it safely high over the net to drop deep near the service line and allow him to follow in to the net. Down fifteen-thirty with the game score at 3–4 or 4–5, he would often whip down three serves, punch away three winning volleys, and leave you wondering what had happened to the tension of a few moments before.

His forehand, a topspin shot, was described as almost Western. Had he used the same face of the racket for his backhand—as his forehand grip would have easily allowed him to do—he would have been called a Western player, but we have already seen that people at this time were reluctant to call a spade a spade unless it was an Eastern one. As it was, Seixas used an Eastern backhand, but the change of grip it required was too large to give him time either to roll the stroke or to have much backswing, and so he cut it. He had good control of it and could keep the

Vic Seixas: English-grip backhand volley despite near-Western forehand

149

ball low over the net against a volleyer, but it was not a strong shot.

Basing his game on serve and volley, Seixas was a Big Game player. For almost a decade he was ranked in the world's first ten players, gaining top ranking in the United States in 1951, 1954, and 1957—a fine performance for anyone and particularly for a man born in 1923.

Tony Trabert was born in Cincinnati, Ohio, in 1930. He made tennis his career, winning amateur championships as a means to an end—professional tennis—and he made an outstanding success of it. Taller than Seixas, he was heavily built, with strong arms and legs, and he played with an all-round weight of stroke. He had a heavy service, a booming flat smash, and powerful volleys, especially when the ball was above the net. For ground strokes he had a solid forehand and an even better backhand, both being hit with plenty of topspin.

With this heavy artillery Trabert pounded the enemy into submission. He usually began well without having to find a delicate touch, and once in front he never needed to pause for rest. At times he could be overwhelming. In three of his greatest triumphs, the 1953 U.S. singles and the 1955 Wimbledon and U.S. singles, he did not concede a set.

Though unobtrusive in manner, he had, when in form, unbounded confidence in his strokes and his ability to win. He had a businesslike approach to match play, a ton of determination, no weaknesses, and well-controlled strokes. He kept the ball bouncing higher than most players, giving his topspin shots (when he was not dipping them against a volleyer) ample net clearance to obtain depth. A smooth-stroking player always found it difficult to get into his groove against him.

Trabert played his forehand with an Eastern or American grip, holding his palm and wrist

Tony Trabert

150

solidly behind the handle. His backhand involved a substantial change of grip, for he placed his hand farther behind the handle for this shot than had been accepted practice for many years. He volleyed in much the same way, taking the ball well in front of his body whenever he could. Though not as quick or as flexible as other players in the top bracket, he was severe on balls

Ashley Cooper

above net height, and he played to get as many of these as possible.

A punishing winner, he was also a good-tempered loser. When top seed in the 1954 Wimbledon he suffered a blistered playing hand, much as Jack Kramer had done in 1946. Concealing his disability to avoid encouraging any of his opponents, he reached the semi-final, where Ken Rosewall, down two sets to one, staged a grandstand finish and put him out. It was a grand match, and Trabert was not the man to spoil a great day for anyone; he made no mention of his handicap.

After Trabert turned pro in 1955 the amateur stage, as we have seen, was dominated for two years by Lew Hoad. In 1958 another Australian emerged as Wimbledon champion. This was strongly built and darkly handsome Ashley Cooper, an Eastern or American player, though not unquestionably so like Tony Trabert, for he had a distinctive Australian stamp on his style. He won the Australian singles and played in a winning Davis Cup team in 1957; and, as already indicated, in 1958 he was singles champion of Australia, Wimbledon, and America—grasscourt champion of the amateur world. Then he, too,

Alex Olmedo: American stylist, but a low-wristed backhand

turned professional (amateur bodies were by this time regarding Kramer as a pirate and his players as defectors), and in 1959 America again returned to the Wimbledon forefront.

The winner that year was an unusual American —Alex Olmedo, of Peru. As well as playing for America, Olmedo, supple and swift, was also basically an American stylist, even if his backhand could have been called English. He was the hero of America's 3–2 Davis Cup victory over Australia in 1958, winning both his singles matches and, with Hamilton Richardson, the doubles as well. Not long after, he became the 1959 Australian champion, entered Wimbledon as the first seeding, and duly won the title. His run of amateur successes was halted by Australia's Neale Fraser, who defeated him in the final of the U.S. National singles in 1959 and also in their Davis Cup singles encounter. By this time, however, the popular "Chief" had taken a string of Australian scalps, including Cooper's and Anderson's, Roy Emerson's and Rod Laver's. He then followed the well-beaten trail into Kramer's troupe.

In that troupe of world champions reigned a monarch whom most tennis-players—even if a number of notable critics disagree—have regarded for more than a decade as our old friend, the greatest player of all time.

Richard (Pancho) Gonzales was born in 1928 of Mexican parents. In 1947 he was ranked seventeenth tennis-player in the United States, and in 1948 first. In 1949 he was ranked as the world's leading amateur. If Ted Schroeder played less tournament tennis than anyone else, Gonzales must have had the shortest amateur career. In 1948 he won the U.S. National singles championship and in 1949 essayed a European tour with singular lack of success. Budge Patty beat him in a semi-final of the French championships, and at Wimbledon, where he was seeded second to Schroeder, he was belted out in the fourth round by Geoff Brown.

Once back in America, however, Gonzales was a different player. Challenged for his title—to everyone's amazement Wimbledon winner Ted Schroeder was entering his second big tournament in one year—Gonzales showed his mettle. Schroeder had defeated him six times previously and was a renowned iron-man fighter over five sets; but this time it was Gonzales who won in

five sets, showing a determination equal to Schroeder's and, being younger by seven years, greater stamina.

Teaming with Schroeder as a singles player and backed by Talbert and Mulloy as doubles pair, Gonzales retained the Davis Cup for the United States against Australia in 1949. Then, turning away from unconquered fields of amateur glory, he was off to join Jack Kramer at the age of twenty-one.

Kramer was at that time king, and remained so for some years. It was he who welcomed Frank Sedgman to the professional ranks in 1952–3 with an individual series of matches throughout America. But when Kramer's duties as promotor began to demand more of his time and energy and an injured back began to hamper his play, it was Gonzales, not Sedgman, who succeeded him as top professional. Gonzales guarded this position year after year against champion after amateur champion, with all succeeding zeal, technical skill, determination and, finally, defiance. Not until about the mid-1960s did anyone else dare to claim his rating.

Gonzales was tall—about 6 feet 2 inches or more—olive-skinned, and lithe as a cat. Just as Frank Sedgman had been Harry Hopman's ideal student for world championship, Pancho Gonzales was the young star most naturally endowed to adopt Kramer's Big Game tactics. His game was built on a wonderful service. With lissom ease he lifted his throwing arm, leaving it poised in line with the ball while he raised his right arm (characteristically wide of his right side), circled the racket behind his back, and from the top of his height and reach crashed down a flat service— flowing in action and terrific in speed. Scorning the safety of either slice or twist, he often delivered his second ball flat as well—a sort of slower cannonball. The impression that he had a flat second service was heightened by his tactic of sometimes delivering his services in reverse of accepted order—a kicker followed by a fast flat second ball. Whatever methods he used, his opponents were always under pressure.

In the 1920s, when Gerald Patterson thundered down his services, there was no one but Tilden to compare to him unless you went back to McLoughlin and his "railroad" delivery; similarly, in the 1930s, Elsworth Vines's blinding speed was compared to that of an earlier player, Patterson. Gonzales, however, played in an era of power services, and his was the greatest of all; little wonder, then, that present-day tennis followers believe Gonzales' service to have been in a class of its own, and its owner unique in the game.

Pancho's long-legged agility and speed carried him well in to the net for his first volley, despite the pace of his service. He was a great volleyer, but behind such a service Gonzales, like Norman Brookes, undoubtedly received many simple volleys to deal with.

Hardly noticed at first by comparison with his serving and volleying, Gonzales' ground strokes, like the rest of his game, were played in the English (or Continental) style. Such a powerful American player might be expected to have been an American stylist, but he wasn't. He held his wrist lower than American-style players do and, with fingers bunched rather than spread, he used a form of English grip commonly called the hammer grip. He did not recommend this bunched grip to younger players, warning that it made control of the racket more difficult. "But in my grip," he said, "my fingers are never spread." He was referring to his forehand grip, and in point of fact he later altered his bunched back-

Pancho Gonzales, 1969

154

hand grip. As an amateur he apparently neglected his ground strokes and they were sometimes erratic, but they improved greatly in his professional days; in a troupe of ex-world champions equipped almost to a man with terrific services, an excellent return of service was essential. Gonzales' forehand was made with a short backswing, as one would have expected of a man who was essentially a volleyer, but, a little surprisingly, he never neglected the follow-through. On the backhand side, like many another player whose concern is to get to the net, Gonzales sliced the ball, and he is one of the few players (Rosewall is another) to have advocated a sliced backhand in print. "Try to give the ball a little underspin," he wrote, and his advice "never put the thumb up" is also pure heresy from an American.

Gonzales modified his hammer backhand grip as late as 1957, when he was almost thirty. Playing a series of matches against Hoad, the latest champion from the amateur world, he was trailing by a clear margin and it seemed that he would be dethroned. Hoad was winning for one reason; in certain positions and under extreme pressure Gonzales preferred to hit his backhand passing shot down the line and could not direct it across court with the same accuracy. This small difference arose from Gonzales' inability to get his racket head round the ball with complete effectiveness. There was no secret about it; each player knew this stroke was making the difference in results between them, and each knew that the other knew. Gonzales, great player though he was, went back to first principles—the grip. In the middle of the series he began to spread his fingers to cover more handle and gain

The young Gonzales

more control of the racket head. Rapidly developing an effective crosscourt backhand, he overhauled Hoad and won the series.

Hoad later expressed admiration for this feat. A new grip is always likely to feel either clumsy or weak, and therefore unnatural and unreliable. It is one thing to practise with a changed grip, another altogether to adopt it successfully while engaged in match play.

Although Hoad regarded this incident as further proof of Gonzales' greatness, others have used it as support for the contention that a series of matches between two champions is not as exacting a test of superiority as winning a major tournament. The case against the series is that it proves only that one player is better than another in a particular series—no more and no less. In a tournament the ultimate winner must win every match he plays or he is out. In a series a player can drop a match that's going badly for him, save his strength and concentration, and level the score next day against a tired opponent.

We shall never know whether Gonzales, if he had stayed longer among the amateurs, would have won a string of major tournaments and so strengthened the claims of those who consider him the greatest player ever. But it's almost certain that he would have, for after having two U.S. National championships and a winning Davis Cup challenge round to his credit by the time he was twenty-one, he beat an impressive list of ex-amateur champions—Sedgman, Trabert, Segura ("Little Pancho"), Anderson, Cooper, Rosewall, Hoad, Laver. Little wonder that many people can scarcely imagine there ever having been a better player.

But here the opinion of Jack Kramer—who has spent a lifetime in tennis as player, promoter, and commentator—comes as something of a shock. After placing Budge, Vines, and Tilden in a class of their own, he chooses Perry and Riggs, allotting Gonzales sixth place. Thus, since Kramer had at the very least proved himself better than Riggs, the great Pancho comes no higher than seventh.

"What of it?" reply Pancho's supporters. "With all due respect to Kramer, he places Riggs higher than anyone else does, so why believe him more than anyone else? As for putting Pancho in a different class from three men who were champions ten, twenty or thirty years before him. . . ."

Once again the intriguing question of who was history's greatest player must be shelved.

19 | Left-handers at Last

WE seem to have kept Wimbledon's 1954 champion, Jaroslav Drobny, waiting an unconscionable time, but this is nothing compared with the time the world waited for a member of the left-handers' club to win the Wimbledon title once more.

In other major tournaments left-handers had had some success, but only now and then. By 1954 the Australian championship list contained the names of Horrie Rice, Norman Brookes, Jack Hawkes, and Mervyn Rose; the French included, besides Drobny, Marcel Bernard; the American, Beals Wright, Lindsay Murray, John Doeg, and Art Larsen.

As we have seen, Norman Brookes was the first left-hander to win at Wimbledon, in 1907; and in 1914 he became the last until 1954. In the intervening forty years only a few left-handers gained seedings: John Doeg of the United States, once (1930); Christian Boussus, of France, twice (1931 and 1935); Mervyn Rose, of Australia, three times (1952–4); and Art Larsen of the United States, five times (1950–54). Drobny was seeded on eight occasions (1947–54) before he won the title, by which time he was practically a forgotten man, and had been seeded as low as eleventh. In all that time people had found left-handers hard to beat and had disliked and sometimes even hated playing against them, yet these same left-handers had not produced a single Wimbledon winner. Even though left-handers were outnumbered, especially in earlier days, it was a poor record. No wonder Ken Rosewall's tennis-loving parents placed the racket in their youngster's right hand or that Maureen Connolly's coach changed her to a right-hander at an early age.

The left-handers' lack of singles championship success is too marked not to have had some direct cause. And this cause was—style.

In theory a left-hander should be simply a right-hander in reverse. In practice this does not necessarily hold true. The average left-hander is decidedly more unbalanced between forehand strength and backhand weakness than a normal right-hander. The reason for this disparity is that left-handers get more forehand play than right-handers do, and far less opportunity to develop a sound crosscourt backhand. Playing a right-hander—and most players are right-handed—a left-hander is able to exploit his forehand considerably. A right-hander's most easily produced ground strokes—whether in rallying or making a net approach—are a straight forehand and a crosscourt backhand; most right-handers therefore have some difficulty in avoiding a good left-hander's forehand. When it comes to backhand play, the left-hander, if he wishes to avoid his opponent's forehand, makes little use of a crosscourt backhand.

Doubles exaggerates this situation. Left-handers almost invariably take the left court, where they have time for a long backswing on the forehand and where, to avoid the opposing net man, they must play a backhand to their off side. This type of stroke tends to become their

Boussus

157

normal backhand in singles as well as doubles and is mostly played square-on with a raised left elbow, in the form of a dropped-racket-head slice.

The typical left-hander makes enormous use of his forehand when returning service in doubles; only later, in championship class, does he encounter opponents capable of consistently reaching his backhand with accurate centre-line services. In his formative years he is able to step round many a service intended for his backhand; he therefore tends to concentrate on his forehand and let his backhand more or less look after itself. Most left-handers are thus strong Eastern or extreme Eastern players, many making little change of grip for the backhand and accordingly using an inadequate grip for this stroke.

This left-handed forehand strength can dominate in doubles, and here left-handers, particularly those who also have strong services, have made big names for themselves. Even in doubles, however, they have been accorded their share of criticism, for they tend to volley erratically, even if often deceptively, to take too long a backswing for forehand volleys, and to play backhand volleys with the same square-on stance and dropped racket head that characterize their backhand ground stroke.

In singles, any vulnerability a left-hander may have on his backhand is obviously more exposed; from the beginning, such a backhand presents an inviting and easily attainable target for a right-hander serving to the right court. Some left-handers are therefore forced to forgo their excellent forehand ground strokes and seek the net not so much as a base of attack as a place of refuge.

A left-hander whose weakness lies in his forehand rather than his backhand is in an even worse plight. Right-handers playing him lose that tied-up feeling they have against a normal left-hander who forces them to use their less natural strokes in an effort to avoid his strong forehand. As previously noted, few right-handers like playing crosscourt forehands and down-the-line backhands, particularly if they are seeking a good length; a left-hander with a weak forehand relieves his opponent of this strain; he also lacks what is usually one of a left-hander's best attacking shots. He may have an attacking backhand instead, and will cope better in receiving serves to the right court, but this is not fair exchange.

As a general rule, championship singles demands a balanced game, and since left-handers did not tend to develop such a game, many students of tennis understandably came to think that the left-handed game was unsound in itself. As Rod Laver has since expressed it, "Many left-handers seem to carry within them the seeds of their own destruction."

It was to avoid this imbalance that Ken

Drobny serving

158

Rosewall and Maureen Connolly were changed from left-handers into right-handers. Although their success cannot be questioned, Laver has thanked his stars that he was allowed to continue in his left-handed way and to develop, as wonderful assets, his natural service and forehand.

It is easy to see why when players change the racket from left hand to right their service is adversely affected, but many observers have wondered why, in addition, their forehand should be weaker than their backhand. The forehand is one of the "natural" strokes, and if it is played with the weaker hand it almost certainly becomes less strong than it need have been; a backhand preference is explainable if we allow that a naturally left-handed person's most comfortable position is probably where his stronger left side is held back in reserve, as though to deliver a blow—i.e., where his right side is forward.

Thus far we have seen that the typical left-hander's strength is his forehand, his weaknesses being the backhand and the consequent imbalance between his two sides. But he has one great compensation: his service is better in practice than a mere theoretical reversal of a right-handed delivery. A left-hander's sliced service can be a deadly weapon with which to attack a right-hander's backhand, whether as a centre-line delivery to the right court that is almost impossible to step round, or as a widely swinging delivery to the left, forcing the receiver beyond the sideline. Surprisingly, many left-handers do not cultivate this swinging service that should be theirs as a gift of nature—a service far more penetrating than the now obsolete reverse spin developed by right-handers in the early days of tennis. They prefer instead to serve towards their off side with an American Twist or kick action. But whichever action the left-hander chooses, he seems to produce more swerve or kick than a right-hander does. Perhaps this is only an illusion caused by the ball swerving or breaking in the opposite direction to the normal, but comparatively more left-handers than right-handers specialize in service spin of some kind.

This leads to the last point of practical difference between left- and right-handers. Over the years the typical left-hander has topspun his long forehand, underspun his short backhand, and swung or kicked his service. He has generally

been a more twisty customer than his right-handed enemies. It is probably fair to say that provided his stroke equipment is equal to his right-handed opponent's, a left-hander will usually win. He has the advantage of being unusual and of thus adversely affecting a right-hander's game. When left-handers fail against right-handers it is because they haven't the all-round stroke equipment of their opponents.

So much for style. It is high time to reintroduce Jaroslav Drobny, surely our most patient stylist to date.

Drobny was a typical left-hander in that he had to carry a backhand that was out of balance with the rest of his game. Short, sturdy, and strong, he had one of the most powerful services of his day (he was also a master of left-handed slice and twist), a terrific overhead in which he had superb confidence, and a wristy and flexible forehand that led the world. As well as power in other departments, he had delicate touch in his volleying and drop-shots. But his backhand—especially when he had insufficient time to play it—was little more than a small cut.

Drobny, however, was untypical of left-handers in having an English or Continental forehand. Since this meant that he needed to make little or no change to have an adequate backhand grip, we can only wonder why he

Drobny: Forehand drive

159

never developed an efficient backhand drive. General opinion was that he simply had a "left-hander's backhand", but the truth may have been that he had a complex about it. Long and hard he practised, time and again he was certain he had mastered this stroke, only to see it collapse in match play on fast grasscourts, forcing him back in desperation to his dependable but relatively ineffective cut. The number of matches this weakness cost him must have been heart-breaking.

Drobny was only sixteen when it took world champion Donald Budge five sets to beat him in the 1938 Czechoslovakian championship. At the same age he was also skilful and powerful enough to become an international ice hockey player. This accounts both for his exceptional stamina in tennis and his wearing of tinted glasses. In one hockey match, steel splinters from an opponent's skate pierced one of Drobny's eyes. A third landmark for sixteen-year-old Drobny was his entry for the Wimbledon championship—the first of eleven. The following year, he had the distinction of being beaten by Bunny Austin, but he won the first of his ten successive Czechoslovakian championships.

At Wimbledon in 1946 he was unseeded, but at least one player recognized his calibre. This was Jack Kramer, who thought that Drobny was the man to beat, and who was duly beaten by him. It was a five-set affair, the second set going to Drobny at 17–15, and the match lasting two and a half hours. This was also the year in which Drobny should have won his first major title, a success that was to elude him for the next five years and cause critics to say that he would never

Drobny: Backhand volley

win one. Opposed to Marcel Bernard in a left-handers' final of the 1946 French championship, he won the first two sets, became overconfident, and eventually lost.

The 1947 Wimbledon quarter-finals provided the first of a series of encounters, later to become famous, between Drobny and Budge Patty. Patty was on the point of exhaustion when he won in five sets, but this was nothing to what was in store for him six years later, in 1953.

The 1948 French championship saw additions to Drobny's list of long matches; after beating Patty in five sets he lost a three-hour final to America's Frank Parker. At Wimbledon he went out before the quarter-finals in a five-set match, including one set of 16–14, to the Italian player Cucelli. Soon afterwards he was engaged with Australia's Adrian Quist in the longest Davis Cup singles ever played. In the usual five sets there were seventy-eight games (forty for Drobny and thirty-eight for Quist), Drobny coming from two sets down to win the third at 18–16 after saving five match points, and the fifth at 7–5. The five match points were also Davis Cup points to Australia. It was all to no avail, however, for Bill Sidwell of Australia defeated Drobny's team-mate Cernik in the final match. To round off his efforts for the year, Drobny went down to Pancho Gonzales at Forest Hills after sharing two sets at 8–10, 11–9.

In 1949 Drobny defeated Patty (by tradition, in five sets) and Australians Geoff Brown and John Bromwich to reach, for the first time, the Wimbledon final. There, despite an unmerciful pounding of his backhand, he stood level with Ted Schroeder at two sets all and three games all; but the title in the end was Schroeder's.

His next battle was a political one, and it turned him into a man without a country. The government of Czechoslovakia ordered Drobny and Cernik to withdraw from the Swiss championship because it contained German and Spanish players. Both men refused to obey, thus choosing exile. Never to be Davis Cup partners again, each went his separate way to make a living from his greatest skill, tennis. It is ironical that this meant amateur tennis, but it in no way detracted from the sadness and loneliness of the situation.

To offset this loneliness to some extent, Drobny had by 1950 become one of Wimbledon's most popular players. Not only was he a regular competitor who had shown considerable courage in his choice of freedom; he was refreshingly different. He was short and square among the usual run of tall and willowy tennis figures; he was European in a scene dominated by Americans and Australians; and he was left-handed in a sport where success had so largely gone to right-handers. Still, 1950 was not to bring him a major title. He was defeated in the French final (almost inevitably by Budge Patty, at 7–5 in the fifth set). At Wimbledon, in a semi-final against Frank Sedgman, he led by two sets to nil, but lost after breaking a string in his racket.* At Forest Hills he went out in an early round to Art Larsen, the eventual winner.

At this time critics began to predict that Drobny would never win a major title; something, they thought, was lacking in his make-up, and his very left-handedness seemed a weakness. Almost immediately Drobny proved them wrong, and then suffered a disappointment.

He began the 1951 season with four successive tournament wins—the Paris International, the French indoor, the Italian and British hardcourts —and, in his fourth appearance in the final of the French championships, captured his first major title. The semi-final and final matches were straight-set victories over, respectively, Frank Sedgman and South African Eric Sturgess. Then came the setback, a severe one in which inspired play by Britain's Tony Mottram caused the upset of the 1951 Wimbledon tournament, in the third round and at Drobny's expense. Playing with a strained shoulder, Drobny battled Mottram in yet another of his long five-set matches, this one containing three advantage sets with the fifth going against him at 6–8.

In 1952 it seemed that Drobny was the world's finest player on hardcourts and that Sedgman had no equal on grass. In the French final it was Drobny over Sedgman; at Wimbledon it was the reverse.

With Sedgman a professional, 1953 seemed certain to be Drobny's Wimbledon, and it could well have been but for his old opponent and opposite in many ways—Budge Patty. In the third round they played a marathon match that dwarfed all their previous clashes. It has already

*This is the third time broken strings have been mentioned. They occurred more frequently in past days; nor was the replacement racket so likely to be an exact replica of the discarded one.

A Drobny backhand

been referred to in connection with Patty's career, but it bears expanding on.

In a centre-court match that lasted four hours and fifteen minutes, the play was continuously daring and ended, almost incredibly, with attacking tennis. Both players injured leg muscles, and since the winner's injury was severe, each effectively put the other out of the tournament. At Wimbledon, as in no other tournament, the rule that "play shall be continuous" applies to the whole match, and there is no break after the third set. The score, to Drobny, read 8–6, 16–18, 3–6, 8–6, and had reached 10–all in the last set— by which time Drobny had saved six match points—when, at 9 p.m., it was decided to play only two more games and then call a halt. Realizing that he would hardly be able to walk next day, Drobny, backing his luck, broke Patty's service and aced his way to victory in the final game. He had won three sets to Patty's two, and forty-seven games to forty-six. Both gladiators had hit plenty of outright winners in these ninety-seven games, and the final point score was 304 for Patty and 301 for Drobny.

Drobny and Patty were given suitable applause —five minutes unbroken—and each later received an engraved silver cigarette case from the All England Club as a token of esteem for an amazing performance.*

Meanwhile Drobny's heart remained set on winning the tournament. Patty released him from their doubles entry, and Drobny, with a damaged thigh muscle and a swollen leg, managed to win two more rounds by courage and racket skill alone; in the semi-final he was defeated by Kurt Neilsen, of Denmark.

After this Drobny began to look played out. In the 1954 French championship he was beaten in the fourth round by Art Larsen—though again the match was a five-set affair—and at Wimbledon his seeding was dropped from fourth to eleventh.

Drobny took this low seeding as an insult and decided to withdraw from the tournament; but fortunately he had married, in 1952, a wife whose tact equalled her knowledge of Wimbledon. Mrs Drobny, a former Wimbledon player as Rita Jarvis, convinced him that withdrawal would prove nothing and could be regarded as poor sportsmanship. Drobny finally entered for the singles event only, and between matches he went fishing.

His first serious test came in the quarter-final against Hoad (and, as Drobny would have put it, Hopman). Hoad did not play badly—his smooth and powerful stroking was always a delight to watch, and he did not miss easy shots— but the ball always seemed to be on Drobny's racket, and he won in straight sets.

Who should be next but Budge Patty. Two hours later, after a 9–7 last set (only the fourth this time), Drobny entered his third Wimbledon singles final. There, in every respect but the odds on his winning, he was the crowd's favourite. It is doubtful whether even an English finalist—and there had been no English winner since Fred Perry in 1936—could have shaken Drobny out of this position. The other finalist could only fill the role of Drobny's opponent.

Ironically, Drobny's opponent was Ken Rosewall, who normally would have got a full measure of any Wimbledon crowd's support. He was an Australian ("the next best thing") and a popular player. He had had bad luck the year before when, seeded first at the age of eighteen, he had been affected by illness. This year he had had a

*Almost unbelievably, Drobny and Patty played the final of the 1955 Lyons covered-courts tournament to an unfinished score of 21–19, 8–10, 21 all. Total games, 100, exceeded the 1953 Wimbledon match, but the time was a mere 3 hours 45 minutes.

Art Larsen: Touch player

Born in 1934, Fraser made the first of eleven consecutive visits to Wimbledon in 1954. That year he was beaten by Mervyn Rose, who was basically a similar type of left-hander, though he

number of long and hard singles matches and, keeping to his doubles and mixed-doubles commitments, had reached the singles final a fairly tired young man. But to a Wimbledon crowd all this was nullified by his being young enough to have all his future before him and by his having won his semi-final against Tony Trabert in such sparkling fashion as to make him the likely winner.

Drobny at last achieved his Wimbledon ambition with a tension-packed win at 13–11, 4–6, 6–2, 9–7 and received a huge emotional ovation. Here was Wimbledon's first left-handed victor since 1914.

There was not to be another until 1960, when Wimbledon saw an all-Australian and all-left-handed final in which Neale Fraser defeated Rod Laver. This time the champion could without reservation be called a typical left-hander. Making full use of his natural advantage, Fraser had, among other deliveries, a swinging service that could force the receiver out of the left court, a powerful long-swinging forehand made with an Eastern or American grip and hit with plenty of topspin, which he could pull sharply across court, and the left-hander's comparatively small and underspun backhand. It is almost needless to add that his volleying was of a high order.

Neale Fraser serving

relied on spin far less than Fraser did, and was a noticeably smooth stroke-maker by any standards. Unlike his younger fellow-Victorian, Rose did not win a Wimbledon singles title, but many critics consider him to have been a better player than Fraser.

Fraser was tall, fair-haired, good-looking, and well-mannered. He was a grand competitor, his Wimbledon record showing that by 1958 he had reached five finals and by 1962 had won every title for which he was eligible—the singles and mixed once each, and the men's doubles (with Roy Emerson) twice. In his earlier years he played in the shadow of Hoad and Rosewall and later of Cooper, and it was not until 1959 that he emerged at full stature. Olmedo won Wimbledon that year, Fraser having been eliminated in

a quarter-final by Barry Mackay of America; then Fraser defeated Olmedo to become U.S. National champion, and a little later beat both Americans when Australia regained the Davis Cup.

In 1960 he was seeded first at Wimbledon. It was his great chance and he took it, defeating America's Earl Buchholz (although most fortunately), India's Ramanathan Krishnan, and finally Rod Laver. He rounded off the year by holding his U.S. title and again playing in a winning challenge-round team.

Fraser had a fine Davis Cup record. He was selected nine times—from 1955 to 1963—and as a leading player on the last five occasions was defeated only once in singles and once (with Roy Emerson) in doubles. Though he will be

Fraser: American forehand

remembered as one of the great left-handed servers, he waited long for the topmost position in world tennis and his championship reign was brief. But just as Wimbledon's first winner, Spencer Gore, may have found solace in giving way to a fellow Old Harrovian instead of some outsider or other, so did Fraser hand over to a young man who had always admired him and was a fellow left-hander. This was his Davis Cup team-mate Rod Laver, five years his junior, slender and on the small side, red-haired, frecklefaced and unassuming, but a player who achieved tremendous success and who has since become a contender for that ethereal title of the greatest player of all time.

The game's greatest player or not, he has certainly been among its most self-effacing. In his younger days he looked shy and even self-conscious on the court; he later gained poise, but in neither his bashful nor his settled period did he display temperament or mannerism; rather was he poker-faced, in the fashion of the players of the 1920s and 30s.

His well-known nickname—like Rosewall's "Muscles"—was born of irony. Harry Hopman, trying out a group of youngsters, pointed to the weediest-looking (Laver's own description) and called out good-humouredly, "All right Rocket, let's see what you can do." He soon saw.

What young Rocket lacked in weight he more than made up for in determination. He himself tells the story of how, in the effort to develop a strong wrist and forearm, he continuously used to squeeze a squash ball in his fingers—in out-of-school hours as well. His success has been variously attributed to one particular stroke or another or to a combination of this and that, but as one player-critic has most pertinently observed, "It's Laver's wrist and forearm that he beats you with; that and his pride."

Laver's career has been so successful that we will confine an outline of it to highlights only. Born in 1939 and brought up in Rockhampton, Queensland, he won the Australian junior title in 1957. In 1959, aged twenty, he competed at Wimbledon as an unseeded player and was beaten by Alex Olmedo in the first of four successive appearances in the final. In the same year he gained Davis Cup selection, he and Neale Fraser providing Australia with two left-handed singles representatives who, with Roy Emerson as a doubles player, won the Davis Cup

from 1959 to 1962—after which period Fraser lost his singles place and Laver turned professional.

In 1960 Laver was Australian singles champion and Wimbledon runner-up again—this time to Fraser. He dominated the Wimbledon finals of 1961 and 1962, beating American Chuck McKinley in less than an hour in the first and

Laver serving

Australian Martin Mulligan with the loss of only five games in the second.

Before the 1962 Wimbledon he had won the Australian and French titles; after it he triumphantly completed the Grand Slam by winning the U.S. National. In the closing stages of this last final, played against Roy Emerson, the nearness of the Slam suddenly made the occasion almost too great for even the level-headed Laver. His game began falling to pieces, and he only managed to reassemble it by consciously going through the drills of stroke-play instilled into him by his early coach, Charles Hollis. The only Grand Slam winner since that other great redhead, Donald Budge, in 1938, Laver that year had also won the Italian and German championships.

After leaving amateur tennis, Laver received some sound beatings from leading professionals such as Gonzales, Hoad, and Rosewall, and this tended to add greater strength to the opinion that even the best of the amateurs were inferior to the pros. But Rosewall has since succeeded Gonzales and Laver has succeeded Rosewall. Some may say that Laver was fortunate not to have had to beat Gonzales at his best, others that Laver's game improved greatly as a professional and that perhaps it was Gonzales' good luck not to have met Laver at his best. Whatever the arguments, Rod Laver—as his winning of the first Open Wimbledon confirmed—became one of the top players in tennis history—and he did it with his left hand.

As much as his success his style opened a new world for left-handers, for it is as balanced between forehand and backhand strength as that of any right-handed champion. In due course we shall see how this came about.

Outstanding among his strokes is his great and thrilling service. Seen for the first time during a pre-match hit-up, Laver can appear a rather small figure in a floppy-brimmed sun hat, but once the umpire announces "Laver to serve, play", up goes the ball in a high throw, Laver's knees are well bent as his racket loops wide behind his back in a long-armed swing and then he seems suddenly to grow about a foot or so in stature, bringing the ball down from a surprising height and at unexpected speed. In an instant one realizes that though he may appear small he plays a very big game.

Confident of getting his service into play, he can use different twists, swerves and breaks almost at will. To the first court he might crack a fast breaking-away service wide of his opponent's forehand, or he might twist the ball down the centreline to kick back confoundingly from his opponent's backhand towards his body, or again, he might slice a swinging service down the centreline, stretching his opponent's backhand to the limit. Such variations, together with those he uses when serving to the second court, are all available in reverse to right-handers, but left-handed mixtures of spin—being less common— have given better results, and left-handers have

Laver overhead

therefore developed them better than right-handers have. Watching Laver serve is not to witness the almost routine matter of yet one more service game held; it is to see an exciting display of varied stroke-plan extracted from one tennis shot.

In his smashing Laver likes to get well into the air, and the higher he can get his red head and outstretched racket the safer he looks, and the more powerful. Like Drobny—and many another left-hander, for that matter—he can smash swingingly across court, but his favourite for weight and speed is the one taken somewhere above his head or right eyebrow and lashed away to the off.

It has already been pointed out that in the Big Game ground strokes are sometimes overlooked. This never happens if the player carries the racket in his left hand. Laver's forehand, though noticeably wristy, is akin to his service in that it can be surprisingly long-armed, giving an appearance of great reach. On the backhand, though he sometimes chooses to chip a ball towards his opponent's backhand with raised elbow and dropped racket head in the left-hander's in-grained way, he is in no way limited to this type of backhand. Attacking from the baseline, rallying or attempting a passing shot either down the line or across his opponent's body, he steps across strongly with his left leg, turns well away from the net and hits a free topspin backhand drive at full arm's length as though this were the stroke he prefers to all others.

Laver is, surprisingly, a Continental or English stylist. Left-handers have so natural a tendency towards the American Eastern or extreme Eastern grips that even Drobny—who learnt his tennis on slow European courts—was unusual in being a Continental or English type of left-hander. Laver, by contrast, began his tennis not only in Australia but on a rock-hard court in tropical Rockhampton.

That Laver indeed uses a Continental or English grip is confirmed by the number of times he has been described as a left-handed version of another acknowledged Continental player, Hoad. This in turn raises the question whether Laver's style could be related to Jack Crawford's, since Hoad's style came almost directly from Crawford.

It is tempting to try to match at least Laver's left-handed forehand to Jack Crawford's right-handed one, but it would be stretching things too far. Laver did not learn his game from seeing Hoad play, much less from seeing Crawford; nor, as in Hoad's case, did he see a local champion whose strokes were a replica of Crawford's. It thus seems that his forehand no more stemmed from Crawford's than had Crawford's from Henri Cochet's or Laurie Doherty's. In any event Laver's forehand does not recall Crawford's; though played with a similar grip, it is almost always hit with topspin and thus bears more resemblance to other left-handers' forehands than to the crisp, flat shot often used by right-handers of the Crawford type.

Still, we may well wonder about Laver's English forehand grip. A hardcourt surface and high-bouncing balls are not conducive to such a grip, and Laver's eagle-eyed coach, Charles Hollis, was, it may be recalled, a devout disciple

Laver forehand

167

of Big Bill Tilden and the Eastern grip. Is the only answer that Laver was a freak? A man less likely to be freakish than down-to-earth Laver would be hard to find. There was a simple explanation.

Charles Hollis was well aware of the left-handers' backhand troubles and consequent lack of balanced strength, but he had no intention of converting young Rod to a right-hander with weakened service and forehand. Setting out to make him a balanced champion, he took Laver's backhand side first and determinedly taught him how to produce a model sideways-to-the-net stroke that would not give way under pressure and could, as occasion offered, be used for attack as much as any other. Young Rod's nondescript little backhand—more a cross between a cut and a mis-hit than anything else—was banished from the court on pain of extreme Hollis displeasure. In its place he was given an adequate backhand grip, shown how to put his left leg well across to the ball, and encouraged to hit flat and as hard as he liked, no matter where his shot landed.

Next came control. Hollis, who was over six feet tall, informed his adoring pupil that he was a little runt who would never be tall enough to play his ground strokes flat with safety and so must base these shots on topspin: "Racket back in line with the ball; come forward from slightly below it; roll hard over the top; *make* it spin. . . ."

Laver backhand

Only when Laver's backhand was thoroughly moulded did Hollis turn to the forehand, Laver's more natural shot, and here the same topspin drill was implanted. Later, when Laver had become a well-known player, in some of his matches he was described as having hit his way out of trouble. What he really did was temporarily set aside accuracy and touch, and lam into the ball with Hollis's topspin drills, confident that if he got the ball past the net it would fall somewhere into court.

But to show how Laver developed his strong backhand, where Drobny did not, is not to explain how Laver came to play with an English forehand grip. The only possible explanation is that Laver learnt his backhand first. He would never have dared to stray from the painstaking instruction he had received on this side. When it came to combining his forehand and backhand, in particular with rising-ball play, he must have found the change from his backhand grip to an Eastern forehand grip too large for his liking and therefore preferred to hit his forehand with an English grip. Charles Hollis would have noticed this, and perhaps he may even have ground his teeth over it a little. But he was too wise a coach to interfere with a strong and natural shot, and Laver kept his English-grip forehand. If Hollis had any doubts about the soundness of this, his favourite pupil must have dispelled them long since, for Laver became a wonderfully free hitter on either side.

English-grip players, in exchange for the advantages of greater flexibility and reach and a handier backhand grip, usually forgo a little power on the forehand. Laver more than took care of this by building up his arm muscles. "It's Laver's wrist and forearm that he beats you with; that and his pride."

20 | In Recent Memory

AMID a welter of American and Australian champions, the leading European player to emerge after Drobny's years at the top was Italy's Nicola Pietrangeli. Winner of the French singles in 1959 and 1960, and Italy's top player in a Davis Cup team that reached the 1960 and 1961 challenge rounds,* Pietrangeli played all-court tennis rather than the Big Game. An American stylist, he was nevertheless stronger on the backhand than the forehand. He was of medium height and although solid in build did not possess the natural throwing arm action that produces so many big servers among the base-balling Americans and cricketing Australians. With ground strokes he had pleasing control over a supple wrist, and treated crowds to the delights of passing shots like those of former days.

Europe offered another fine player in Andres Gimeno, probably the best player Spain has produced. In 1960, at the age of twenty-two, Gimeno in one tournament (at Queen's Club, preceding Wimbledon) defeated players of the calibre of Krishnan, Laver, and Emerson, and in the same year he became a professional. Unlike Pietrangeli, Gimeno has as his main weapons a powerful match-winning American forehand, a strong serve and, on fast surfaces, Big Game tactics.

The three most outstanding ladies of recent times have been Maria Bueno of Brazil, Margaret Smith Court of Australia, and Billie Jean Moffitt King of America. The slender and dainty Maria Bueno was queen of Wimbledon and Forest Hills in 1959 and again of Wimbledon in 1960. Severe illness halted her career until 1963, between which year and 1966 she won her third Wimbledon and three more U.S. titles. Her strokes were as attractive as her appearance; very much an all-court player, she advanced to the net behind either flat rising-ball shots or a well-produced service to volley neatly and effectively.

Margaret Smith became the greatest woman player in Australian tennis history, surpassing both Daphne Akhurst of the 1920s and the popular, hard-hitting Nancye Wynne Bolton, who had been Australian champion at the outbreak of the war and four times after it. Beginning in her teens, Margaret won the Australian championship seven times in succession from 1960 to 1966, and again in 1969, her other major successes being three French titles, two Wimbledons, and three U.S. Nationals.

Andres Gimeno

*Australian Davis Cup players of about this time (1959–62) were Fraser, Laver, Emerson, Stolle, Bob Mark, and Ken Fletcher.

170

Since the Australian championships, held in January each year, are off the beaten track for players from other countries, Australians have generally a better chance than others of winning the Grand Slam. Margaret Smith set her sights on this target several times; she was unsuccessful, but twice won three of the four titles.

Tall and rangy, she was somewhat coltish in her early career, making up with power what she lacked in smoothness and control. As she settled down into a tall and beautifully built world-class player of the net-attacking type, her backhand and volleying became nicely grooved and almost always reliable as well as strong. On service and forehand she hits the ball hard and appears a complete player, but, work on them as she would, these two shots (wild in her early years) have never responded sufficiently to be rock-like in crisis.

Service and forehand. These two shots mentioned together in the context of unreliability have a familar ring. And isn't her service action —hard as she may hit the ball—less smooth than her other strokes? Sure enough, Margaret

Nicola Pietrangeli

Maria Bueno

171

Smith, rushed by a flock of schoolgirls at the end of a victorious championship, would sign autograph after autograph with her left hand.

As a girl in Albury, New South Wales, Margaret began to play tennis with her left hand. Girls were no competition, so Margaret—tomboy and accepted member of a gang of boys anyway—took to playing against young males. Fearing to be thought odd by being left-handed as well as female, she played with her right hand, and, defeating the boys, remained a right-hander. No left-handed lady had yet won **Wimbledon**, but perhaps the performances of such great players as Little Mo Connolly and Margaret Smith provided the left-handers with at least a moral victory.

As for Margaret's well-known attacks of nerves, which many a critic has found inexplicable in a girl of such high courage, it seems reasonable to ascribe them to an unsound service and a brittle though powerful forehand—heritages of a left-handed right-hand player.

Billie Jean Moffitt King does not possess the advantages of either the fleet-footed Maria Bueno or the tall and lithe Margaret Smith Court. Short, stocky and bespectacled, she seemed at first to be in a lower class than the other two, and likely to beat them only if either suffered a lapse. But Billie Jean, with her strong, compact ground strokes and her serve-and-volley game, has won the U.S. and Australian championships, and the Wimbledon title three years in succession.

Margaret Smith

Margaret Smith Court

extreme extension of the forefinger along the racket handle. McKinley, short and sturdy, was a bounding player full of vigour; the tall, fair-haired Stolle was rather stiff in movement and often appeared deceptively tired. McKinley, thumping his forehand with great confidence, recorded America's first Wimbledon win since Alex Olmedo's in 1959. Stolle was to become Wimbledon runner-up for the next two years, French champion in 1965, and American in 1966.

Unless some truly great player like Tilden, or some astounding youngster like Hoad or Rosewall brings them out of their seats in excitement, tennis followers tend to sigh over the great

It thus seems, so far as tactics are concerned, that Little Mo Connolly's hard-driving baseline game, which dominated women's tennis on any type of surface in the early 1950s, was merely a temporary return to the past. In recent memory fast-surfaced championship women's tennis, like men's, has been most successfully played from the net position.

Men's tennis in the same period was dominated by Australians, except in 1963, when American Chuck McKinley won the Wimbledon title and teamed with Denis Ralston to take the Davis Cup from Australia. The final match of McKinley's Wimbledon provided a good contrast of styles and stylists. McKinley's style was American; that of his opponent, Fred Stolle of Australia, was English—the most noticeable feature of Stolle's grip, however, being the

Billie Jean Moffitt King

173

Denis Ralston

them yards start in a sprint, and at the age of thirty he seemed as fit as ever.

Big Bill Tilden in the 1920s and Frank Sedgman some thirty years later won title after title, but in this respect Emerson excelled both. Over Tilden he had the advantage of air travel, and he remained an amateur longer than Sedgman did, but his record—noticeably similar to Margaret Court's—of six Australian singles titles and two each in the other three major championships speaks for itself. In Davis Cup challenge rounds between 1961 and 1967 he played twelve singles matches for eleven wins, his only loss (to Manuel Santana of Spain, in 1965) being sustained after the tie had been decided.

Emerson is a Continental or English stylist in a more pronounced fashion than any other champion except Fred Perry. His service grip is extreme, giving the impression that his palm is even more on top of the racket handle than in its backhand-grip position. His service is severe, and because of his physical fitness he has been able to maintain this severity for five sets and for match after match in a tournament. But it

personalities of the past and to take their current champions for granted. This for a long time was the fate of Roy Emerson, but several distinctive aspects of this highly successful champion show him to be anything but run-of-the-mill.

Neale Fraser played in the shadow of a list of famous players; Emerson waited for the same players to pass, then two more—Fraser himself, and Laver. When at last his chance came he not only took it but remained at the top of the tree for years. Born in 1936, he won his first Australian singles title when almost twenty-five and his last to date at thirty. His total of six Australian championship wins is a record.

Harry Hopman made a name for himself in producing the fittest players the tennis world has seen. Sedgman, McGregor, Rose (reluctantly), Hoad, Rosewall, Hartwig, Cooper, Anderson, Fraser, and Laver—they made an athletic line to gladden the heart of any fitness fanatic, but Emerson was the fittest of them all. At any stage of their careers he could have given the rest of

Chuck McKinley

174

lacks the smoothness of the rest of his strokes. This is noticeable only in preparation, however, and not during the delivery action; standing ready to serve, racket strings resting against the balls in his left hand, he indulges in a kind of rapid circular wind-up, suggestive of a falter, before parting his arms to throw up the ball and take his racket back.

As a young player Emerson's backhand was much superior to his forehand. It remained a strong, flexible, and completely natural stroke while he built up a forehand so effective that he became a powerful right-court doubles player. Tall and springy, with a Continental player's natural aptitude for low volleying, he is a wonderful net man.

Triumph and disaster have figured at all stages of tennis's long history, and Emerson has shared both in full measure. Wimbledon champion in 1964 and 1965, in 1966 he was favoured to become the first man since Fred Perry to win the title three years running. In an early round he was playing Owen Davidson (Wimbledon's present official coach) when he badly injured his shoulder in a fall, and from that moment was virtually out of the tournament.

Manuel Santana, the Wimbledon winner that year, took over from Pietrangeli as the finest player in Europe. His tournament successes included the French (twice) and U.S. championships and he was mainly responsible for Spain's reaching the Davis Cup challenge rounds of 1965 and 1967. Typifying the present inter-

Fred Stolle: English grip, with forefinger spread less than usual for Stolle

Manuel Santana

175

national flavour of styles that once were national, Santana, though a Spaniard and a Continental, played in the American style. Sportsmanship is also international, and Santana, after winning the 1966 Wimbledon final, graciously acknowledged that "Emerson remains the real champion".

1966 was also India's year of greatness, the year Ramanathan Krishnan, ably supported by team-mates Mukerjea and Lal, led his country to the Davis Cup challenge round. Krishnan had obtained his highest world ranking (third) seven years before, but despite an appreciable increase in his weight, his smooth and powerful American-style groundstroking made him still a force to be reckoned with.

Australia returned to the Wimbledon forefront in 1967, but not through Roy Emerson or the English style; the winner was twenty-three-year-old John Newcombe, large and powerful both in physique and in application of the Big Game. He has been a model of the American style, getting well behind the ball and hitting it in strong, firm-wristed and straight-ahead fashion. Even on service he uses little wrist-snap by comparison with other big servers, his great speed coming from good timing, weight distribution, and height. Handsome, strong, and composed, Newcombe has always looked dependable and his appearance has been well backed by performance. He won the New South Wales schoolboy championships at every age level, and from sixteen to eighteen won the Australian junior singles title from 1961 to 1963. Emerson barred him from major titles for a time, but by 1967 his Wimbledon and Forest Hills wins came as no surprise.

By the end of 1967 Newcombe's compatriot

Roy Emerson

Tony Roche, a year his junior, had won only the French championship, which seemed to bear out the contention that his game was more suited to hardcourt tennis than to grass. Prevented from gaining a Davis Cup singles position by the superior play of Emerson, Stolle, and Newcombe, Roche had to be content with doubles representation, and his early transfer to the professional ranks with so little behind him was somewhat unusual. His potential for professional success was nevertheless high. Fair-haired and sturdy in build, he is a left-hander with all his breed's propensity for spin and twist. Though all too often he merely chips his backhand return of service, he can, in the Laver manner, produce a rolled backhand passing shot almost equal to his forehand. Grip and style are probably responsible for this balance between forehand and backhand strengths, for Roche does not belong to the Eastern or American class of left-hander with forehand grip behind the handle and an inadequate backhand grip; nor does he use the English or Continental grip of Drobny and Laver. He may be classed as the first Australian-style left-hander.

1967 closed quietly with Australia defeating Spain in the Davis Cup challenge round; 1968 opened in similar fashion with the Australian championship won by Bill Bowrey. A year or two older than Newcombe and Roche, Bowrey had played below them and had yet to achieve Davis Cup selection. An English stylist, his backhand is his outstanding ground stroke, but like practically all champions dating back to Jack Kramer and the year 1947 (with Krishnan the most notable exception), on fast surfaces he is perforce a Big Game player and an excellent volleyer.

Thus far, champions of recent memory will appear to have been dealt with rather summarily. The girls' styles have not received the attention given to those from Suzanne Lenglen to Maureen Connolly, Emerson has not been portrayed in the detail devoted to Jean Borotra, and there is no description of a great Newcombe match. This has been intentional—to accord with the sense of declining interest which in Australia at least accompanied the tennis of the period. A number of explanations, varying from the philosophical to the technical, have been offered for this decline. Sociologists have informed us that affluence has diverted our former direct concern with ball games to a wider interest in surfboards, skis, and racing cars. Australia's overlong success in the Davis Cup has made us blasé and seriously lowered attendances at all our championships, State and even national. Administrators of amateur tennis assured us for a time that professional tennis had ruined the game; and public opinion to some extent supported this view, since tennis seemed the only sport in which it was not possible to see the best players compete for the major titles. Tennis lovers—especially those of an age to have seen all-court tennis played as an efficient and match-winning game

Ramanathan Krishnan

177

rather than as a generous but tame exhibition of a player's range of strokes—have blamed the

monotony of Big Game tennis.

Then—suddenly, it seemed—in 1968 England,

John Newcombe

who has contributed so much to lawn tennis that it seems no more than plain justice to name a style in her honour, prized loose a card tightly buttoned under administration's sleeve. Open tennis was introduced, and (whatever attendant disadvantages it may possibly bring) at least the top tournaments again became open to the top players. The 1968 French championship—unexpectedly won by Rosewall rather than Laver—created great interest, but it was to the following Wimbledon, with its head-on meeting of the world's leading professionals and amateurs, that all eyes were turned.

For some of the former great players since turned professional this first open Wimbledon came too late. In early rounds professionals and amateurs alike crashed to defeat and an uneasy impression grew that perhaps after all open

Tony Roche

Bill Bowrey

ably free and casual American stylist brings to life the well-known American phrase "loose as ashes". A most versatile player who seems able to call instinctively on almost any shot demanded by the occasion, Ashe serves many aces from a deceptively easy action, and already there have been claims that he serves faster than Pancho Gonzales. Is the game progressing at this rate, or is memory short?

The world ranking list for 1968 was open, comparing for the first time the merits of both

tournaments would not necessarily bring significantly better tennis and greater spectator interest. By the end of the tournament this doubt was settled, for with the exception of the mixed doubles the professionals captured all titles and provided most of the runners-up as well. A fresh breeze was blowing, scarcely tempered by the fact that all winners were confined to the two dominant tennis nations, Australia and America.

Somewhere or other we must make an end to descriptions of our stylists. It is appropriate to do so with the first open Wimbledon champion. Rod Laver, who defeated Tony Roche in a stirring left-handed final, has already been well met and thus would seem to make any further description of players unnecessary. But time does not stand still, and only a few months later Arthur Ashe achieved a noteworthy double by winning the 1968 U.S. National singles and the newly staged U.S. Open singles. The play, and by quaint coincidence the name, of this remark-

Arthur Ashe

180

An Ashe smash

Cliff Drysdale

promising, contained no players ranked in the world's first ten. Interest was not high and, disappointingly, Ashe scarcely lived up to his reputation. It was noticeable, however, how different the styles of the two nations had become. All four U.S. players—Ashe and Graebner in singles, Lutz and Smith as a doubles pair—played in some form of American style, contrasting strongly with the English style of Australians Bowrey and seventeen-year-old John Alexander. The remaining Australian, Ray Ruffels, was naturally seen at first as a left-hander with a typical swinging service and crosscourt topspin forehand drive, but his strong backhand soon showed him to be in the balanced, palm-towards-

professionals and amateurs. Tom Okker, European and amateur, gained third placing—below professional Laver and amateur Ashe and ahead of such professional champions as Rosewall, Newcombe, and Roche. The same list recorded the return of an "orthodox" double-hander (right-handed with a two-handed backhand, and the first since Vivian McGrath) in the person of Cliff Drysdale of South Africa.

The 1968 season wound up with a "closed" Davis Cup challenge round in which the U.S.A. defeated an Australian team which, while

Tom Okker

182

Clark Graebner

John Alexander

(1) The public wanted open tennis. The total attendance for the New South Wales championships was twenty-five times greater than that of the previous year.

(2) The professionals were good. They dominated the various tournaments, sometimes from as early in the draw as the quarter-finals.

(3) Australia could not afford professionals and registered amateurs *en masse*. The Australian

Ray Ruffels

the-top company of Laver and Roche.*

1969 brought open tennis to Australia, focusing world attention on a leading tennis country that had long opposed open tournaments. Its belated arrival stirred the Australian public after long years of apathy. The professionals were well represented, and three things were soon amply demonstrated:

*A second outstanding junior, Phil Dent, was included in the Australian team. An American stylist, he did not play in the tie and thus obliged by not interfering with the contrast in styles just described.

championship meeting, held in Brisbane, lost a record $13,500 or more, and even the heavily attended New South Wales championship only managed to secure a profit by generous commercial sponsorship. A short summary of Australia's first open season might be: public—aroused; administrators—duty done; treasurers—heartache.

On the courts the hero was Tony Roche. He defeated Laver for the New South Wales title, and in the Australian semi-final forced him to the longest men's singles match in the history of the championship—an encounter of ninety games over four hours of exciting play, a struggle worthy of comparison with the Drobny-Patty encounter at Wimbledon in 1953. Laver's normally telling attack to his opponent's backhand side was reduced—by another left-hander.

Each succeeding championship alters the game's statistics, and even as our story goes to press Wimbledon has produced its first left-handed lady winner—Britain's Ann Haydon Jones. Similarly, each tournament changes the champions' records, altering our conceptions of their relative merits. Existing champions' performances will vary, and new champions will continue to march by. But we must call a halt. It is now time to survey the field that has paraded before us, and to make some awards for meritorious conduct.

21 | Blue Ribbons

THE first award should be for the best of the various styles of play.

Once this would merely have meant deciding between the Eastern style and two unconventional styles—the Western of Little Bill Johnston and the Continental of Fred Perry. There could have been only one horse in such a race—the Eastern. But as we have seen in the chapter "Eastern Octopus", styles need to be classified more realistically than this if players are to be described by their styles of play. The contest must be among what we have finally called the Western, American, Australian, and English styles.

The Western's entry is purely a matter of form. Only a handful of great players used it, the best known being Maurice McLoughlin, Little Bill Johnston, and George Lott, a master of doubles play. Norman Brookes and Gerald Patterson played some of their backhand shots in the Western manner, and J. O. Anderson almost all of them, but none of these players could be classed as Western. This style, like chopping, slicing, or cutting on the forehand side, was developed to meet exceptional rather than normal conditions, and since the development of better-quality tennis balls it has long been out of favour.

By contrast, the American or Eastern style, from its earliest days of probably somewhere in the 1890s to the present time, has provided many champions. But this style, once distinctively Eastern at all points, has by evolution moved closer to the English style. An Eastern player's service, and often his volley as well, is almost always made with an English grip, so that while serving and volleying in doubles or playing Big Game tactics in singles he may be practically indistinguishable from an English-style player.

It may be remembered that the Eastern backhand, since about the 1930s, has been accepted as involving a change of only forty-five degrees from the forehand position, with the thumb extended diagonally across the back of the handle, in place of the earlier ninety-degree change with the thumb straight along the back of the handle. This makes the modern Eastern backhand grip no different from the English grip, though an Eastern stylist may play the stroke differently by not holding his wrist so low and by using distinct topspin. The most positive identification of the Eastern style is its forehand, where a grip with palm and wrist behind the racket handle tends to produce a strong shot, naturally flat, rolled or topspun rather than sliced. A soundly based and powerful forehand must always be an effective weapon, and in order to produce it the Eastern stylist is prepared to adopt a special grip for the forehand, even though this includes the disadvantage of a larger change for the backhand than is demanded by any other style.

But just as the very strong Eastern backhand of earlier days was forced to give way to a more flexible shot, so too have inroads been made on the powerful Eastern forehand. The backhand grip cannot be moved any closer to the forehand without becoming inadequate and making the shot unacceptably weak; thus we find that for both greater flexibility and a smaller change to the backhand, the forehand grip moves closer to the backhand. This gives what we have chosen to call the Australian grip, since it has been used most noticeably by Australian players.

The styles of Australian and American players of recent years, even though both may have been generally referred to as Eastern, have been recognizably different from each other. The recent overwhelming superiority of Australian players in world tennis would indicate that the Eastern style, in championship tennis at least, has given way to the Australian. Thus we are in effect saying something that would have sounded unbelievable a few years ago: that the inviolable Eastern—given to the world almost by the Pilgrim Fathers, modified and handed down to us by the mighty Tilden, and revered by us thenceforth—has been superseded and is no longer the best style in tennis. Some will flatly refuse to believe this; others will feel that perhaps it has been done by a swift change of name somewhere or other.

What we are saying is that the Eastern style has been superseded. We have not shirked the issue or sweetened the pill; we have used the name "Eastern" to avoid any misunderstanding.

The English style, involving little or no change of grip for any stroke, has given the world some beautifully fluent and low-wristed stylists. But unless its user has either an exceptionally strong wrist or has developed exceptionally good timing, the English forehand is weaker than others in forward power for the basic waist-high forehand drive, and often weaker than its user's own backhand; also, it often induces the use of a stiff wrist and unwanted underspin. The English style has thus shown itself to be a style of extremes, associated on the one hand with rapier brilliance and on the other with patient retrieving and rallying on slow European courts. Its recent comparative return to favour may be attributed to the same factors that have influenced the change from the Eastern to the Australian style—namely, that the crowding serve-and-volley tactics of the Big Game have forced the man at the receiving end to adopt a quicker and more flexible style. One's first thought was that the Big Game would produce big tennis in all departments, including big Eastern forehand driving, but it has not given players enough time for this; instead it has demanded a more flexible game.

But whatever the future may hold, results to date do not dispose us to offer the Blue Ribbon for Style to the English game, even though for a time during the past few years it claimed the world's leading amateur and professional—Emerson and Laver.

It seems in poor taste for an Australian to award the first prize to the Australian style. It's only a name, however, and as indicated earlier, it could scarcely be called by such outlandish names as "modified Eastern American", "modified Continental", "Eastern-left-of-Centre", or worst, "near-English". Perhaps it would be better to say that in a contest between palm-behind-handle and palm-on-top, both have been defeated by a grip having the palm *towards* the top.

Our next task, equally controversial, is the award for the greatest stylist.

The Dohertys were elegant, R.F. having a graceful backhand drive and H.L. an outstanding forehand. Tilden's form was so correct that even in the tightest match most of his strokes could have been taken as models for coaching demonstrations. Cochet brought economy of effort to a pitch that critics agree has never been equalled. Austin's ground strokes were near-perfection.

Von Cramm: American style

186

Sedgman: Australian

Crawford's grace won world renown and made him the favourite of countless followers. Von Cramm's long and flowing strokes with their characteristic lifting of the racket head at the end, combined with their power and constant use for attack, were acclaimed by Tilden as the most beautiful he had seen. Budge's magnificent back-hand lives to this day. Kramer and Gonzales backed smooth and venomous serving with piston-like volleys. The powerful forearms and supple wrists of Hoad and Laver brought a new joy to lovers of forehand driving. Rosewall's backhand was calm and clean cut. . . .

To avoid making our judgement among these and other masters entirely one of personal preference, let's try a first selection by styles.

Little Bill Johnston, with his wonderful timing and smoothness of movement that gave him terrific power in spite of his lightness of build, must surely be the Western style's nominee. One can scarcely choose other than Gottfried von Cramm for the American style or Frank Sedgman for the Australian. In the English style Jack Crawford encounters a strong challenge from the more modern play of Hoad, but one cannot discard the original master for his nearest descendant.

The left-handers should be considered as having a style of their own, since they always manage to look more left-handed than Western, American, Australian, or English. Here Laver is the choice.

From this exalted company Johnston must at once depart, for the Western style, no matter how well executed, is ungainly to the modern eye. Similarly Laver must go, for left-handers never seem to have achieved the crispness of the best right-handed stylists. Sedgman, too, must go, for with all his power and freedom, he cannot match the fluidity of the remaining two.

Between von Cramm and Crawford it becomes, after all, a matter of personal choice. Allowing the judge, namely the author, a personal preference, the stylist's blue ribbon goes to Jack Crawford.

Style alone was probably a bigger part of Crawford's total game than of any other player's. The Dohertys had their charming and dashing presence. Tilden was a master tactician and strategist. Cochet had his nonchalance, Kramer his Big Game, Sedgman his superb fitness, von Cramm his flair for attack, Hoad his power. But Crawford was the supreme racket-handler, making beautiful strokes from almost every ball he received. Even when he was well past his prime people flocked to see him in action. Swung from steady shoulders with the straightest of arms,

Cochet: Nonchalance

187

yet never stiffly, his racket head would flash in the sunlight, whipped round by superb wrist control; the ball would shoot low across the net, looking like a broad white tape stretched over the green turf, and you saw another forehand or backhand that some onlookers thought casual, some crisp, some most stylishly produced, and some the most natural thing in the world. Crawford's game was almost an anthology of such shots, and it seemed a matter of complete indifference to him where his opponent's shot landed. More than any other player's, his games were watched for their style alone.

Our award to Crawford may not be the correct one, but few indeed will begrudge it.

Styles and stylists having been covered, we are not obliged to become involved in further controversy. It would be unpardonable, however, not to try to select the greatest player of all time—especially after making so many provocative references to this title.

One way or another, a number of players have been mentioned or indicated as having a claim to this highest of all honours—H. L. Doherty, Brookes, Tilden, Cochet, Vines, Budge, Kramer, Gonzales, Hoad, Laver. These ten great players of different eras are not necessarily the ten best players of all time, but they provide an interesting group from which to begin our elimination.

It seems to be the fate of any player of Tilden's

Laver: From the left

188

Crawford: Blue ribbon English

player's welfare that concerns us; we never seem to think that the later player needs help.

Budge equalled Tilden's capacity for playing on any type of surface, and his all-court game probably had the beating of Tilden's all-stroke technique. Without further discussion, therefore, we can in conscience name Donald Budge as the greatest player of the whole pre-World War II era.

One confesses, however, to a sense of relief at having ended the tricky business of disposing of the great Tilden, and at knowing that he is not alive to read about it. His devotees will nonetheless declare that they cannot imagine Tilden not beating Budge, and anyone else who crossed his path. Remembering how Tilden refused to accept defeat, we may well hesitate to say they're wrong.

Among the Big Game players of post-war tennis, Hoad had possibly more potential than

long era or earlier to be eliminated by him. Thus Doherty and Brookes of the early days disappear from the contest, and Cochet too, despite his many magical displays for the greater glory of France. It seems that even Vines must share this fate. Tilden regarded him as the greatest player ever, and it does seem that on a fast court and on his day he could produce better tennis than anyone. If we were awarding a title of King for a Day he would have few serious rivals. But Tilden's long reign, his ability late in his career to hold Vines over three sets, and his mastery in all conditions seem to place him above Vines.

Budge's time put him beyond the reach of Tilden's levelling scythe, thus making a choice between these two more difficult.

In comparing older players with those of later times, most critics try to be fair to a grand old man, providing him, for example, with modern equipment and conditions. But it must be allowed that there is such a thing as improvement due to progress. With his many books Tilden ensured that his vast knowledge and the results of his experiments were known to the tennis world by Budge's time. In other words, Budge had the opportunity of beginning where Tilden left off. It should also be noted that it is always the older

Tilden: Man for all seasons

189

Budge: Where Tilden left off

are that these two players exerted even greater service pressure, and Kramer, as well, greater pressure on return of service; relying less on topspin, they were more accurate; and would not Laver, fast and long-armed though he is, have been at some disadvantage against such tall players?

Reluctantly, Laver, Australian and present world idol, is eliminated. But a heavy storm is brewing. Frenchman are not the only patriots, and the author is uneasily aware that he has suddenly lost many friends.

If our criterion is class of opposition rather than number of titles won, Jack Kramer has

Gonzales: Fighting qualities

any. Behind his terrific power and ease of stroke production lay a range of shots second only, as Sir Norman Brookes has said, to Tilden's. As an amateur he was to some extent held back by making too many errors; when he turned professional it was expected that constant hard play would make him the greatest player ever, but his back injury intervened before this could be proved.

Any Australian attempting to challenge Rod Laver's claims is likely to be accused of treason, especially after his 1969 U.S. Open win—a stop-press item for this book. Completing a second, and Open, Grand Slam, he has recorded one of the greatest feats in the history of sport, and modern tennis followers will support him as strongly as an older generation may champion Tilden. And with good reason, since Laver's tournament record is the greatest of any.

However, that's not to say he is the best player ever, if we are matching man to man. There are a number of well-based critics—champions who know tennis inside out—who are convinced that despite Laver's complete game and wonderful record he could not have defeated either Kramer or Gonzales at their top. The main reasons given

190

probably the greatest record of all. He outclassed a strong amateur field and then, as a professional, defeated Riggs, Budge (though no longer at his best), Gonzales, and Sedgman. With constant play Gonzales' game improved later, but that does not necessarily mean it eventually became better than Kramer's.

Pancho Gonzales is the choice of many observers. He lacked amateur success outside America, but this can reasonably be ascribed to his having turned professional very early in his career. His professional successes over Sedgman, Trabert, Rosewall, Hoad—to say nothing of Segura, McGregor, Cooper, and Anderson—together with his terrific service and dynamic all-

Hoad: Power and ease

King Kramer

round play, stamped him for a number of years as unquestionably the greatest player in the world.

Our next task, then, is to decide between Kramer and Gonzales. Kramer is regarded as having been the better volleyer, but it could be argued that Gonzales, having the faster service, did not need to volley as well as Kramer; in other words, that on total results of serve-and-volley the two were equal. Even so, many players who opposed them both have said that although Gonzales had the faster cannonball, Kramer's serve could place them under more pressure. There was, for example, Kramer's fast sliced service to the first court; when he swung this away viciously and followed in after it to blanket the net it seemed almost as though the only place to hit a passing shot was somewhere between the umpire's stand and the net post. Disregarding this, and allowing the combined serve-and-volley of the two men to have been equal, Kramer could be judged the better player because of his superior ground strokes.

Supporters of Gonzales will be disgusted with such a colourless and mathematical assessment. Their man had tremendous fighting qualities, stamina (as shown by his long reign at the top), and a relentless "killer instinct". They will claim passionately that Gonzales would have beaten Kramer. In turn, Kramer's supporters would disallow this claim as being unsubstantiated.

But a decision has to be made, and it is taken in favour of Kramer, leaving our final choice between him and Budge.

In this final confrontation it would be useless to seek the views of either participant. Kramer has placed Budge at the top of his own list, and said after playing him that certain Budge shots were beyond his own powers. Similarly, Budge recounts Kramer's attributes and refuses to be drawn into discussing his own.

Australian Davis Cup players Crawford, Quist, and Sproule choose Budge—though Quist adds that any choice between Budge and Kramer is no more than a matter of personal opinion. All these players, however, were members of Budge's era rather than Kramer's.

A player indisputably of Kramer's time was Ted Schroeder, from whom we receive a no-nonsense "Jake would have killed every one of them" decision. But there can be no question of a knock-out. In a split points decision the author's

verdict goes to Kramer, the forehand player.

Now that the decision has been made—or has evolved, rightly or wrongly—everyone probably wants to speak at once. Tilden disciples remain convinced that he would have found a way of beating not only Budge but all the Big Game players as well, King Kramer included; they also argue that against these players Tilden would have played the Big Game himself—and he certainly had the service, size, power, or whatever else it takes, to do so. Others heatedly say that there have been a dozen Big Game players who would have beaten Tilden or any other pre-war player, Vines and Budge thrown in. They disagree that Kramer, the first of the modern Big Game players, was likely to have been the best of them. Many consider any choice other than Gonzales ridiculous or even insulting. Others demand to know what more Laver has to do to be properly recognized, and some simply stick to Hoad.

The author, attempting a diplomatic half-change of subject, recalls that such is Wimbledon's stature that one sometimes hears discussion over "the greatest player never to have won Wimbledon". Contenders for this title would include McLoughlin, McGrath, von Cramm, Bromwich, Gonzales, Rosewall. About to suggest Gonzales for this award, the author is sharply reminded that we have been speaking of blue ribbons and told that he can keep his red ones.

Does the final battle between Kramer and Budge, to say nothing of Tilden and Vines—all Eastern American stylists—mean that we should revise our previous award to the Australian style and give it instead to the Eastern American? Perhaps, but only if the choice of the greatest players was more firmly settled. Many tennis followers hold that the above four immortals should be replaced by Gonzales, Hoad, Laver, and Sedgman—Australian and English stylists.

If the truth be known, most people who support, say, Gonzales as the greatest player, would in contradiction also be supporters of the Eastern American grip. We can't have it both ways. Or can we? In a renewed debate the author's best hope is that not too many life-long friendships will be broken beyond mending.

The opinion was offered earlier that it would be unforgivable not to attempt to name the greatest player of all time. One now wonders whether the awarding of this bluest ribbon of all has been worth it.

The unkindest cut is yet to come. With the tumult and the shouting dying, and the captains and kings all ready to depart, a quiet English voice inquires with deadly politeness: "Excuse me, but do you by any chance remember a gentleman named Frederick Perry?"

Fred Perry

22 | Tomorrow

*The greatest disloyalty one can offer
to great pioneers is to refuse to move
an inch from where they stood*

MANY tennis followers of today may see tomorrow only in terms of the pros and cons of open tennis—that is, merely as a question of politics to be fought out for the most part between professional promoters in control of the top players and amateur L.T.A.s in control of the grounds, the major championships, and the Davis Cup, with skirmishes on the outside by freelance professionals and registered amateurs; and, whichever way it goes, the public paying. Paying willingly, many may think, for won't the best tournaments be open to the best players? And who could ask for more?

Let's leave all that to conference tables and committee rooms, where it belongs. We have been talking of styles and stylists. Let's look at the game.

Henri Cochet was once asked what he saw for tomorrow. "Closer to the ball," he replied, "always closer to the ball." He meant that the ball would be taken earlier, and that championship tennis would become a more and more polished rising-ball game. He can hardly be called right. There may have been more early-ball play since his time, but no one has taken the ball earlier than Cochet himself.

Tilden saw the tennis of his tomorrow as the early-ball game of Cochet with more variations of stroke and spin. He too was astray. No one since Tilden has seen fit to employ Tilden's range of strokes—though Hoad, as we have seen, could probably have done so.

Both Cochet and Tilden prophesied more artistry. From the spectator viewpoint, in the grasscourt world of England, America, and Australia, and on fast indoor surfaces in any country, the game the champions adopted has been, as everyone knows, the Big Game. Instead of artistry we have seen power serving, agile blockading of the net, and points so short that almost any form of rally evokes marked applause.

We have now had the Big Game for over twenty years. Will it continue into our tomorrow?

If not, what can we expect?

However uninspiring the Big Game may have become after the excitement of its early years, no one can gainsay its efficiency on fast surfaces, where the world's top tennis has been played. For the immediate tomorrow, therefore, we can expect the Big Game to become bigger. Champions will probably be tall, and there are likely to be fewer Rosewalls to stem their advance. Propelled from polished metal rackets, or plastic models of equally low air resistance and high whip, services will become faster; the service of tomorrow's greatest player of all time must be expected to outdo Gonzales' or anyone else's; and, whether it does or not, future critics will refuse to believe that any player of the 1960s or earlier could have hit really hard using an old wooden racket.

If a cannonball can be served on the second ball as well as the first—as it was by America's John Doeg in the 1930s, usually whenever he was a point ahead—the service can be expected to become so dominant that tomorrow's game, counting one shot for each player, could come to be described as the serve-and-lunge game. Since lunging is likely to be a losing proposition, a possible death-or-glory alternative might be to take all serves within reach on the half-volley.

In this vein, the English grip will become the only one used, as it gives the greatest reach for a retrieval or lunge and requires no change of grip for a half-volley on either side. One would hesitate, however, to call its accompanying style English, for unless this picture has been greatly overdrawn, style will be scarcely discernible.

Tennis will continue to be open, so we shall have the best players competing in the best tournaments. This will give the game a tremendous fillip for the time being, but once it is accepted as the normal pattern the game itself will come under closer scrutiny, and the game must inspire or die away.

Long after *le grand Henri* and the mighty Big

Bill gazed speculatively into the future, a shrewd young promoter named Jack Kramer took a calculating look at his immediate tomorrow—and what he saw was not artistry so much as falling gate receipts. Denied the stimulus that open tournaments would have provided, he sought to maintain spectator interest by various ways of eliminating the Big Game—the game on which he himself had ridden to greatness and the game that was not attracting the paying public.

Kramer realized in the 1950s that before tennis can be of enthralling interest it must provide an equal chance for net and baseline, for volley and ground stroke—just as the All England Club did in 1878, after the first Wimbledon had been won by Spencer Gore's unseemly behaviour of planting himself behind a net too high to allow a passing shot an even-money chance. With the game in its infancy, the Club was able to redress the balance by lowering the official height of the net for the comparatively few courts then in existence. But only makeshift measures were open to Kramer's professionals. In one experiment a single service instead of two was allowed; in another the service had to be delivered from an extra line marked about a yard behind the baseline. Since such rules would never suit players below championship class (not that they suited the champions, either), they had no chance of becoming law. Another experiment—disallowing the server to volley until he had made at least one ground stroke—seemed to have possibilities, but in practice it put the game off key and aroused no enthusiasm.

Kramer's experiments are mentioned in case anyone who has seen no other form of championship tennis should imagine that the Big Game is acceptable as the basis of men's tennis and that ground strokes have rightly been relegated to women's matches. The sterile Big Game is not acceptable. No responsible person wants exciting serving or daring volleying to be taken out of tennis, but we cannot have these without the possibility of the groundstroke counter that makes them exciting or daring. We cannot have one-way traffic and still expect the champions to inspire and the game to survive.

A better way of cutting the service down to size might be to reduce the compression of the ball. This would perhaps be acceptable if it could be guaranteed that all over the world the balls would be at the compression most suited to the conditions in which they were used—meaning, in effect, low-compression balls for fast court surfaces and high-compression balls for slow ones. But no such guarantee can be given. Tennis balls can only be at any required compression in countries and circumstances where they can be delivered direct from factory to courtside; since they are filled with air and have a porous rubber core, they inevitably lose compression with age.

If instead of being too hard the balls used in a tournament are altogether too soft, play can be ruined; this happened in the French championships as recently as 1957, when some otherwise astonishing victories and defeats were recorded. It probably also explains an epic match at Bordighera, in Italy, in 1930 between Mrs Satterthwaite of England and Signora Valerio of Italy, for one point of which the ball crossed the net 450 times in a rally that lasted nineteen minutes. (There must have been other endurance rallies before this one, or nobody would have bothered to make a special count.) The court was probably en-tout-cas, heavily watered, and the balls very soft. One also suspects that each participant was determined not to be beaten by a lady from the other side of the Channel.

The moral here is that as well as net/baseline balance we must also have a balance between rallies that are too short for interest and those that are boringly long. Though a player needs to be able to keep the ball in play to be worth watching, the game cannot be reduced to consistency alone; there must be incentive for initiative and dash and the sparkle of clean winners.

It may be wondered why Kramer did not arrange for his professionals to play with balls of lower compression. The probable answer is that it would have been one thing for a promoter to restrict the famous serves of his power players in obvious ways and another altogether to have them appear disappointingly less devastating than spectators expect. Certainly one cannot imagine Pancho Gonzales suffering such a fate in silence.

Fortunately for the tennis-players and followers of this world, another race of people, inventors, inhabits the earth. Already in use in Sweden, and certain to become exclusively used everywhere in our tomorrow, is a pressureless tennis ball. Its weight, bounce, and resilience against racket strings are contained in its core and covering, and having no internal air pressure to lose, it will in time be developed so as to have a long store life. It will then become possible to manufacture a ball a little less hard than today's, without the risk of its deteriorating and becoming far too soft.

Tomorrow's International L.T.A. will thus be able to decree that the balls used in Australian, Wimbledon, and American championships shall be less hard than those used in the corresponding hardcourt championships on the Continent. This difference will be only a small one, or players moving from one tournament to another will never be able to get the feel of the ball against their rackets satisfactorily. It is therefore unlikely that tomorrow's grasscourt tournaments will be rid of Big Game tactics simply by the introduction of a slightly softer ball.

This brings us to the vexed question of court dimensions and surfaces. Court dimensions were laid down in 1882, when surfaces were relatively soft, and there is no doubt that given the much faster surfaces of today—and the harder balls, and often the extra height and reach of many of the players—the dimensions of the court are now too small.* Everyday players who have often suspected that the court was too small for them (the worse the player, the deeper the suspicion) may be gratified to learn that a group of champions in America have proved it to their own exalted satisfaction. A court six inches wider at each sideline was found to redress the volleyer/ baseliner balance for passing shots, while an extra foot at the baseline not only allowed drives a little more length but greatly improved the chance of putting successful lobs over a volleyer's head; at present a lob played from anywhere near midcourt against a well-positioned volleyer and hit out of his reach usually has nowhere else to go but out. On fast-surfaced courts the dimensions are now inadequate for the best tennis.

Is anyone greatly surprised at this? Apart from a relaxation of the foot-fault rule, the basic laws of tennis are now about ninety years old. Although this speaks well for the early committeemen who drew them up, it is a sorry reflection on the apathy of their descendants—which, of

*Long since, many people have thought the doubles game to be overcrowded and its tactics resultantly monotonous. However, we shall keep discussion to singles, for simplicity.

course, means all of us. Would anyone today dare to draw up rules for a new game and expect them to satisfy players in about the year 2060? Once set in motion, our tomorrow will probably see the laws of tennis re-examined every five years or so. This will not be done with a view to turning the game upside-down twice a decade; it will be concerned with adjustments, such as the degree of ball hardness.

It is not being suggested that the immediate remedy for inadequate court dimensions would be to pass a world law increasing them, or else lowering the height of the net. To do either of these things on other than a fast-surfaced court could well produce a new wave of Mrs Satterthwaites and Signora Valerios who, on the dampened *en-tout-cas* of the Continent, would make their ancestors' record of 450 strokes and nineteen minutes to one point look like a speed record.

The existence of varying court surfaces makes it most difficult to apply any general legislation for improvement. The remedy for early tomorrow thus lies in the use of pressureless balls backed, for later tomorrow, by uniform court surfaces. These new courts will be made of synthetic grass, the surface speed of which can be regulated by varying the length of the nap to allow for climatic conditions in different countries or regions.

All this comes down to saying that tomorrow's significant change will stem not from either style or stylist but from equipment, principally balls and court surfaces. This statement has a familiar ring about it. Didn't someone once place the Doherty brothers at the peak of tennis art and say that up to their retirement players improved more than equipment and that after their departure the reverse applied? History has a way of pointing to the future, and just as we consider the players after the Doherty era to have improved along with their equipment, so too may we expect tomorrow's players to surpass all who have gone before them. But it will be controlled balls, reliable surfaces, and rules altered as necessary that will ensure this.

There are some who won't listen to such talk. They don't see that modern players, in physical size and greater athletic ability, have outgrown the static dimensions of faster courts. They don't want to mess about with the rules of a grand old game. They see the Big Game as a real advance, in keeping with modern and future times. If those who think like this are at present in the great majority, there could be death in the game's tomorrow.

The true concept of tennis includes exciting groundstroke play. This concept has been lost in Australia and elsewhere, and falling attendances have shown it to be a change for the worse. Open tournaments will give respite from its effects, but it would be highly dangerous to allow another period of decline to occur if tennis courts are to remain in land-hungry cities.

It has long been evident that champions need the backing of rank-and-file players and of the public; it is equally true that rank-and-file players and the public need the champions for inspiration. Champions must be permitted to inspire, to provide the sort of tennis that is not only attended but remembered, relived, even passed down in golden reminiscence from one generation to another.

What of tomorrow's styles and stylists? If the balance the game needs is to be returned by means of controlled pressureless balls and eventually by synthetic grass surfaces, it becomes possible to make a number of specific predictions about style. To obtain speed, harder hitting will develop, and this, to be done effectively, will induce smoothness, free stroking, and eventually —though at first glance it seems contradictory— economy of effort. With pressureless balls allowing greater control, rallies will be longer and strokes flatter; and the truer bounce of the court will make finer placements worth attempting. This in turn suggests that the Western style will remain out of favour, that there will be time for pounding drives to be made in the Eastern style with its change of grip between forehand and backhand, and that players seeking more flexibility will continue to use either the Australian or the English grip—as one hopes they will be called tomorrow.

As for stylists, we shall hear far more of players from Europe, where the game's popularity is steadily growing. Italy and Spain have already advanced; Germany and France can be expected to follow suit. Tennis is highly organized in Russia, and the improvement her players have already shown at Wimbledon and elsewhere will continue. Tennis is played in most parts of Asia. The feats of Krishnan and company have developed great enthusiasm in India. Japan, with

thousands upon thousands of players, must soon return to the world position it once held; the line that ran from the old Western (or Japanese) players Shimizu, Kumagae, and Harada to the more polished play of Satoh, Nunoi, and Yamagishi cannot remain interrupted for ever. South America will make its presence felt. Ecuador gave us "Little Pancho" Segura, and Peru "Chief" Alex Olmedo; where they came from there must be more. Brazil and Argentina are sleeping giants. Africa? Apart from the South Africa of Eric Sturgess and Cliff Drysdale, her time is more likely to be the day after tomorrow.

Before all these countries can hope to come to the fore the holders of the Davis Cup must play through the competition each year instead of standing out and playing only the challenge round. This in turn is likely to accelerate standardization, as far as possible, of playing conditions; meanwhile Australia and America, the leading grasscourt nations so far as players are concerned, will realize, as their earlier Davis Cup players did, that they may not after all be the world's chosen races of tennis-players.

What, then, of grasscourts? They cradled the game, and developed, from the solid weight of the ball and its comparatively low bounce, not only an attractive style but practically all that is best in the game. They *are* lawn tennis, and all other surfaces are substitutes. But after the first few years of the game's near-century history they have been giving way to other surfaces, and one can only see this trend continuing. It need not be hastened; championship grasscourts have—mistakenly, one feels—been shorn too closely and made too fast; they can be allowed to have a little more growth and thus play their part in discouraging Big Game play.

Finally, what of dear old Wimbledon? The Wimbledon tournament is the championship of the world. Let other countries lay down what surfaces they will, and let Davis Cup matches be played only on standard surfaces, players and crowds alike will continue to flock to Wimbledon and its turf. Long may it be so. Eventually this sacred turf may disappear, but it will never give way to red dust or soulless concrete. Synthetic grass, thank Heaven, is green.

Time has shown the forecasts of our betters, Cochet and Tilden, to have been inaccurate. Our picture may come nearer the mark, if only because it has been painted on a wider canvas. If so, then what a background for a rising star! The champions have always been willing to play their part, and those of tomorrow can be confident that they will capture our imagination and our loyalties. If yesterday and today influence tomorrow, if history points the way to the future, lawn tennis will always provide a proud place for its styles and stylists.

Grips and Styles

STYLE is basically concerned with stroke-making rather than tactics, and hence is directly connected with the type of grip used.

The various lawn tennis styles had their origins in the conditions existing in different countries where the game was first played, but by now they are all completely international; an Australian champion, for instance, can be described as a Continental player.

Grips and styles are illustrated and broadly outlined in the pages immediately following. Since many other shots are now played in a similar manner in various styles, it is the manner in which the forehand is played that technically denotes a player's style. Although differences in the forehand grips illustrated may at times appear small, the resulting styles of play are clearly distinguishable, and each has its own characteristic strengths and limitations.

The names Continental, Eastern, and Western are really groupings. Individual grips have been known, over the years and in different localities, by a variety of names. Some of these are descriptive and a few even picturesque.

To cover all types of play, five classifications of grips and styles have been given instead of the basic three, together with a suggested name, or change of name, for each.

Note: In the following photographs the grips are seen from directly above the top surface of the racket handle, the racket being held in front of the player with its longer strings parallel to the ground.

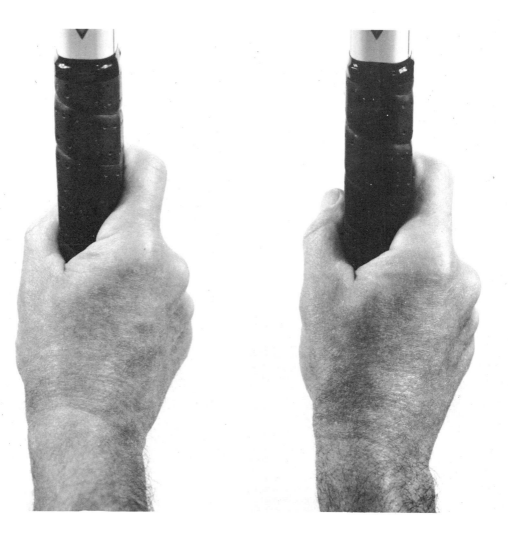

Palm and wrist above top surface of racket handle.
Large knuckle of index finger on right-hand bevel of handle.
Thumb and forefinger "V" somewhere on left bevel.
Other names used for forehand grips within the Continental group:

Racquets	Hammer
English	Hatchet
Doherty	Perry
All-stroke	Full Continental
No-change	Table Tennis
Crawford	Squash

Suggested name: English.

CONTINENTAL STYLE

The term Continental is of fairly recent origin, and for various reasons is now unpopular. Formerly references were made to the "English grip and style". The English grip in lawn tennis derived in part from the grip used in two older games, Tennis (or Real Tennis) and Racquets (later Squash). The style was well suited to the comparatively heavy conditions in which lawn tennis was first played in England, the open racket face meeting the need to lift low-bouncing balls over the net.

Regardless of conditions, the Continental is the most flexible of all grips, allowing its users to deal easily with balls of normal and low bound and those wide of or behind the receiver. As a result, Continental-type players tend to be attractive stylists. There is flexibility between forehand and backhand, too, as little or no change of grip is needed. The forehand, however, lacks power against high balls.

Whatever style they use, most players serve and smash with a Continental grip and many also use it for low-volleying and retrieving.

After being largely outmoded by the introduction of the Eastern American style (in which specialist forehand and backhand grips are used for driving power), the Continental style has made a remarkable comeback in modern championship tennis, where the speed of play demands flexibility.

Assuming the player's body to be sideways to the net, the Continental forehand meets the ball a little behind the left hip, the backhand a little in front of the right hip.

DOUBLES

Service returns. The Continental grip allows the greatest reach for covering wide serves. It also best permits the receiver to stand in close and play rising-ball returns without knowing whether the service will be to forehand or backhand. Except for strong-wristed players, however, it is the least suitable grip for producing angled topspin returns or for taking full advantage of a weak service.

Volleys. The Continental is the most suitable grip for low-volleying, and for rapid exchanges involving both forehand and backhand volleying.

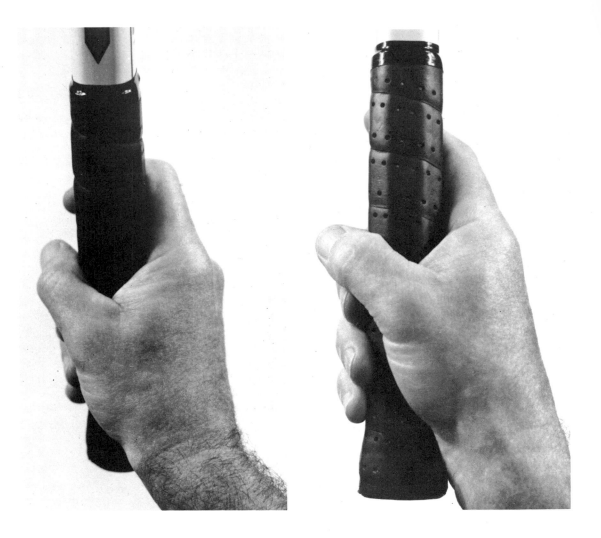

Palm and wrist solidly *behind* racket handle.
Large index knuckle on rear surface of handle.
"V" in centre of top surface of handle or somewhere right of centre.
Third and little fingers well up front surface of handle.
With the full Eastern (second picture) arm and racket are almost in line when viewed from in front.
Other names used for forehand grips within the Eastern group:

American	Full Eastern
Eastern American	Standard Eastern
Tilden	Modified Eastern
Shake-hands	Standard

Suggested name: American.

204

EASTERN STYLE

The Eastern style was developed in America, where stress was placed on power rather than flexibility. Specialist forehand and backhand grips were used to provide forward power on both wings and at the same time to keep the ball down better.

The Eastern has been regarded for some years as the standard style, although one inherent disadvantage is that it requires a marked change of grip for the backhand. In the earliest Eastern style this backhand change was as large as a quarter of a circle, and the thumb was advanced along the back of the handle for support. Such a change was found to be unacceptably large, and somewhere in the 1930s the Continental backhand position was adopted, the thumb being placed diagonally across the back of the handle for Eastern solidity.

The Eastern forehand grip also provides a safe service grip, but because it does not allow the wrist snap available from the Continental grip it does not develop maximum speed, spin, or twist.

The Eastern forehand meets the ball a little in front of the left hip, and the backhand, in its modern form, a little in front of the right hip.

DOUBLES

Service returns. Though all players are more or less basically committed to one style or another, many Eastern players choose to cover an opponent's first services with the Continental grip and to attack the second services strongly with their normal Eastern grip.

Volleys. The Eastern volley is normally more powerful than the Continental, but many Eastern players prefer to low-volley with a Continental grip.

Palm mainly under handle and wrist behind it.
"V" on right bevel, or even on rear surface.
Middle knuckles of all fingers point forwards.
Other names:

Western American	Poidevin
Californian	Johnston
Reverse	Hardcourt
Carpet-beater	Topspin
Frying-pan	Old-fashioned
Japanese	

Suggested name: Western.

WESTERN STYLE

The Western style was developed on the West Coast of the United States to cope with the high bound produced by concrete court surfaces and fast-wearing balls. The basic Japanese style, it was also largely used in Australian hardcourt tennis up to the early 1930s.

Great power and heavy topspin can be applied to high balls met well in front of the player. Overall, however, the grip is inflexible and restrictive in reach, and is largely outdated in men's tennis.

Besides its undoubted power, the Western style has the advantages of needing only a small change of grip for the backhand, of providing a natural balance between forehand and backhand strengths, and of exerting little strain on the wrist. For these reasons it is still in wide use in women's tennis, though without heavy topspin. The backhand grip is achieved by turning the racket head over the top and using the same face of the racket as for the forehand.

The original Western style included a reverse type of service, either Reverse Spin or Reverse Twist.

The Western forehand and backhand meet the ball well in front of the left and right hips respectively.

DOUBLES

Service returns. The Western grip provides the most devastating service returns of all—provided the ball is above net height and within comfortable reach.

Volleys. High volleys become a slaughter of the innocent. But to get a low volley over the net with a Western grip, particularly with the backhand, the ball has to be taken so far in front of the player as to reduce appreciably the amount of time available for the stroke.

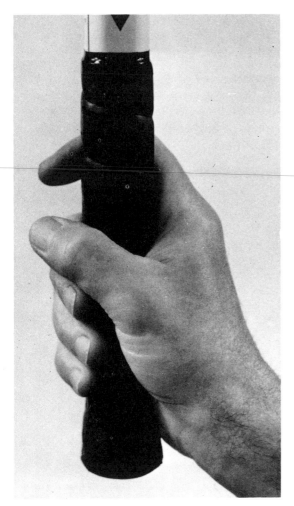

EXTREME EASTERN STYLE

Many early Americans and Australians played in this style, and it is still used today, particularly by hardcourt players.

A powerful topspin forehand can be produced, but a large change of grip is needed if the backhand grip is to be adequate. If this large change is made, the player is vulnerable to fast shots directed close to his body, particularly on the volley. If sufficient change is not made, the backhand is usually weak.

Because this style can involve the largest possible change of grip between forehand and backhand strokes, it can be called an extreme Eastern. Most of its characteristic strengths and weaknesses lie somewhere between those of the normal Eastern and the Western.

For the forehand, the ball is taken in front of the left hip, the backhand position depending upon how far the grip is changed.

Palm and wrist farther behind racket handle than in other Eastern grips.
Large index knuckle on rear surface.
"V" on right bevel.
Suggested name: Included in "American".

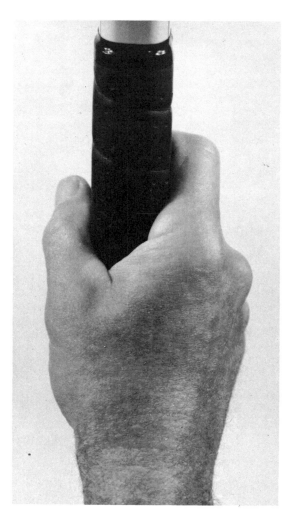

AUSTRALIAN STYLE

The intention being to have a specialist forehand grip and to change grip for the backhand, this style has Eastern associations; since it is used by many Australians it could perhaps be regarded as the Australian adaptation of the Eastern American style.

However, because the palm and wrist lie towards the top of the handle and no longer solidly behind it, and because the backhand change is very small, this grip and style are probably more accurately described as modified Continental. A compromise name would be Eastern/Continental, but this is a contradiction in terms.

An individual name seems desirable; a suitable one would be "Australian".

Characteristic strengths and weaknesses lie somewhere between those of the Continental and the Eastern styles.

The forehand is taken about opposite the left hip, the backhand a little in front of the right hip.

Palm and wrist towards top surface of racket handle.
Large index knuckle near ridge between right bevel and rear surface.
"V" somewhere between centre of top surface (Eastern) and left bevel (Continental)—in this picture, "V" position is close to that shown in second Continental photograph.
Suggested name: Australian (to date has had no name of its own).

Championship and Davis Cup Honour Rolls

MEN

Year	Australia	France	Wimbledon	United States	Davis Cup*
1877			S. W. Gore		
1878			Hadow		
1879			Hartley		
1880			Hartley		
1881			W. Renshaw	Sears	
1882			W. Renshaw	Sears	
1883			W. Renshaw	Sears	
1884			W. Renshaw	Sears	
1885			W. Renshaw	Sears	
1886			W. Renshaw	Sears	
1887			Lawford	Sears	
1888			E. Renshaw	Slocum	
1889			W. Renshaw	Slocum	
1890			Hamilton	Campbell	
1891		Briggs	Baddeley	Campbell	
1892		Schopper	Baddeley	Campbell	
1893		Riboulet	Pim	Wrenn	
1894		A. Vacherot	Pim	Wrenn	
1895		A. Vacherot	Baddeley	Hovey	
1896		A. Vacherot	Mahony	Wrenn	
1897		Aymé	R. F. Doherty	Wrenn	
1898		Aymé	R. F. Doherty	Whitman	
1899		Aymé	R. F. Doherty	Whitman	
1900		Aymé	R. F. Doherty	Whitman	U.S. d. Br. Isles, 3–0. Whitman, Davis; Davis and Ward
1901		A. Vacherot	A. W. Gore	Larned	U.S. No challenge
1902		M. Vacherot	H. L. Doherty	Larned	U.S. d. Br. Isles, 3–2. Whitman, Larned; Davis and Ward
1903		Decugis	H. L. Doherty	H. L. Doherty	Br. Isles d. U.S., 4–1. R. F. and H. L. Doherty
1904		Decugis	H. L. Doherty	Ward	Br. Isles d. Belgium, 5–0. H. L. Doherty, Riseley; R. F. and H. L. Doherty
1905	Heath	Germot	H. L. Doherty	Wright	Br. Isles d. U.S., 5–0. H. L. Doherty, Smith; R. F. and H. L. Doherty
1906	Wilding	Germot	H. L. Doherty	Clothier	Br. Isles d. U.S., 5–0. H. L. Doherty, Smith; R. F. and H. L. Doherty
1907	Rice	Decugis	Brookes	Larned	A/asia d. Br. Isles, 3–2. Brookes and Wilding
1908	Alexander	Decugis	A. W. Gore	Larned	A/asia d. U.S., 3–2. Brookes and Wilding
1909	Wilding	Decugis	A. W. Gore	Larned	A/asia d. U.S., 5–0. Brookes and Wilding
1910	Heath	Germot	Wilding	Larned	A/asia. No challenge

*Players named are those who contested the challenge round for the winning team. Where only two players are named, they contested both singles and doubles.

Year	Australia	France	Wimbledon	United States	Davis Cup
1911	Brookes	Gobert	Wilding	Larned	A/asia d. U.S., 5–0. Brookes, Heath; Brookes and Dunlop
1912	Parke	Decugis	Wilding	McLoughlin	Br. Isles d. A/asia, 3–2. Parke, Dixon; Parke and Beamish
1913	E. Parker	Decugis	Wilding	McLoughlin	U.S. d. Br. Isles, 3–2. McLoughlin, Williams; McLoughlin and Hacket
1914	A. O'Hara Wood	Decugis	Brookes	Williams	A/asia d. U.S., 3–2. Brookes and Wilding
1915	Lowe			Johnston	
1916				Williams	
1917					
1918				Murray	
1919	Kingscote		Patterson	Johnston	A/asia d. Br. Isles, 4–1. Patterson, Anderson; Patterson and Brookes
1920	P. O'Hara Wood	Gobert	Tilden	Tilden	U.S. d. A/asia, 5–0. Tilden and Johnston
1921	Gemmell	Samazeuilh	Tilden	Tilden	U.S. d. Japan, 5–0. Tilden, Johnston; Williams and Washburn
1922	J. O. Anderson	Cochet	Patterson	Tilden	U.S. d. A/asia, 4–1. Tilden, Johnston; Tilden and Richards
1923	P. O'Hara Wood	Blanchy	Johnston	Tilden	U.S. d. Australia, 4–1. Tilden, Johnston; Tilden and Williams
1924	J. O. Anderson	Borotra	Borotra	Tilden	U.S. d. Australia, 5–0. Tilden, Richards; Tilden and Johnston
1925	J. O. Anderson	Lacoste	Lacoste	Tilden	U.S. d. France, 5–0. Tilden, Johnston; Williams and Richards
1926	Hawkes	Cochet	Borotra	Lacoste	U.S. d. France, 4–1. Tilden, Johnston; Williams and Richards
1927	Patterson	Lacoste	Cochet	Lacoste	France d. U.S., 3–2. Lacoste, Cochet; Borotra and Brugnon
1928	Borotra	Cochet	Lacoste	Cochet	France d. U.S., 4–1. Lacoste, Cochet; Cochet and Borotra
1929	Gregory	Lacoste	Cochet	Tilden	France d. U.S., 3–2. Borotra and Cochet
1930	Moon	Cochet	Tilden	Doeg	France d. U.S., 4–1. Borotra, Cochet; Cochet and Brugnon
1931	Crawford	Borotra	Wood	Vines	France d. Gt.Britain, 3–2. Borotra, Cochet; Cochet and Brugnon
1932	Crawford	Cochet	Vines	Vines	France d. U.S., 3–2. Borotra, Cochet; Cochet and Brugnon
1933	Crawford	Crawford	Crawford	Perry	Gt. Britain d. France, 3–2. Perry, Austin; Lee and Hughes
1934	Perry	von Cramm	Perry	Perry	Gt. Britain d. U.S., 4–1. Perry, Austin; Lee and Hughes

Year	Australia	France	Wimbledon	United States	Davis Cup
1935	Crawford	Perry	Perry	Allison	Gt. Britain d. U.S., 5–0. Perry, Austin; Hughes and Tuckey
1936	Quist	von Cramm	Perry	Perry	Gt. Britain d. Australia, 3–2. Perry, Austin; Hughes and Tuckey
1937	McGrath	Henkel	Budge	Budge	U.S. d. Gt. Britain, 4–1. Budge, Parker; Budge and Mako
1938	Budge	Budge	Budge	Budge	U.S. d. Australia, 3–2. Budge, Riggs; Budge and Mako
1939	Bromwich	McNeill	Riggs	Riggs	Australia d. U.S., 3–2. Quist and Bromwich
1940	Quist			McNeill	
1941		Destremau		Riggs	
1942		Destremau		Schroeder	
1943		Petra		Hunt	
1944		Petra		Parker	
1945		Petra		Parker	
1946	Bromwich	Bernard	Petra	Kramer	U.S. d. Australia, 5–0. Kramer, Schroeder, Mulloy; Kramer and Schroeder
1947	Pails	Asboth	Kramer	Kramer	U.S. d. Australia, 4–1. Kramer and Schroeder
1948	Quist	Parker	Falkenburg	Gonzales	U.S. d. Australia, 5–0. Schroeder, Parker; Talbert and Mulloy
1949	Sedgman	Parker	Schroeder	Gonzales	U.S. d. Australia, 4–1. Schroeder, Gonzales; Talbert and Mulloy
1950	Sedgman	Patty	Patty	Larsen	Australia d. U.S., 4–1. Sedgman, McGregor; Bromwich and Sedgman
1951	Savitt	Drobny	Savitt	Sedgman	Australia d. U.S., 3–2. Sedgman, Rose; Sedgman and McGregor
1952	McGregor	Drobny	Sedgman	Sedgman	Australia d. U.S., 4–1. Sedgman and McGregor
1953	Rosewall	Rosewall	Seixas	Trabert	Australia d. U.S., 3–2. Hoad, Rosewall; Hoad and Hartwig
1954	Rose	Trabert	Drobny	Seixas	U.S. d. Australia, 3–2. Seixas and Trabert
1955	Rosewall	Trabert	Trabert	Trabert	Australia d. U.S., 5–0. Hoad, Rosewall; Hoad and Hartwig
1956	Hoad	Hoad	Hoad	Rosewall	Australia d. U.S., 5–0. Hoad and Rosewall
1957	Cooper	S. Davidson	Hoad	M. Anderson	Australia d. U.S., 3–2. Cooper, Anderson; Rose and Anderson
1958	Cooper	Rose	Cooper	Cooper	U.S. d. Australia, 3–2. Olmedo, Mackay; Olmedo and Richardson
1959	Olmedo	Pietrangeli	Olmedo	Fraser	Australia d. U.S., 3–2. Fraser, Laver; Fraser and Emerson
1960	Laver	Pietrangeli	Fraser	Fraser	Australia d. Italy, 4–1. Fraser, Laver; Fraser and Emerson

Year	Australia	France	Wimbledon	United States	Davis Cup
1961	Emerson	Santana	Laver	Emerson	Australia d. Italy, 5–0. Laver, Emerson; Fraser and Emerson
1962	Laver	Laver	Laver	Laver	Australia d. Mexico, 5–0. Laver, Fraser; Laver and Emerson
1963	Emerson	Emerson	McKinley	Osuna	U.S. d. Australia, 3–2. McKinley and Ralston
1964	Emerson	Santana	Emerson	Emerson	Australia d. U.S., 3–2. Emerson and Stolle
1965	Emerson	Stolle	Emerson	Santana	Australia d. Spain, 4–1. Emerson, Stolle; Newcombe and Roche
1966	Emerson	Roche	Santana	Stolle	Australia d. India, 4–1. Emerson, Stolle; Newcombe and Roche
1967	Emerson	Emerson	Newcombe	Newcombe	Australia d. Spain, 4–1. Emerson, Newcombe; Newcombe and Roche
1968	Bowrey	Rosewall	Laver	Ashe	U.S. d. Australia, 4–1. Ashe, Graebner; Lutz and Smith
1969	Laver	Laver	Laver	Laver	

LADIES

Year	Australia	France	Wimbledon	United States
1884			Miss Watson	
1885			Miss Watson	
1886			Miss Bingley	
1887			Miss Dod	Miss Hansell
1888			Miss Dod	Miss Townsend
1889			Mrs Hillyard (Bingley)	Miss Townsend
1890			Miss Rice	Miss Roosevelt
1891			Miss Dod	Miss Cahill
1892			Miss Dod	Miss Cahill
1893			Miss Dod	Miss Terry
1894			Mrs Hillyard	Miss Helwig
1895			Miss Cooper	Miss Atkinson
1896			Miss Cooper	Miss Moore
1897		Mlle Masson	Mrs Hillyard	Miss Atkinson
1898		Mlle Masson	Miss Cooper	Miss Atkinson
1899		Mlle Masson	Mrs Hillyard	Miss Jones
1900		Mlle Prevost	Mrs Hillyard	Miss McAteer
1901		Mme Girod	Mrs Sterry (Cooper)	Miss Moore
1902		Mlle Masson	Miss Robb	Miss Jones
1903		Mlle Masson	Miss Douglass	Miss Moore
1904		Mlle Gillou	Miss Douglass	Miss Sutton
1905		Mlle Gillou	Miss Sutton	Miss Moore
1906		Mme Fenwick	Miss Douglass	Miss Homans
1907		Mme Kermel	Miss Sutton	Miss Sears
1908		Mme Fenwick	Mrs Sterry	Mrs Wallach
1909		Mlle Mathey	Miss Boothby	Miss Hotchkiss
1910		Mlle Mathey	Mrs. L. Chambers (Douglass)	Miss Hotchkiss
1911		Mlle Mathey	Mrs L. Chambers	Miss Hotchkiss
1912		Mlle Mathey	Mrs Larcombe	Miss Browne
1913		Mlle Broquedis	Mrs L. Chambers	Miss Browne
1914		Mlle Broquedis	Mrs L. Chambers	Miss Browne

Year	Australia	France	Wimbledon	United States
1915				Miss Bjurstedt
1916				Miss Bjurstedt
1917				
1918				Miss Bjurstedt
1919			Mlle Lenglen	Mrs Wightman (Hotchkiss)
1920		Mlle Lenglen	Mlle Lenglen	Mrs Bjurstedt Mallory
1921		Mlle Lenglen	Mlle Lenglen	Mrs Bjurstedt Mallory
1922	Mrs Molesworth	Mlle Lenglen	Mlle Lenglen	Mrs Bjurstedt Mallory
1923	Mrs Molesworth	Mlle Lenglen	Mlle Lenglen	Miss Wills
1924	Miss Lance	Mlle Vlasto	Miss McKane	Miss Wills
1925	Miss Akhurst	Mlle Lenglen	Mlle Lenglen	Miss Wills
1926	Miss Akhurst	Mlle Lenglen	Mrs McKane Godfree	Mrs Bjurstedt Mallory
1927	Miss Boyd	Mlle Bouman	Miss Wills	Miss Wills
1928	Miss Akhurst	Miss Wills	Miss Wills	Miss Wills
1929	Miss Akhurst	Miss Wills	Miss Wills	Miss Wills
1930	Miss Akhurst	Mrs Wills Moody	Mrs Wills Moody	Miss Nuthall
Year	Australia	France	Wimbledon	United States
1931	Mrs Buttsworth	Frl. Aussem	Frl. Aussem	Mrs Wills Moody
1932	Mrs Buttsworth	Mrs Wills Moody	Mrs Wills Moody	Miss Jacobs
1933	Miss Hartigan	Miss Scriven	Mrs Wills Moody	Miss Jacobs
1934	Miss Hartigan	Miss Scriven	Miss Round	Miss Jacobs
1935	Miss Round	Frau Sperling	Mrs Wills Moody	Miss Jacobs
1936	Miss Hartigan	Frau Sperling	Miss Jacobs	Miss Marble
1937	Miss Wynne	Frau Sperling	Miss Round	Sen. Lizana
1938	Miss Bundy	Mme Mathieu	Mrs Wills Moody	Miss Marble
1939	Mrs Westacott	Mme Mathieu	Miss Marble	Miss Marble
1940	Miss Wynne			Miss Marble
1941		Mlle Weivers		Mrs Palfrey Cooke
1942		Mlle Weivers		Miss Betz
1943		Mme Lafargue		Miss Betz
1944		Mlle Veber		Miss Betz
1945		Mme Payot		Mrs Palfrey Cooke
1946	Mrs Bolton (Wynne)	Miss Osborne	Miss Betz	Miss Betz
1947	Mrs Bolton	Mrs Todd	Miss Osborne	Miss Brough
1948	Mrs Bolton	Mme Landry	Miss Brough	Mrs Osborne du Pont
1949	Miss Hart	Mrs Osborne du Pont	Miss Brough	Mrs Osborne du Pont
1950	Miss Brough	Miss Hart	Miss Brough	Mrs Osborne du Pont
1951	Mrs Bolton	Miss Fry	Miss Hart	Miss Connolly
1952	Mrs Long	Miss Hart	Miss Connolly	Miss Connolly
1953	Miss Connolly	Miss Connolly	Miss Connolly	Miss Connolly
1954	Mrs Long	Miss Connolly	Miss Connolly	Miss Hart
1955	Miss Penrose	Miss Mortimer	Miss Brough	Miss Hart
1956	Miss Carter	Miss Gibson	Miss Fry	Miss Fry
1957	Miss Fry	Miss Bloomer	Miss Gibson	Miss Gibson
1958	Miss Mortimer	Mrs Kormoczy	Miss Gibson	Miss Gibson
1959	Mrs Reitano (Carter)	Miss Truman	Miss Bueno	Miss Bueno
1960	Miss Smith	Miss Hard	Miss Bueno	Miss Hard
1961	Miss Smith	Mrs Haydon Jones	Miss Mortimer	Miss Hard
1962	Miss Smith	Miss Smith	Mrs Susman	Miss Smith
1963	Miss Smith	Miss Turner	Miss Smith	Miss Bueno
1964	Miss Smith	Miss Smith	Miss Bueno	Miss Bueno
1965	Miss Smith	Miss Turner	Miss Smith	Miss Smith
1966	Miss Smith	Mrs Haydon Jones	Mrs Moffitt King	Miss Bueno
1967	Miss Richey	Mlle Durr	Mrs Moffitt King	Mrs Moffitt King
1968	Mrs Moffitt King	Miss Richey	Mrs Moffitt King	Mrs Court (Smith)
1969	Mrs Court (Smith)	Mrs Court (Smith)	Mrs Haydon Jones	Mrs Court (Smith)

213

Australian Davis Cup Players

Brookes (10)	1905, 1907, 1908, 1909, 1911, 1912, 1914, 1919, 1920, 1924	Turnbull	1933, 1934, 1935
		Bromwich (7)	1937, 1938, 1939, 1946, 1947, 1949, 1950
Wilding (6)	1905, 1906, 1907, 1908, 1909, 1914		
Dunlop (6)	1905, 1908, 1909, 1911, 1912, 1914	Schwartz	1938
Poidevin	1906	Pails	1946, 1947
Sharp	1909	Long	1946, 1947, 1948
Heath	1911, 1912, 1920	Brown	1947, 1948
Rice	1911, 1913	Sidwell	1948, 1949
Jones	1912, 1913	Sedgman	1949, 1950, 1951, 1952
Doust	1913, 1914	McGregor	1950, 1951, 1952
Patterson (6)	1919, 1920, 1922, 1924, 1925, 1928	Worthington	1950
Anderson, J. O. (5)	1919, 1921, 1922, 1923, 1925	Rose (6)	1950, 1951, 1952, 1953, 1954, 1957
Thomas	1919	Ayre	1951
O'Hara Wood, P.	1920, 1922, 1924	Hoad (5)	1952, 1953, 1954, 1955, 1956
Hawkes	1921, 1923, 1925	Rosewall	1953, 1954, 1955, 1956
Peach	1921	Hartwig	1953, 1954, 1955
Todd	1921	Fraser (9)	1955, 1956, 1957, 1958, 1959, 1960, 1961, 1962, 1963
Wertheim	1922		
Schlesinger	1923, 1924	Cooper	1956, 1957, 1958
McInnes	1923	Anderson, M.	1957, 1958
Kalms	1924	Laver (5)	1958, 1959, 1960, 1961, 1962
Crawford (9)	1928, 1930, 1932, 1933, 1934, 1935, 1936, 1937, 1939	Emerson (9)	1959, 1960, 1961, 1962, 1963, 1964, 1965, 1966, 1967
Hopman (5)	1928, 1930, 1932, 1938, 1939. Non-playing captain each year from 1950	Mark	1959, 1960
		Stolle (5)	1961, 1963, 1964, 1965, 1966
		Fletcher	1962
Moon	1930	Newcombe (5)	1963, 1964, 1965, 1966, 1967
Willard	1930	Roche	1964, 1965, 1966, 1967
Sproule	1932, 1936, 1937	Davidson	1964
Clemenger	1932	Ruffels	1968
Quist (9)	1933, 1934, 1935, 1936, 1937, 1938, 1939, 1946, 1948	Bowrey	1968
		Alexander	1968
McGrath (5)	1933, 1934, 1935, 1936, 1937	Dent	1968

Index

216

Picture Credits

The following list is necessarily incomplete because it has been impossible to trace all pictures used to their original sources. Author and publishers offer their apologies to the copyright-owners of any pictures that may have been reproduced without prior permission.

Pages 8, 10, 11, 13, 16-18 (col. 1), 29, 30, 54-56 — All England Tennis Club.

Pages 2, 5, 6 — Lord Aberdare.

Pages 9, 60, 69 — Central Press Photos Ltd, London.

Pages 1, 18 (col. 2), 26, 35-39, 42, 57, 58 (col. 1), 63 (col. 2), 65, 78, 81, 84-88, 90, 91, 97-99, 101, 103, 104 (col. 2), 105, 108, 110, 116-18, 121, 128, 135-38 (col. 1), 141, 142 (col. 2), 143, 144, 146, 149, 163 (col. 1), 165, 166, 170-73 (col. 2), 174 (col. 2), 175 (col. 1), 178, 180 (col. 2), 181-83 (col. 1), 183 (top col. 2), 192 — *Herald-Sun*, Melbourne.

Pages 27, 154, 155, 183 (bottom col. 2), 189 (col. 2) — *Sydney Morning Herald*.

Page 32 — A. Huxley.

Pages 41, 45, 46, 48, 50, 52, 72, 74, 75 — Wide World Photos, U.S.A.

Pages 58 (col. 2), 63 (col. 1), 66, 76, 158, 159, 162, 186, 187 (col. 2), 194 — M. Philippe Chartrier.

Pages 71, 140 — P. A. Reuter

Pages 92, 93, 94, 95, 96, 119, 157, 190 (col. 1) — A. K. Quist.

Page 104 (col. 1) — G. P. Hughes.

Pages 107 (col. 1), 109 — J. Donald Budge.

Page 114 — Hans Nusslein and Riebicke (Berlin).

Pages 125, 127, 142 (col. 1), 151, 152, 163 (col. 2), 164, 167, 168, 173, (col. 1), 175 (col. 2), 179, 180 (col. 1) — Australian News and Information Bureau.

Pages 126, 187 (col. 1) — Associated Press, London.

Page 129 — William Talbert and *Sports Illustrated*

Page 130 — Gardnar Mulloy.

Page 160 — United Press, London.

Pages 174 (col. 1), 176, 189 (col. 1) — Australian Consolidated Press.

Page 177 — Baker's Tennishop, Sydney.

Pages 202, 204, 206, 207, 208 — Paul Metzler.